LUCASFILM

PHILOSOPHICAL FILMMAKERS

Series editor: Costica Bradatan is a Professor of Humanities at Texas Tech University, USA, and an Honorary Research Professor of Philosophy at the University of Queensland, Australia. He is the author of *Dying for Ideas: The Dangerous Lives of the Philosophers* (Bloomsbury, 2015), among other books.

Films can ask big questions about human existence: what it means to be alive, to be afraid, to be moral, to be loved. The *Philosophical Filmmakers* series examines the work of influential directors, through the writing of thinkers wanting to grapple with the rocky territory where film and philosophy touch borders.

Each book involves a philosopher engaging with an individual filmmaker's work, revealing how it has inspired the author's own philosophical perspectives and how critical engagement with those films can expand our intellectual horizons.

Other titles in the series:
Eric Rohmer, Vittorio Hösle
Werner Herzog, Richard Eldridge
Terrence Malick, Robert Sinnerbrink
Kenneth Lonergan, Todd May
Shyam Benegal, Samir Chopra
Douglas Sirk, Robert B. Pippin

Other titles forthcoming:
Christopher Nolan, Robbie Goh
Leni Riefenstahl, Jakob Lothe

LUCASFILM

Filmmaking, Philosophy, and the *Star Wars* Universe

Cyrus R. K. Patell

BLOOMSBURY ACADEMIC
LONDON • NEW YORK • OXFORD • NEW DELHI • SYDNEY

BLOOMSBURY ACADEMIC
Bloomsbury Publishing Plc
50 Bedford Square, London, WC1B 3DP, UK
1385 Broadway, New York, NY 10018, USA
29 Earlsfort Terrace, Dublin 2, Ireland

BLOOMSBURY, BLOOMSBURY ACADEMIC and the Diana logo
are trademarks of Bloomsbury Publishing Plc

First published in Great Britain 2021

Copyright © Cyrus R. K. Patell, 2021

Cyrus R. K. Patell has asserted his right under the Copyright,
Designs and Patents Act, 1988, to be identified as Author of this work.

For legal purposes the Acknowledgments on p. x constitute
an extension of this copyright page.

Cover image: *Daisy Ridley is Rey and Adam Driver is Kylo Ren in STAR WARS: THE RISE OF SKYWALKER* © 2019 and TM Lucasfilm Ltd. (LucasFilm / Photofest)

All rights reserved. No part of this publication may be reproduced or transmitted in any form or by any means, electronic or mechanical, including photocopying, recording, or any information storage or retrieval system, without prior permission in writing from the publishers.

Bloomsbury Publishing Plc does not have any control over, or responsibility for, any third-party websites referred to or in this book. All internet addresses given in this book were correct at the time of going to press. The author and publisher regret any inconvenience caused if addresses have changed or sites have ceased to exist, but can accept no responsibility for any such changes.

A catalogue record for this book is available from the British Library.

Library of Congress Cataloging-in-Publication Data
Names: Patell, Cyrus R. K., author.
Title: Lucasfilm : filmmaking, philosophy, and the Star Wars universe / Cyrus R.K. Patell.
Description: London : New York : Bloomsbury Academic, 2021. | Series: Philosophical filmmakers | Includes bibliographical references and index. |
Identifiers: LCCN 2021004252 (print) | LCCN 2021004253 (ebook) | ISBN 9781350100619 (paperback) | ISBN 9781350100602 (hardback) | ISBN 9781350100596 (ePFD) | ISBN 9781350100626 (eBook)
Subjects: LCSH: Lucasfilm, Ltd.–History. | Lucas, George, 1944- | Star wars films.
Classification: LCC PN1999.L78 P38 2021 (print) | LCC PN1999.L78 (ebook)|
DDC 791.4302/33092–dc23
LC record available at https://lccn.loc.gov/2021004252
LC ebook record available at https://lccn.loc.gov/2021004253

ISBN:	HB:	978-1-3501-0060-2
	PB:	978-1-3501-0061-9
	ePDF:	978-1-3501-0059-6
	eBook:	978-1-3501-0062-6

Series: Philosophical Filmmakers

Typeset by Integra Software Services Pvt. Ltd.

To find out more about our authors and books visit www.bloomsbury.com
and sign up for our newsletters.

For
Caleb, Liam, and Deborah

Contents

List of Images viii
Acknowledgments x

Introduction 1

1   Filmmaking and Philosophizing 17

2   From Lucas to Lucasfilm 41

3   Reversal and Recognition, Exile and Return 67

4   Melodrama 93

5   Individualism 109

6   Technophobia 129

7   Cosmopolitanism 161

8   Fallibilism 191

9   Moral Compass 205

Notes 219
Bibliography 231
Index 242

List of Images

Cover Lightsaber duel between Rey and Kylo on the ruins of the second Death Star in *The Rise of Skywalker*

1. New York premiere xi
2. The *Star Wars: Identities* exhibition 15
3. Comparing crawls 34
4. *The Force Awakens* premiere 59
5. VHS Rental Edition of *Star Wars* 63
6. Still from *The Story of Anakin Skywalker* by Lego 69
7. Stills of Han Solo shooting Greedo: original 1977 version and 2011 Blu-ray version 100
8. Still of stormtrooper bumping his head on a door in *Star Wars* (1977) 106
9. Princess Jedi 122
10. Luke Skywalker's first lightsaber 136
11. Boris Karloff as the Monster in *The Bride of Frankenstein* (1935) 143

List of Images

12 Press kit for the "Special Edition" rerelease of the original *Star Wars* trilogy 178

13 Celebrating *Star Wars* 190

14 Luke and Yoda watching the sacred Jedi tree burn 201

15 Princess Jedi grows up and grows dark 206

16 Rey is fierce 212

17 Rey's skills are complete 218

Acknowledgments

Some years ago—never mind how long precisely—Costica Bradatan invited me to participate in the *Philosophical Filmmakers* series that he was curating for Bloomsbury and was enthusiastic about my proposed contribution: "Believe it or not," he wrote back, "George Lucas has not been taken, so he is all yours." I am deeply grateful for his support through the proposal, review, and drafting process—and I'm particularly grateful for his and Bloomsbury philosopher editor Liza Thompson's willingness to let me bend the model for the series by treating a corporate person—Lucasfilm—as a "filmmaker and philosopher." I'm also grateful for their willingness to let me sit on the first draft for a year so that I could incorporate ideas from *The Rise of Skywalker* into the book. As I wrote the first draft, the importance of what we might dub "Next-Gen Lucasfilm" became evident, so it made sense to wait for the completion of the sequel trilogy.

Star Wars is closely associated with various periods in my education and intellectual development. I've been thinking about *Star Wars* since that spring day in 1977 when I saw the first film for the first time in what was once New York's largest single movie screen—the cavernous Loew's Astor Plaza in Times Square—which ceased to be a movie theater in 2004 and is now the Playstation Theater (see Figure 1). I remain deeply grateful to Al Quintero for taking me to see it, one of many adventures we shared together. Those high school years bring to mind many friends—particularly Warner Fite, Gregory Fletcher, Ted

Harris, Cynthia Tougas Penney, Tanja Sablosky, and Les Wacker—and teachers who taught me to think: Paul Bolduc, Mary Evelyn Bruce, Alice Horton, Donald Hull, Gregory Lombardo, Jane Mallison, Frank Smith, Gilbert Smith, and Thomas Squire. *The Empire Strikes Back* came out just after exams finished in my first year of college, and *Return of the Jedi* capped off my senior year. Jonathan Kolber came with me to *Empire* and bought my ticket to *Return* to pay off a first-year bet. Susan Rakov accompanied us to *Return* and is linked to so many memories from college and beyond. I continue to cherish my friendships with Melissa Block, Cabot Brown, Ann Corbett, Joseph Hershenson, Dave Kennedy, Ingrid Jacobson, Stefan Pinter, Jack Rippey, Ed Rogers, Mark Saltveit, and Andy Whitney. Some of these friends and mentors have left us; other friendships are dormant. I take to heart the multiple meanings of Luke Skywalker's perspective in *The Last Jedi*: "No one's ever really gone."

Figure 1 New York premiere. The Loew's Astor Plaza in New York during the premiere run of *Star Wars* in May 1977. Photo credit: Paul Slade. Getty Images.

I've been thinking about the intersections of literature, film, and political theory since beginning work on my dissertation in the late 1980s; I owe a particular debt of gratitude to Sacvan Bercovitch and Philip Fisher. After joining New York University (NYU) in 1993, my scholarly interests have included theories of cosmopolitanism and representations of technology. I'm very grateful that this book gives me an opportunity to bring all these interests together.

I am grateful to audiences at the American Comparative Literature Association, the American Literature Association, the American Studies Association, the American Studies Association of Korea, Ewha Womans University, the Modern Language Association, NYU, NYU Abu Dhabi (NYUAD), the NYUAD Institute, Sogang University, and the University of Pittsburgh, who have heard and commented on some of the arguments that I make here. I owe a profound debt of gratitude to the many NYU students and teaching assistants over the years who have helped me to test ideas presented here; I am particularly grateful to the students at NYUAD who discussed many of these topics in seminars on "The Cosmopolitan Imagination," "Speculative Fiction," "Global Text: *Star Wars*," and "Technophilia and Its Discontents."

I am grateful to NYU Abu Dhabi for vital research support and for leading me to expand my scholarly horizons in ways that have helped to shape the account present in this book. I am indebted to the administrative staff who have been invaluable in making NYUAD's Art and Humanities Division a fruitful place for the pursuit of scholarship and teaching: Nisrin Abdulkhadir, Alana Barraj, Gemma Chance, Rosa Choi, Julie Cowans, Tina Galanopoulos, Suze Heinrich, Caitlin Newsom, and Jesusita Santillan. I am grateful to the Arts & Humanities deans Reindert L. Falkenburg and Judith Graves Miller, who helped us navigate the first few years at NYUAD. The NYU Abu Dhabi experience has been enriched for me in ways too numerous to detail by our colleagues Marzia Balzani, Ron Berry, Linsey Bostwick,

Bill Bragin, Carol Brandt, Saba Brelvi, Alide Cagidemetrio, Aysan Celik, Una Chaudhuri, John Coughlin, Tishani Doshi, Renee Dugan, Toral Gajarawala, Chuck Grim, Katya Grim, Deborah Kapchan, Maya Kesrouany, Philip Mitsis, John O'Brien, Lisa Philp, Rubén Polendo, Maurice Pomerantz, Charles Siebert, Stephanie Smith-Waterman, Werner Sollors, Justin Stearns, Kate Stimpson, Miguel Syjuco, Lisa Taylor, Tomi Tsunoda, Bryan Waterman, Katherine Schaap Williams, and Shamoon Zamir.

Four members of the NYUAD community in particular have helped me think about *Star Wars* during the past decade: Vishwanath Chandrasekar, Class of 2018; Chani Gatto-Bradshaw, a member of NYUAD's inaugural class of 2014; Matthew Silverstein, a member of the philosophy faculty; and Josh Taylor, now Associate Vice Chancellor, Global Programs and Mobility Services at NYU. Bhrigu Bhatra provided superb research assistance. Saka Naka, Aishah Shafiq, Jamie Uy, and Eva Zhang offered valuable advice on a full draft of the manuscript. Bloomsbury Saka Assistant Philosophy Editor Lucy Russell and project manager Suriya Rajasekar at Integra Software Services expertly guided me through the production process.

Earlier versions of material in Chapter 6 appeared in the essay "Star Wars, Star Trek, and Other Sites of Technocultural Anxiety," *Journal of American Studies* 34 (2002); in revised form in "Star Wars and the Technophobic Imagination," in *Myth, Media, and Culture in Star Wars*, edited by Douglas Brode and Leah Deyneka (Scarecrow, 2012); and in my *Cosmopolitanism and the Literary Imagination* (Palgrave, 2015). I am grateful to the Executive Committee of the American Studies Association of Korea and to Douglas Brode, Leah Deyneka, and the Scarecrow Press for permission to adapt that material for use here. I am grateful to the NYU English Department for a grant from the Abraham and Rebecca Stein Faculty Publication Fund in support of this project.

My late parents—my mother, Estrella Raña Patell, and my father, Rusi Kaikhusroo Nanabhoy Patell—took me to the movies a lot when I was a kid growing up in New York, and I owe my love of film (and many, many other things) to their guidance. It's been one of the pleasures of our growing older that my sister, Shireen, and I now both count literary scholarship and blockbuster films like *Star Wars* among our common interests.

My sons, Liam and Caleb, fell in love with the prequel trilogy and the lore of the Jedi when they were little. It's been deeply rewarding to share *Star Wars* with them in a variety of ways: building Lego sets, inventing our own expanded universe of *Star Wars* stories on the way to school, watching the films and the television series, and now discussing the ideas that I investigate in these pages. I owe a particular debt to my wife, Deborah Lindsay Williams, who is not a *Star Wars* fan but is a good sport and has put up with my interest in the saga—and the DVDs, Blu-rays, books, memorabilia, and Lego pieces that have accompanied it—over the years. She is also my best critic, and my pursuit of scholarship would be unthinkable without her as interlocutor. This book is for the three of them.

Introduction

It's unsurprising that the first book in a series called *Philosophical Filmmakers* was devoted to Eric Rohmer, film critic-turned-director and a central figure in the French *Nouvelle Vague*, which (according to that book's back cover) "reconstituted French cinema based on the theoretical principles articulated in the *Cahiers du Cinéma*." Rohmer is routinely described as an *auteur*, a label that he himself embraced: he told an interviewer in 2008, "The public often tell me that I make films that resemble each other and they are right, but it is normal because I am a complete auteur, that is someone who creates the film, looks at the subject and at the same time I am also the man who creates the image."[1] The next books in the series treated legendary *auteurs* Werner Herzog and Terrence Malick.

You might expect, therefore, this book to be called *George Lucas: Filmmaker and Philosopher*. Despite having cinematic aims that are more oriented toward commercial success than the other directors I've named, Lucas would seem to fit the auteurist bill, both early in his career, before he turned over the directing duties for *The Empire Strikes Back* (1980) to Irvin Kershner, and later when he returned to the director's chair for the *Star Wars* prequel trilogy (1999–2005).[2] In the introduction to a collection of interviews with Lucas that appeared just before the release of *The Phantom Menace* (1999), Sally Kline writes,

As director, producer, writer, editor, technology innovator, and entrepreneur, the controversial George Lucas may well be the most identifiable and popular film maker in the history of the medium. ... Along with his close friend and colleague Steven Spielberg, he established the modern blockbuster phenomenon. For good or for ill, Lucas has revolutionized an industry and created the most successful film series of all time.[3]

Such a description makes Lucas sound like the ultimate *auteur*. I think that's a misrepresentation of what George Lucas has achieved as the creator of the *Star Wars* universe, however, and also a misrepresentation of how he achieved it.

In substituting "Lucasfilm" for "George Lucas" in the book's title, I am deliberately cutting against the grain of the auteurist model that is implicit in the series description's emphasis on "engaging with an individual filmmaker's work." If *Star Wars* arose in the 1970s from the imagination of a single individual, four decades later it has become the province of the corporate person known as "Lucasfilm," which employs more than 2,000 people. Lucasfilm's website offers this description of the company's aims:

> Founded by visionary filmmaker George Lucas in 1971, Lucasfilm established itself as a "rebel base" of sorts in San Francisco's Bay Area, a place the filmmaker chose to "shake up the status quo ... of how movies were made and what they were about." It was a defiant departure from the Hollywood mainstream and a more conducive atmosphere to cultivate his independent spirit of filmmaking.
>
> With money earned from his third motion picture, 1977's blockbuster *Star Wars*, Lucas was able to construct Skywalker Ranch in San Francisco's North Bay in the early '80s, a place where filmmakers could work together sharing ideas and experience.

Treating "Lucasfilm" as if it were a person that can imagine things and make films isn't as odd as it sounds, especially in the aftermath of the Supreme Court's 2010 decision in *Citizens United v. Federal Election Commission*, which reaffirmed the idea that corporations are legally considered to be "persons"; in fact, their status as artificial persons entitles them to First Amendment protection, which the Court's majority interpreted to mean that a corporation could make more or less unlimited expenditures to disseminate its views on political elections.

The idea, however, that a corporation is an artificial person is a legal fiction that dates back to at least the Middle Ages.[4] In an influential lecture delivered at Oxford in 1904, A. V. Dicey argued that "when a body of twenty or two thousand or two hundred thousand men bind themselves together to act in a particular way for some common purpose, they create a body which, by no fiction of law but from the very nature of things, differs from the individuals of whom it is constituted."[5] Arthur Machen noted in the *Harvard Law Review* in 1911 that "a corporation exists as an objectively real entity, which any well-developed child or normal man must perceive: the law merely recognizes and gives legal effect to the existence of this entity." Seeking to avoid philosophical hair-splitting about whether such an entity should be designated a "person," Machen argues in favor of "the truth that a corporation bears some analogy or resemblance to a person, and is to be treated in law in certain respects as if it were a person, or a rational being capable of feeling and volition."[6] Headlines like "How Lucasfilm Reimagined Classic Moments in *Star Wars Galaxy of Adventures*" for a piece that is actually an interview with Josh Rimes, director of animation and live action series development at Lucasfilm, suggest that imagining Lucasfilm the corporate person to be a "filmmaker" is a widely shared—and uncontroversial—convention.[7]

This book takes that convention seriously and explores its implications: it is about the collective approach to filmmaking that Lucasfilm embodies and the kinds of philosophizing that it has engendered through its creation, first and foremost, of the *Star Wars* universe and, secondarily, of the special-effects company Industrial Light and Magic.[8] It examines not just the films that Lucas himself might be said to have "made," but also subsequent works made by other filmmakers and even works in other media inspired by the *Star Wars* films. Pull down the "What We Do" tab on the Lucasfilm website, and you get the following choices: "Movies. Series. Toys, Books, & Stuff. Games. Immersive Entertainment. Visual Effects. Sound." All of these activities, I will argue, are worth considering if we are going to think about what *Star Wars* has to offer to those who are interested in the disciplines of philosophy and cultural theory. My hope is that the analyses presented below will offer readers ways of thinking about different philosophical issues that the film saga and its offshoots open up and will provide a set of conceptual frames that can be productively applied not only to the films, books, and other media that have been released to date, but also to future works set in the *Star Wars* universe.

To be clear: the focus of this book is not on George Lucas as a philosopher, nor on the philosophical positions dramatized by the original 1977 film and its sequels and prequels, but rather on *Star Wars* as an ongoing platform for public philosophy. It isn't, in other words, primarily about philosophical thinking that can actually be attributed to George Lucas—that he might be said to have "put into" the films that he wrote, cowrote, or directed—though I will discuss some of that thinking at the outset. I see Lucas as not only mobilizing philosophical thinking in the films he himself made, but also creating, in what has now come to be known as "the *Star Wars* universe," a vehicle for philosophical thinking by others. These others include the directors and writers of subsequent *Star Wars* films, and all of the other participants in the development of the *Star Wars* universe in other media, as well as the fans of the series. One press reviewer for my original book proposal complained about the "glut of books—scholarly and coffee table—on George Lucas and *Star Wars*" and asked why we needed to have another. That very "glut of books," however, is not a liability for the book you are about to read, but rather one of its subjects. The proliferation of *Star Wars* books—both imaginative texts that have become part of the "*Star Wars* canon" and "secondary" studies about aspects of the phenomenon—attests to the fact that *Star Wars* raises "philosophical issues" that "have a major intellectual and existential significance" and that they are already "part of a larger, trans-disciplinary public conversation [taking] place beyond the ivory towers of academia" (to quote Costica Bradatan's proposal for the *Philosophical Filmmakers* series). This book aims to investigate that conversation, but also to channel it in new and, I hope, productive directions.

The Shared Universe

It is part of Lucasfilm's achievement that in *Star Wars* it created what a *New York Times* review of *The Last Jedi* (2017) called "a franchise that deliberately resists individual authorship."[9] *Wired* magazine writer Adam Rogers offers a useful way of thinking about how and why this approach works when he invokes the concept of the "paracosm," a term drawn from social psychology to denote "the detailed imaginary world inside one's mind."[10] Rogers describes it as "a complete world populated with autonomous characters."[11] What Lucas did in creating the first *Star Wars* film was to translate a paracosm onto a pad of paper and then onto the big screen. According to Rogers, Lucas's nascent paracosm, about a universe where a farm boy with preternatural skill as a pilot could turn out to be a messianic warrior-priest, didn't exactly fit in with the gritty, violent stories his peers (or even his mentor, Francis Ford Coppola) wanted to tell. All he had was a document laying out the long arc. It was naive and nostalgic, but amid the weird names and clichés was a real vision.[12]

What made the paracosm persuasive onscreen was its retro feel, both in the allusion it made to older cinematic forms and in the used, lived-in look of its props, costumes, and sets. This mise-en-scène emphasizes that we've entered into a world with a history and an unhappy present, a point made by Obi-Wan Kenobi early on in *A New Hope* (1977) when he tells Luke, "For over a thousand generations the Jedi Knights were the guardians of peace and justice in the Old Republic. Before the dark times, before the Empire."[13] Rogers suggests that this built-in "nostalgia … for the days before the dark times of the Empire [makes] the *Star Wars* universe [feel] like it exists even when you're not looking at it."[14]

Hollywood has translated the idea of the paracosm into the idea of the "shared universe," and Rogers claimed in 2015, "The shared universe represents something rare in Hollywood: a new idea." He notes that "it evolved from the narrative techniques not of auteur or blockbuster films but of comic books and TV, and porting that model over isn't easy. It needs different kinds of writers and directors and a different way of looking at the structure of storytelling itself. Marvel prototyped the process; Lucasfilm is trying to industrialize it."[15] While I think that this insight has merit, I believe that we can find precursors to the shared universe in two imaginative spheres that, as we will see, were important influences on Lucas as he conceived the *Star Wars* universe: the world of Greek tragedy and the world of the Hollywood Western. Robert Fagles describes classical Athenian tragedy in this way:

The first three plays of the day's performance were tragedy, and here, with very few exceptions, the figure who walked the stage, far from being contemporary, were men, women and gods from the far-off past, from the dim beginnings of the youth of the race—an age of heroes and heroines, the legends of the beginnings of the Greek world. The stuff from which the tragic poet made his plays was not contemporary reality but myth.[16]

Writing about the Western, David Lusted describes a game of Cowboys and Indians that he used to play as a child and then comments:

While we played, the images in our heads were drawn not from any real West—we had few history books and historical images, and The West was not a topic on the school curriculum—but from the fictional West of Western films, comics and television series. This popular representation of the West is The West to most people, even in the American West today, and it affords an otherworldly, imaginary space of dramatic excitement, film star glamour and pictorial splendour.[17]

This imaginary world comes with a set of recurring motifs—Jane Tompkins identifies them as "death, women, language, landscape, horses, cattle"—and a set of ideological associations that shape its makers and consumers into an interpretive community.[18]

Though not himself a *Star Wars* aficionado, the legendary auteur Werner Herzog summed up the aspirations behind the saga and its offshoots at the premiere of Jon Favreau's live-action television series, *The Mandalorian* (2019), which features Herzog in a supporting role:

What you are creating is an entire universe. ... This universe is filled with new mythology. Not very often in cultural history have we had new mythologies. We had it with ancient Greek mythology, we had it in antiquity, but very rarely ... and it's also a world filled of fantasy, full of fever dreams, full of new characters you never expected so it's a wonderful possibility for filmmaking.[19]

Novelist Delilah S. Dawson, author of the canonical novels *Phasma* (2017) and *Galaxy's Edge: Black Spire* (2019), as well as a fairy-tale retelling of the first eight Skywalker films entitled *The Skywalker Saga* (2019), described what it is like to create stories within the shared universe in the aftermath of criticisms leveled at *The Rise of Skywalker*. Writing *The Skywalker Saga* required her to watch the films in numerical order for the first time, leaving her struck by "the echoes, heartbreak, failure, redemption! And also the clunky dialogue, the plot holes, the WTFery! It's as beautiful and messy as we are." She describes writing within a shared universe as "nuts," requiring "a rare skill set. The author is not God. It's a group project! We have so many constraints and rules! It's not easy." Ultimately, she argues, "*Star Wars* is a patchwork story crafted by the combined talents and love of hundreds of people over 42 years (so far). Everyone who participates in the *Star Wars* story is a fan. Like the Force, writing it requires balance and restraint. What I saw last night was a triumph."[20]

To do justice to the significance of the modern shared universe exemplified by *Star Wars*, filmmakers and writers have needed to find a new model for collaboration. Likewise, film scholarship needs to find a new model, beyond the traditional auteurist approach with its emphasis on intentionality.[21]

A Note on Methodology

In this book, I use an expansive notion of reading that encompasses what we do when we read novels, poems, essays, or plays, but also what we do when we watch plays or films. I will treat all of these artistic forms as "texts" that can be "read." What such an approach will reveal is that what underlies the *Star Wars* universe is a cosmopolitan philosophical project, which works both by creating a narrative framework that promotes liberalism, tolerance, and inclusiveness and by creating a platform for the kinds of conversations about cultural values that lie at the heart of cosmopolitanism. The narrative framework is something that both traditional film studies and more recent film-and-philosophy studies are used to examining, but understanding the platform calls for a more contextualizing approach reminiscent of cultural studies.

Originating in the idea of the world citizen and conceived in contradistinction to nationalism, cosmopolitanism has more recently been described as an alternative to universalism, pluralism, and multiculturalism, ideas upon which it draws but with which it also takes issue. In other words, cosmopolitanism mediates between the claims of sameness (drawing on the idea of universalism) and the claims of difference (drawing on pluralism and its offshoot multiculturalism). Cosmopolitans have been described as those who are at home everywhere (because their identities are not rooted in particular nations, regions, or group identities) and also at home nowhere (because they are rootless). In my view, cosmopolitanism is about the interplay of both of these kinds of experiences—of being at home and not at home, of feeling comfort and discomfort—and a truly cosmopolitan perspective actively cultivates whichever experience does not immediately arise when it encounters something new. A cosmopolitan who finds herself at home in a given situation will look for ways to make it different and strange; she will likewise search for the familiar within situations that present themselves at first as different and strange, as Other.

Cosmopolitanism is best understood as a perspective that regards human difference as an opportunity to be embraced rather than a problem to be solved. This perspective might be said to lie behind all "great" literature, which asks its readers to experience otherness by opening themselves up to another person's words and thoughts.[22] If, as I'm arguing, writers or filmmakers create out of something that might be called a cosmopolitan impulse, then it may be part of the philosophical work of their texts to encourage readers to engage in a concomitantly cosmopolitan reading practice. The cosmopolitan reader recognizes that reading is a social practice. Whenever we encounter a piece of imaginative work, we are encountering words, images, or thoughts that aren't ours. It's the closest thing, given our self-enclosed minds, to letting our consciousness merge with someone else's. We can then realize that meaning-making is a collaborative process: meaning is the result of a conversation between the author and the reader through the medium of the text.

A cosmopolitan reading practice requires us to attune ourselves constantly to the interplay of sameness and difference, of comfort and discomfort in the acts of writing, reading, and performing texts. I offer this advice to those who wish to pursue a cosmopolitan reading practice: when you find a text familiar and comforting, look for ways to make it feel strange, unfamiliar, and different; produce discomfort in yourself. And when a text makes you uncomfortable, try to locate aspects of sameness and to make yourself comfortable with its difference. Be at home with all the texts you encounter—and with none of them.

Such a practice hinges, in part, on understanding that texts (whether written or cinematic) have a reciprocal relationship with the culture that produces them. In other words, readers can learn something about the culture from which a text springs by reading the text, but can also read the text more effectively if they already know something about that culture. Cosmopolitan readers must learn to become comfortable with the idea that the boundary between "text" and "context" is porous, the relationship between them fluid. Furthermore, particularly when we are discussing global works of art such as *The Odyssey*, Shakespeare's plays, *The Ramayana*, or *Star Wars*, these texts also exist in a reciprocal relationship with the culture that consumes them, which may be remote in time and space from the text's culture of origin.

Citing such different forms as "folktales, drama, opera, novels, short stories; biographies, histories, ethnographies; fiction or nonfiction; painting, music, sculpture, and dance," Kwame Anthony Appiah argues that "every human civilization has ways to reveal to us values we had not previously recognized or undermine our commitment to values that we had settled into."[23] To uncover these values fully within a text, we must learn to be attuned to the effects produced by artistic form and to understand the ways in which form itself is informed by cultural practices and perspectives. Every work of narrative art dramatizes a system of values that it asks its reader to discern and evaluate. These values are encoded through the use of figurative language and rhetorical devices, some obvious to the casual reader, some apparent only with the kind of reading that literary scholars have called "close reading." Stephen Greenblatt offers us a way of thinking about how works of art encode a culture's "values" by drawing our attention to the symbiotic relationship between close reading and "cultural analysis." In his essay "Culture" (1995), Greenblatt begins by calling our attention to two poetic genres in which moral stances and cultural values are generally readily apparent, at least to the audiences for whom they were originally written: satire (poems of blame) and panegyric (poems of praise). Greenblatt then advises readers to look for the ways in which structures of praise and blame are at work in every text, asking a set of questions designed to highlight the "beliefs and practices" that these structures implicitly enforce:

> What kinds of behavior, what models of practice, does this work seem to enforce?
>
> Why might readers at a particular time and place find this work compelling?
>
> Are there differences between my values and the values implicit in the work that I am reading?
>
> Upon what social understandings does the work depend?
>
> Whose freedom of thought or movement might be constrained implicitly or explicitly by this work?
>
> What are the larger social structures with which these particular acts of praise or blame might be connected?

Greenblatt presents these questions in order to encourage readers to read not only closely, but also self-consciously, and to think about the ways in which cultural values are encoded into literary form. "Eventually," Greenblatt argues, "a full cultural analysis will need to push beyond the boundaries of the text, to establish links between the text and values, institutions, and practices elsewhere in the culture. But these links cannot be a substitute for close reading."[24] For Greenblatt, texts are "cultural" not only because they make "reference to the world beyond themselves," but also, and perhaps most importantly, because they have "successfully absorbed" the set of "social values and contexts" from which they spring. That "sustained absorption" is, according to Greenblatt, what "enables many literary works to survive the collapse of the conditions that led to their production."

What Greenblatt wants us to realize is that many "cultural" aspects of a text that were once regarded as "extrinsic" to the text can now be seen as intrinsic and integral to the text's formal qualities.[25] And it is in those "formal qualities" that a significant portion of the philosophical content of a work of art may well be embedded. As Martha Nussbaum argues, "Literary form is not separable from philosophical content, but is, itself, a part of content—an integral part, then, of the search for and the statement of truth."[26] Learning to read closely, attuned to the ways in which both literary form and cultural context influence the production of meaning in a text, is a way of unlocking the philosophical components of the text.

To do justice to the shared universe that Lucasfilm has created, however, requires us to read and interpret not only the *Star Wars* films, but also the other storytelling forms that have emerged from them. The commitment to caring for George Lucas's shared universe has led Lucasfilm to establish the Lucasfilm Story Group, which ensures that not only the films but also all of the other media that the universe includes—television shows, books, comic books, games, theme park attractions, and (soon) hotels—are coordinated with one another. Lucasfilm president Kathleen Kennedy suggests that *Star Wars* worked because it "was deeply personal to [Lucas]. He was looking for meaning. It was authentic to who he was."[27] What the careers of both Lucas and Lucasfilm demonstrate is that the shared universe succeeds when it transcends the personal and individual and becomes communal. Rogers notes the plan for the Galaxy's Edge *Star Wars* lands at Disney's theme parks in California and Florida (the latter of which will also have a *Star Wars*–themed hotel) is to enable visitors "to assume a *Star Wars* character, and the 'cast' of the Land and hotel will react to them in-story." Given that "the *Star Wars* Land is regulated by the Story Group and, ostensibly, in canon, this means that our universe now at least crosses over with—and in fact may be a sub-universe of—*Star Wars*. We are all canon."[28]

The creation of these immersive *Star Wars* experiences is the logical extension of the ways in which fans have been encouraged to participate in the *Star Wars* universe. The action figures licensed by Lucasfilm that belatedly accompanied the 1977 film set in motion an industry of *Star Wars* toys, costumes, and other forms of merchandise.

Star Wars cosplay is encouraged at the periodic "Star Wars Celebration" conventions that Lucasfilm organizes, and Lucasfilm has sought to use its stories as the basis for pedagogy. George Lucas himself experimented with the idea that his stories could be used to teach history, with his television series *The Young Indiana Jones Chronicles* (1992–1993), a set of historical fictions in which the young Indy met real-life historical characters like Winston Churchill, Ernest Hemingway, T. E. Lawrence, Pablo Picasso, Theodore Roosevelt, and Leo Tolstoy. The Smithsonian Institution's National Air and Space Museum presented an exhibition called *Star Wars: The Magic of Myth* (1997–1999) that was designed to introduce viewers to the idea of comparative mythology discussed by Joseph Campbell in his study *Hero with a Thousand Faces* (1949), which was a primary inspiration for the narrative of the *Star Wars* saga. A later touring exhibition, *Star Wars: Identities* (2012–) uses theories of identity drawn from social psychology and biology to illuminate the *Star Wars* saga and vice versa (see Figure 2). The *Star Wars Galaxy of Adventures* (2018–) cartoon shorts have an explicitly pedagogical motive, featuring such tag lines as "Through Han and Chewie, we can talk to our younglings about the meaning of friendship," or "Talk with your younglings about our favorite rebel princess and what it means to be a leader—with some help from StarWars.com and *Galaxy of Adventures*!"

The end result is the transformation of the shared universe of *Star Wars* into something even more: a platform for philosophy that enables its participants to engage in the kinds of conversations about hard questions that philosophers like Appiah have described as the bedrock of a truly cosmopolitan experience. In *The Ethics of Identity*, Appiah argues that "cosmopolitanism imagines a world in which people and novels and music and films and philosophies travel between places where they are understood differently, because people are different and welcome to their difference. Cosmopolitanism can

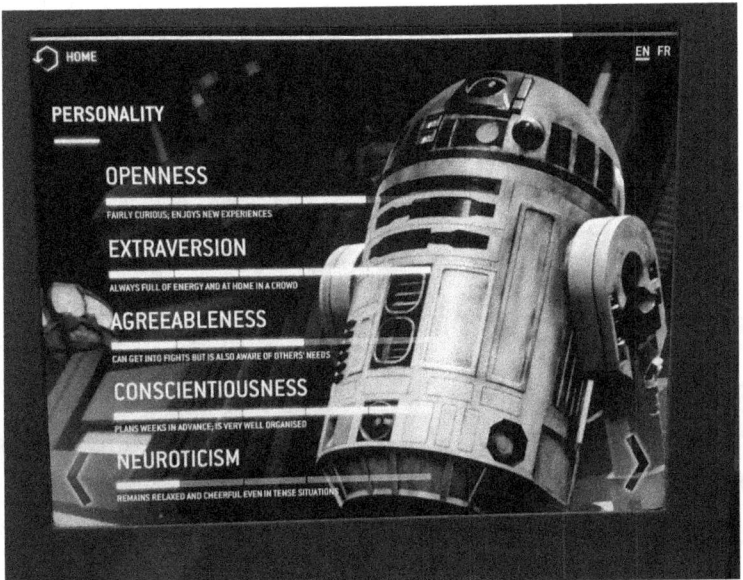

Figure 2 The *Star Wars: Identities* Exhibition. Screen describing R2-D2's personality, O2 Arena, London, 2017. Photo credit: Cyrus R. K. Patell.

work because there can be common conversations about these shared ideas and objects."[29]

Star Wars, I contend, promotes these kinds of common conversations and indeed even creates a set of ideas and objects that can be shared. Moreover, the mixed responses among fans of the saga to Lucasfilm's sequel trilogy and anthology films dramatize the fact that cosmopolitan conversations are rarely easy, particularly when cherished meanings, practices, and values are at stake.

1

Filmmaking and Philosophizing

Philosophy and Storytelling

Star Wars, Episode VIII: The Last Jedi (2017) ends with a coda that dramatizes the power of storytelling. Two downtrodden children who work in the fathier stables on Canto Bight listen with rapt attention as a third tells the story of Luke Skywalker's climactic encounter with Kylo Ren and the forces of the fascistic First Order, a scene that we have witnessed earlier in the film. The storytelling party is broken up by the cruel stable manager, and one boy—who has earlier in the film aided Resistance heroes Rose and Finn—goes outside into the night. He pulls a broom to his side from against a wall—seemingly by using the Force—brushes some straw and then, as the Force theme begins to play, watches a ship streak in the heavens. He turns his hand to reveal the ring with the Resistance symbol that Rose has given him and, in the film's final shot, we see him from behind, raising his broom handle as if it were a lightsaber. He's seemingly inspired by what he has heard. The scene recalls another moment of storytelling that involves the adventures of Luke Skywalker: C-3PO's recounting of the destruction of the Death Star to the Ewoks in *Return of the Jedi*

(1983) on the eve of the Battle of Endor. This story inspired the Ewoks to fight with the Rebellion against the Empire's vastly superior destructive technology. *The Last Jedi*'s conclusion suggests this legacy of heroism can continue, that there are others in the galaxy like this young boy, who have the power to resist oppression, if only they can be inspired to act by hearing the right stories.

Star Wars, it seems, knows something that professional philosophy might have forgotten. In a 2017 article entitled "Philosophy Needs a New Definition," Costica Bradatan urges philosophers to remember philosophy's roots in storytelling traditions, arguing that "with every new story we make the world anew. Storytelling pushes the boundaries of what it means to be human: envisions and rehearses new forms of experience, gives firm shape to something that hasn't existed before, makes the unthought-of suddenly intelligible. Storytelling and philosophy are twins."[1] That's been true for more than 2,000 years in the Western philosophical tradition. After all, Plato's dialogues are stories of conversations between Socrates and his students, in which Socrates himself frequently makes use of stories such as the *Republic*'s "allegory of the cave" or the invention of writing by the Egyptian god Theuth in the *Phaedrus*. Aristotle argues that the pursuit of *mimesis* (imitation) is one of the ways in which human beings are distinct from animals, because mimesis is linked to understanding, which "is extremely pleasant, not just for philosophers but for others too in the same way, despite their limited capacity for it."[2] Mimesis is a crucial component of what the *Poetics* presents as the highest form of storytelling: the tragic drama. Philosophy leads to understanding; mimesis, in a different way, also leads to understanding, perhaps in a way that is more accessible to the nonphilosopher.

It's possible, of course, that if storytelling and philosophy are twins, to pick up Bradatan's metaphor, then they are fraternal twins. In his "Letter on Art in Reply to André Daspre," the French neo-Marxist philosopher Louis Althusser uses the term "science" instead of "philosophy," but his attempt to characterize what art does offers a useful way of thinking about how art might serve as either a supplement to philosophy or even an alternative form of philosophy. Science, Althusser writes, gives us "the conceptual knowledge of the complex mechanisms which eventually produce the 'lived experience'" portrayed by art, as in the novels of Balzac and Solzhenitsyn that Daspre has mentioned to Althusser, prompting the letter. "The peculiarity of art," writes Althusser, "is to 'make us see' …, 'make us perceive', 'make us feel' something which alludes to reality." He then clarifies: "What art makes us see, and therefore gives to us in the form of 'seeing', 'perceiving' and 'feeling' (which is not the form of knowing), is the ideology from which it is born, in which it bathes, from which it detaches itself as art, and to which it alludes." Althusser famously defined "ideology" in his essay "Ideology and Ideological State Apparatuses" as "a 'representation' of the imaginary relationship of individuals to their real conditions of existence."[3] In the "Letter," he argues that

> Balzac and Solzhenitsyn give us a "view" of the ideology to which their work alludes and with which it is constantly fed, a view which presupposes a retreat, an *internal distantiation* from the very ideology from which their novels emerged. They make us "perceive" (but not know) in some sense from the inside, by an internal distance, the very ideology in which they are held. (italics in original)[4]

In other words, because both ideology and art are mimetic—they both create representations of reality—Althusser suggests that art somehow manages to create a disjunction between itself and the ideology from which it springs that the reader or viewer can experience ("see," "perceive," "feel").

Coming from a rather different philosophical tradition, Martha Nussbaum argues not only that novels can be said to do philosophical work, but also that literary texts have a particular contribution to make to philosophical discourse, precisely because they do not take the form of argumentation commonly associated with philosophical discourse. Nussbaum suggests that

> there may be some views of the world and how one should live in it—views, especially, that emphasize the world's surprising variety, its complexity and mysteriousness, its flawed and imperfect beauty—that cannot be fully and adequately stated in the language of conventional philosophical prose, a style remarkably flat and lacking in wonder—but only in a language and in forms themselves more complex, more allusive, more attentive to particulars.

Moreover, for Nussbaum, there is something about the way that storytelling can make use of the unexpected that might help readers to grasp ideas more effectively than through "the expositional structure conventional to philosophy, which sets out to establish something and then does so, without surprise, without incident." Narrative can take a "form that itself implies that life contains significant surprises" and helps us to understand "that our task, as agents, is to live as good characters in a good story do, caring about what happens, resourcefully confronting each new thing."[5] There is something that happens in the tragic drama, for example, when it makes use of what Aristotle calls "reversal" and "recognition," that enables both the characters in a drama and the viewers of the drama to confront truth in a way that eludes philosophical argumentation. Perhaps that confrontation lies at the heart of the experience of *katharsis* that Aristotle describes so enigmatically.

The philosopher Thomas Wartenberg wonders whether a similar claim might be made for film as philosophical discourse. Raising the examples of three very different films—"Akira Kurosawa's 1950 art film masterpiece, *Rashomon*; Ridley Scott's 1982 science-fiction classic, *Blade Runner*; and Woody Allen's 1989 tour de force, *Crimes and Misdemeanors*"—Wartenberg notes that all three films "pose philosophical questions and even take stabs at answering them," which leads him to ask the general question: "To what extent are films capable of actually doing philosophy?"[6] Wartenberg presents two possible answers, which he believes constitute the ends of a spectrum: "One option is to make the strong claim that films are capable of actually doing philosophy in something like the sense we think of the classical texts of the Western tradition—such as Plato's *Republic* and Descartes' *Meditations on First Philosophy*—doing philosophy." Such a view is aligned with Nussbaum's view of the novel and with the kind of analysis she performs of Satyajit Ray's adaptation of Rabindranath Tagore's novel *The Home and the World*.[7] At the opposite end of the spectrum is the view that while "some films do have a relationship to philosophy," it is not "anything like that exhibited by the founding texts of the Western tradition. Here, the contention might be that film is a medium that is very adept at popularizing philosophical issues but lacks the capacity to actually produce original philosophy itself."[8]

Wartenberg himself defends what he calls "a moderate form of one of them: that films can do philosophy." This view is predicated on the idea that not only is it "quite natural to think of films as sometimes addressing philosophical issues," but also that an important way of thinking about what the term "philosophy" means is to see it as "the name given to the most basic issues that concern us as human beings."[9] Thinking about Nussbaum's claims for the novel, Wartenberg argues that "a fiction film [*sic*] can address a philosophical issue in as interesting a manner as a great novel," though he stresses that "one reason for this is that films are capable of giving philosophical ideas a liveliness and vivacity that some may find lacking in the written texts of the tradition."[10] Stephen Mulhall also argues that "that films can be seen to engage in systematic and sophisticated thinking about their themes and about themselves—that films can philosophize."[11] Thinking about the films that constitute the *Alien* quadrilogy begun by Ridley Scott, Mulhall writes:

> I do not look to these films as handy or popular illustrations of views and arguments properly developed by philosophers; I see them rather as themselves reflecting on and evaluating such views and arguments, as thinking seriously and systematically about them in just the ways that philosophers do. Such films are not philosophy's raw material, nor a source for its ornamentation; they are philosophical exercises, philosophy in action—film as philosophizing.[12]

Film, in other words, doesn't simply dramatize philosophical ideas and debates, though that's one of the things it can do: it can also, through the cinematic equivalent of the formal resources of language and structure that Nussbaum identifies, persuade its viewers to adopt a position toward ideas and debates.

I will argue below that Lucasfilm's *Star Wars* saga does just that: it dramatizes debates about the nature of individual identity, freedom, fate, and the ordering of the ideal society that are typically regarded as philosophical topics, but it does so in a way that uses the persuasive mechanisms of film to frame the debates around these issues. But because the persuasiveness of these mechanisms depends in part on a set of socially determined factors, they are not going to be equally persuasive to all members of the saga's audience.

What distinguishes the *Star Wars* saga from other films is that Lucasfilm has engineered it to transcend the medium of film and consciously transformed it into a platform for various kinds of philosophical thinking.

Film and Persuasion

The persuasive mechanisms of film are not those of analytic philosophy, which relies heavily on a logic of argumentation that is rational and teleological. Although film can make use of teleological thinking when it tells a story from beginning to end, the logic through which it "persuades" is associative rather than teleological, which enables it to work through emotion as well as reason. In *Moving Viewers: American Film and the Spectator's Experience* (2009), Carl Plantinga argues that "any satisfactory account of film reception and its implications for ideology, rhetoric, ethics, or aesthetics had better be able to take film-elicited affect and emotion into account." For Plantinga, "the viewing of a narrative film is not merely an intellectual or cognitive exercise, but one colored by affect and emotion." The effects of the emotions conjured by a film are, Plantinga suggests, both short term and, at least potentially, long term: "In the short term, the function of emotion and affect is to make film viewing powerful, rather than merely an intellectual exercise. In the long term, such experiences may burn themselves into the memories of audiences and may become templates for thinking and behavior." A real-world example of the experience that Plantinga describes can be found in the Twitter thread of the actress Mary Chieffo, who played a major role as the Klingon Chancellor L'Rell in the first two seasons of the television series *Star Trek: Discovery* (2017–2018). After watching *The Rise of Skywalker* three times, she posted (on Christmas Day):

> I have loved watching this trilogy. Even when I am frustrated with creative choices made, they push me to examine why they frustrate me. At its best, art forces us to look at ourselves and decide how we can be better. … I want to be better. I want to go deeper. Rewatching *Star Wars* this past week has reminded me of who I want to be and

the kind of art I want to put out into the world. For that, I am forever grateful.[13]

Plantinga's work is part of a trend within the field of film studies to think more about "how ... emotions at the movies are used for rhetorical or persuasive ends," and he reminds us that "Aristotle found the elicitation of emotion to be one of the key strategies of persuasive discourse."[14] Plantinga calls his approach to film "cognitive-perceptual," because he seeks "to draw attention to its recognition not only of conscious cognitive processes in affective experience, but also to preconscious cognition and automatic, 'cognitively impenetrable' processes."[15] Robert Sinnerbrink suggests, however, that theorists like Plantinga, despite their interest in "the interplay of cognitive, emotional and generic factors," tend to overstress "the role of character, action and narrative content in their analyses of affective and emotional engagement with film." Sinnerbrink argues that "it is not just character action and narrative content that elicits emotion, but the entire repertoire of cinematic-aesthetic devices (lighting, composition, montage, rhythm, tempo, colour, texture, gesture, performance, music and sound). Emotion is elicited and communicated aesthetically as well as cognitively." Citing the work of Greg Smith, Sinnerbrink proposes that we pay greater attention to the ways in which films create "mood," which "cues the background affective dispositions that enable us to experience emotional engagement with characters in the narrative."[16] In other words, these "cinematic-aesthetic devices" are part of film's mechanism of persuasion, and they work in large part by generating emotional responses. In the case of *Star Wars*, we might point to a number of devices that work in this way: the "lived-in" feel of the films' universe due to the use of practical special effects; the cyclical patterns of the narrative, which Lucas described in a documentary on the making of the Phantom Menace as being "like poetry," in which "every stanza kind of rhymes with the last one";[17] the recurrence of the line "I have a bad feeling about this"; and, perhaps above all, the music of John Williams.

Plantinga tells us that "one of the principle motivations for the viewing of movies" is to experience emotion, but he reminds us that the value of this experience can be "both intrinsic (emotions that are enjoyable in themselves) and extrinsic (emotions that lead to pleasing meta-emotions, social communication, or some other use value)."[18] Plantinga's notion of extrinsic value here points to the idea that the emotional responses that film generates are to a great extent social responses. I suggest that in this respect the mechanisms of persuasion in films closely resemble what scholars working in the area of cultural studies have identified as the mechanisms of *ideology*.

The term "cultural studies" arose, or at least was institutionalized, in Great Britain in the 1960s at the University of Birmingham. According to the anthropologist James Clifford, "Cultural studies in Britain emerged with the New Left and a theoretically supple neo-Marxism. It has been associated with adult and popular education movements, working-class politics, and more recently with new social movements based on gender, sexuality, ethnicity, anti-racism and anti-militarism."[19] In the United States, cultural studies retained some of these associations but tended to focus on the democratizing impulses of the discipline (rather than the leftist political agenda of its British counterpart). Although occasionally identified with ethnic studies (providing a generic rubric for the interdisciplinary work of African American Studies, Latinx Studies, Indigenous Studies, and LGBTQIA+ Studies, to name a few), what became the dominant trend in US cultural studies in the late twentieth century was the effort to break down the traditional distinctions between highbrow and lowbrow culture. During the 1980s, the literary critic Gerald

Graff provided a very useful description of this trend, arguing that the point of cultural studies was

> not to scrap the classics and substitute "Westerns as lit" for "Western lit," or to declare, "Say goodnight, Socrates," as some ill-informed news reports have ... complained. The point is not to get rid of the classics but to teach the classics in relation to the challenges being posed to them. It is not, in other words, a question of substituting Rambo for Rimbaud so much as putting highbrow and lowbrow traditions back into the dialogical relation in which they have actually existed in our cultural history.[20]

Cultural studies urged its students to be able to talk about *both* Rambo and Rimbaud and to understand how the cultural traditions that each represented are interrelated.

Cultural studies in both Great Britain and the United States has frequently taken as its object of study the relationship between representation and ideology. Like early Marxist thinkers, when cultural studies scholars speak of "ideology" they are talking about consciousness, but (in contrast to the Marxists) they do not see it necessarily as "false" consciousness: what they stress is that an ideology is an internalized mode of consciousness that serves as a kind of social glue. Ideology acts as an interpretive lens or filter that enables people to make sense of each other and the world.

A good working definition of ideology comes from the historian David Brion Davis, who uses the term to mean

> an integrated system of beliefs, assumptions, and values, not necessarily true or false, which reflects the needs and interests of a group or class at a particular time in history. By "interest" I mean anything that benefits or is thought to benefit a specific collective identity. Because ideologies are modes of consciousness,

containing the criteria for interpreting social reality, they help to define as well as to legitimate collective needs and interests. Hence there is a continuous interaction between ideology and the material forces of history. The salient characteristic of an ideology is that, while it is taken for granted by people who have internalized it, it is never the eternal or absolute truth it claims to be. Ideologies focus attention on certain phenomena, but only by arbitrarily screening out other phenomena in patterns that are not without meaning.[21]

This conception of ideology is indebted to Althusser's interpretation of Karl Marx's *Capital*. Althusser claimed that although Marx does not explicitly name the concept of ideology in *Capital*, it is implicit throughout the book. Althusser described ideology as "a system (with its own logic and rigour) of representations (images, myths, ideas or concepts, depending on the case) endowed with a historical existence and role within a given society."[22] Elaborating upon Althusser's theory, the sociologist Stuart Hall writes that "ideologies do not operate through single ideas"; rather, "they operate, in discursive chains, in clusters, in semantic fields, in discursive formations. As you enter an ideological field and pick out any one nodal representation or idea, you immediately trigger off a whole chain of connotative associations. Ideological representations connote—summon—one another."[23] Each of the representations generated within an ideological field derives from one or more associations, but these representations are themselves linked to one another as sequences of thought. Within an ideological field, certain dominant strands, certain characteristic patterns of reasoning, eventually emerge, becoming evident throughout a broad range of different discourses.

Ideologies thus create what the literary theorist Stanley Fish called "interpretive communities," which are made up of individuals who share similar assumptions about how texts should be interpreted. In

Fish's famous formulation, "interpretive strategies are not put into execution after reading: they are the shape of reading; and because they are the shape of reading, they give texts their shape, making them rather than, as is usually presumed, arising from them." According to Fish, "Since the thoughts an individual can think and the mental operations he can perform have their source in some or other interpretive community, he is as much the product of that community (acting as an extension of it) as the meanings it enables him to produce."

The idea of the interpretive community explains why texts are thought to have stable meanings—not because they do, but rather because the meanings have been generated by members of the same interpretive community. Fish suggests that

> members of the same community will necessarily agree because they will see (and by seeing, make) everything in relation to that community's assumed purposes and goals; and conversely, members of different communities will disagree because from each of their respective positions the other "simply" cannot see what is obviously and inescapably there. This, then, is the explanation for the stability of interpretation among different readers (they belong to the same community). It also explains why there are disagreements and why they can be debated in a principled way: not because of a stability in texts, but because of a stability in the makeup of interpretive communities and therefore in the opposing positions they make possible.[24]

This notion of the interpretive community became a cornerstone of "reader-response theory," which emphasized the vital role that readers played in the creation of textual "meaning." Juxtaposing reader-response theory to ideology theory suggests that the construction of meaning is less a function of logical reasoning than the influence of patterns of association that readers bring to the texts that they encounter.

As we will see in greater detail below, *Star Wars* fans as a whole may be said to constitute an interpretive community that was formed by the success of the 1977 film and then extended through the subsequent films and other forms of media that Lucasfilm created around them. Over time, however, that interpretive community became so large that it came to contain many overlapping communities, some with very different ideas of what "*Star Wars*" was about in 1977 and what it should be about in 2019, with the completion of the sequel trilogy and thus the end of the Skywalker saga. For example, one interpretive community insists that the version of the first film released in theaters is *the* authentic *Star Wars* and considers Lucas's revised versions, to which special effects and a few additional scenes were added, to be desecrations. An overlapping interpretive community believes that *Star Wars* has always been about the power of white masculinity and has excoriated Lucasfilm for creating the sequel trilogy around a female hero and a multicultural cast of human characters.

Interpretive communities are formed through what the literary theorist Hans Robert Jauss called "the horizon of expectations." According to Jauss, when we read a new text, we read with certain expectations and rules in mind, which are the products of our social, cultural, historical, aesthetic, and personal contexts. "The new text evokes for the reader," writes Jauss, "the horizon of expectations and rules familiar from earlier texts, which are then varied, corrected, altered, or even just reproduced." In short, the "meanings" of a text are a function not only of its author's intentions but also of what Jauss describes as "the milieu, views and ideology of [the] audience."[25] Generic expectations are a part of this milieu: when you tell an audience that it's going to be seeing a science-fiction film, certain associations formed by previous encounters with films dubbed "science fiction" come to mind. At the same time, an audience's responses to what it sees on the screen are going to be shaped by other contextual factors from the realms of politics or culture. A writer or filmmaker creates new work with an implicit understanding that these horizons of expectations are in place and can choose to work with them or cut against them: a new work can attempt to create a new horizon of expectations. As we'll see, *Star Wars* did just that.

The Horizon of Expectations, circa 1977

Let's think for a moment about how the first *Star Wars* film both responded to and reset viewers' expectations in 1977. After the familiar fanfare of the Twentieth-Century Fox opening music and the segue from the Fox logo to the Lucasfilm production credit, we see, in silence, blue letters that locate us in time and space: "A long time ago in a galaxy far, far away …." If the title led us to expect a science-fiction film, these lines both affirm and shift that expectation: "a galaxy far, far away" evokes science fiction, but science fiction tends to be associated with futurism, and that is not where we are. Instead, we are told, we are in the distant past. There's a complicated act of interpretation going on in just that moment: we've made an association of the film to a genre, invoked the expectations that accompany that genre, and then had those expectations shifted by the film. Lucas knows that we're going to have those expectations, and he deliberately means to shift them. The fairy-tale sound of the opening words is not at all accidental.

Lucas was well aware of the horizon of expectations for a "science fiction" film in 1977, which were formed around the conventions established by Stanley Kubrick's *2001: A Space Odyssey* (1968). Lucas himself said in 1977, "Kubrick made the ultimate science fiction movie. It is going to be very hard for someone to come along and make a better movie, as far as I'm concerned." Lucas did note that the pace of Kubrick's film and the movements of its spaceships were a little slow.[26] He could change that. In 1977, most audiences expected a science-fiction future to look clean and new. He could change that too.

Viewers who had seen the trailer for *Star Wars* that was released in December 1976 would have formed certain expectations about the film. The trailer was put together hurriedly, before many of the special-effects sequences had been completed. In the documentary *Empire of Dreams* (2004), Ken Ralston remembers, "What was really cool about the trailer was that we were still working on the movie. It was more about the spirit of it. It introduced a lot of different characters [including] the robots. One thing they did have was a couple of the early lightsabers. It was cool."[27] In contrast to the way the film would eventually present itself, the trailer began, "Somewhere in space, this might all be happening right now. Twentieth-Century Fox and George Lucas, the man who brought you *American Graffiti*, now bring you an adventure unlike anything on your planet: *Star Wars*." Interspersed with scenes of TIE fighters, the *Millennium Falcon*, the droids, Luke and Leia, Vader, Chewbacca, the Tusken Raiders, and the Jawas, the trailer's voice-over described the film as "the story of a boy, a girl, and a universe. It's a big sprawling space saga of rebellion and romance." Rebellion would indeed prove to be a major theme in the film, romance (as the audience was likely to understand the term) a little less so, though in retrospect the film clearly draws on the tradition of chivalric romance. In addition to introducing the term "saga," which would eventually be commonly used to describe the sum total of the *Star Wars* stories, the trailer described the film as a "spectacle light years ahead of its time" and an "epic of heroes and villains and aliens from a thousand worlds." The trailer not only showed viewers snippets of content, but also attempted to create a horizon of expectations for the film.

Even before the trailer was released, however, Lucasfilm was working hard to shape expectations over against the knowledge that a science-fiction film was likely to be a hard sell. According to *Empire of Dreams*, "Industry insiders had been predicting doom for *Star Wars*, but a small army of fans had been building, thanks to the foresight of Lucasfilm." The company hired Charles Lippincott, a science-fiction fan who, according to producer Gary Kurtz, had "contacts with the fan base that were critical" to create a marketing strategy for the first film, which proved to be highly successful. Kurtz believed that "science fiction fans were going to be the big supporters of this film, regardless of its popularity with any other audience. So that was the key target audience to start with."[28] Lucasfilm did most of the prerelease marketing itself, and Lippincott signed a comic book deal with Marvel Comics and convinced Del Rey Books to publish a novelization of Lucas's script in November 1976. By the following February, the print run of 500,000 copies had sold out.[29]

When the film was finally released, it was clear that *Star Wars* had an appeal that far outstripped that base of science-fiction fans. In a conversation with George Lucas at the 2015 Tribeca Film Festival, Stephen Colbert recalled his reaction as a thirteen-year-old boy seeing the film when it first came out:

> As soon as [the trumpet kick] came on and "Star Wars" appeared, we knew that everything was different. From the moment that those words appeared on screen and then the scroll came, and when the whole thing was over—we got to school on Monday … we couldn't explain to anyone how the world was different now! There was no way to convey a fresh representation of what sci-fi battles were, or what a space epic was. There wasn't a word for that, for us, we had no vocabulary for what you showed us.[30]

Lucas had shifted the horizon of expectations for a science-fiction film. He and Lucasfilm would go on to shift many more expectations as the *Star Wars* series continued.

The "scroll" to which Colbert refers, with its slanted letters receding upward into the distance, recalls the opening crawls of the Buck Rogers and Flash Gordon serials, particularly the 1940 serial *Flash Gordon Conquers the Universe*, which was one of Lucas's inspirations for *Star Wars* (see Figure 3). Like classical epic or tragedy, it places us in medias res—in the middle of an ongoing story, as if we were watching an episode from a longer serial:

> It is a period of civil wars in the galaxy. A brave alliance of underground freedom fighters has challenged the tyranny and oppression of the awesome GALACTIC EMPIRE.
>
> Striking from a fortress hidden among the billion stars of the galaxy, rebel spaceships have won their first victory in a battle with the powerful Imperial Starfleet. The EMPIRE fears that another defeat could bring a thousand more solar systems into the rebellion, and Imperial control over the galaxy would be lost forever.
>
> To crush the rebellion once and for all, the EMPIRE is constructing a sinister new battle station. Powerful enough to destroy an entire planet, its completion spells certain doom for the champions of freedom.[31]

In the sequel, *The Empire Strikes Back* (1980), the crawl is preceded by the words "Episode V," indicating that although this is only the second *Star Wars* film, it should be thought of as the fifth episode in a longer series. When the first film was re-released in the spring of 1981, the words "Episode IV" and the title "A New Hope" were added to the top of the crawl. The crawl would become one of the formal features that audiences would expect to see with each successive *Star Wars* film, and the stand-alone "anthology" films *Rogue One* (2016) and

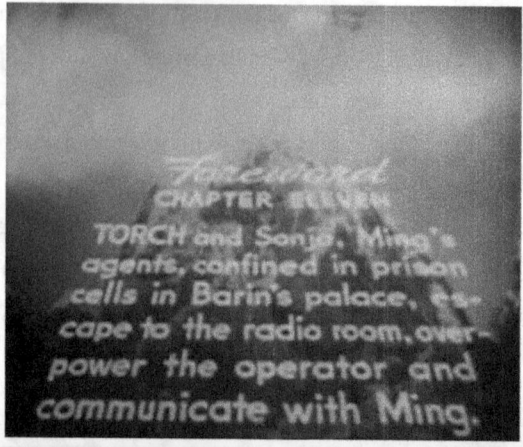

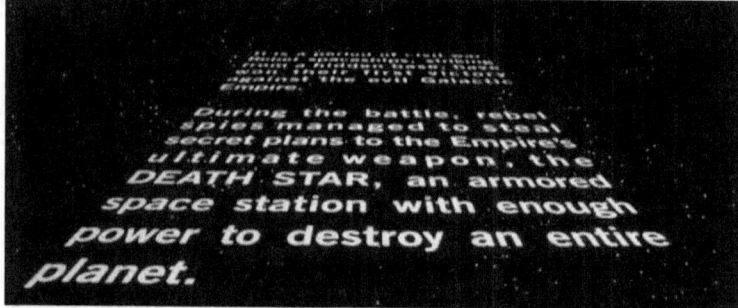

Figure 3 Comparing crawls. *Top:* The opening crawl from the eleventh episode of the 1940 serial *Flash Gordon Conquerors the Universe*, one of Lucas's inspirations for *Star Wars*. Photo credit: Universal Pictures. *Bottom:* The crawl from the original theatrical release of *Star Wars* in 1977. Photo credit: Lucasfilm. *Star Wars: Episode IV—A New Hope* directed by George Lucas © 1977 Walt Disney Pictures/Lucasfilm Ltd. All rights reserved.

Solo (2018) distinguished themselves from the nine-film Skywalker arc by not using a crawl at the opening.

The grand symphonic music that accompanies the crawl also links the film to the Flash Gordon serials, which used themes from "Les Preludes" by Franz Liszt to accompany its main title and other key moments. The music would prove to be a crucial mechanism for generating an emotional bond between *Star Wars* and its viewers, though it also required Lucas once again to challenge the prevailing horizon of expectations. In *Empire of Dreams*, composer John Williams says,

> I do remember George talking about the fact that what we were going to see in the film represents worlds that we hadn't seen, but that the music should give us some kind of emotional anchor. We heard a romantic melody for Princess Leia, we heard bellicose music for the battle scenes, and some very heavy declamatory thing for Darth Vader.[32]

At the same time, however, the use of the kind of music that Lucas believed could provide an "emotional anchor" was risky in the context of the movie music prevalent in the 1970s. According to *Empire of Dreams*, "Like *Star Wars* itself, the music in the film defied conventional wisdom. At a time when disco was burning up the charts, having a traditional symphonic soundtrack was another huge risk on Lucas's part."[33]

The information that the opening crawl conveys to us is important as well: we understand that the story we are about to watch is a story about a "brave alliance" of freedom fighters who are rebelling against a Galactic Empire that rules through "tyranny" and "oppression": it is a story, in other words, about the fight between liberalism and fascism that recalls not just the serials of the 1940s but also the world war that took place in those years as well. After a quiet moment in which we see only a dark star field, the camera pans down to reveal the bright surface of a planet, its curve filling the bottom of the screen. And then the screen explodes with sound and color as we see a spaceship flying from the upper right of the screen to a vanishing point near the center, pursued by laser bolts and then an enormous ship that keeps coming and coming, dwarfing the first ship and filling the area above the planet. This story may be taking place a long time ago, but the technology is what we associate with the future.

It's the technological sublime, but unlike the slow-moving spaceships in Kubrick's *2001*, which are accompanied by Johann Strauss's lilting "Blue Danube Waltz," *Star Wars* gives us an awesome technological vision that is kinetic, accompanied by Williams's ringing score. Once the camera cuts to the interior of the rebel ship, we hear the first lines of dialogue, spoken by a golden robot with a fussy voice, whose commentary reinforces the idea that we are watching one adventure in a series: "Did you hear that? They've shut down the main reactor. We'll be destroyed for sure. ... There'll be no escape for the Princess this time." The rebels, it seems, are led by a princess dressed in flowing white robes, while the Empire is led by a huge man—perhaps a cyborg—wearing a black helmet that recalls the armor worn by samurai and accompanied by the sounds of artificial breathing and melodramatic music. There's no question about who the viewer is supposed to root for.

At the outset, then, *Star Wars* presents itself as a story about political turmoil, about the fight for freedom, in which one side is clearly coded "good," the other "evil." The formal qualities of the opening scenes create a genealogy for the film but also set up a system of values for the audience. Only later in the film does the story take on the mythological resonances that Lucas studied in the work of Joseph Campbell.

The opening scenes create the kind of spectators that Martha Nussbaum associates with both tragic drama and the novel. In *Poetic Justice*, Nussbaum argues that the literary text can help us to cultivate a just public discourse within democratic societies:

> I make two claims, then, for the reader's experience: first, that it provides insights that should play a role (though not as uncriticized

foundations) in the construction of an adequate moral and political theory; second, that it develops moral capacities without which citizens will not succeed in making reality out of the normative conclusions of any moral or political theory.[34]

Nussbaum argues that "the literary imagination is a part of public rationality, and not the whole" (hence her remark above that literary reading cannot serve as an "uncriticized" foundation for moral and political theory). In this connection, she valorizes the novel above other forms because she believes "that the genre itself, on account of some general features of its structure, generally constructs empathy and compassion in ways highly relevant to citizenship."[35] For Nussbaum, "the mainstream realist novel" creates spectators in the same way that Aristotle argued for classical Greek tragedy:

> Like tragic spectators, novel-readers have both empathy with the plight of characters, experiencing what happens to them according to their point of view, and also pity, which goes beyond empathy in that it involves a spectatorial judgment that the characters' misfortunes are indeed serious and have indeed arisen not through their fault.

I suggest that these are exactly the kinds of spectators that the first *Star Wars* film creates as it presents its dramatic context and introduces us to its central characters—the droids, the Princess, Darth Vader, Obi-Wan Kenobi, and above all, Luke Skywalker—in its first act.

Although, as we will see, the creation of these kinds of spectators would prove to be a double-edged sword for the *Star Wars* franchise, understanding the ways in which the link between philosophy and storytelling hinges on forms of persuasion that arise from the associative logic of stories enables us to see what Lucas, Abrams, Jon Favreau, Dave Filoni, and their colleagues at Lucasfilm have sought to achieve in the *Star Wars* saga. Cinema can further enhance the associative logic of stories through its use of forms of persuasion that visual and musical representations make possible. Lucas knew how to manipulate the techniques of melodrama so that, for example, as soon as Darth Vader enters in *A New Hope* the audience has no doubt that he is a villain: Vader's character is conveyed not through exposition but through his black costume set against a predominantly white scene and through the use of a musical fanfare that signals "bad guy!" At that moment, what's important to the film is not how Vader became Vader but rather what it's like to encounter him as an antagonist. Chris Terrio, who cowrote the screenplay for *The Rise of Skywalker*, notes that "George Lucas has often said" that in *Star Wars* "you want to be dropped right into the action, in the tradition of those old 1930s Republic serials. The crawl is there to catch you up, but you just want to be dropped into the story."

In *The Rise of Skywalker*, Terrio and Abrams would keep exposition to a bare minimum, even going so far as to edit out lines of dialogue indicating that the resurrected Palpatine was a clone.[36] These are the kinds of details that some fans craved, but that Abrams deliberately omitted from the final edit. The film instead focuses the viewer's attention on what's important to Kylo as he confronts the resurrected Emperor: not how he was resurrected, but rather the fact that he *is* resurrected and still dangerously powerful. Describing *The Rise of Skywalker* as a revolutionary piece of "post-cinema," Travis Bean wrote in *Forbes* magazine that the film is built on the belief that "at the end of the day, 'plot' and 'logic' are not the reasons people deeply connect with movies. Those are standards critics have largely set for movies. But when you truly connect with a movie, it's because of the characters, the action, the philosophy of the film." In the *Star Wars* shared universe, those kinds of narrative details can be filled in by the supplementary forms of storytelling that accompanies the film (and

Rae Carson's novelization provides explanations that fill in most of what the film's critics regarded as "plot holes"). Bean argues that

> movies that are part of the post-cinematic movement tend to be much more reflective of reality and how we live our lives day to day. Oftentimes, we aren't concerned with where we are or how we got there, but instead with what we're doing and where it will lead. We live from moment to moment, and only afterwards are we able to contextualize our journey and find meaning.

That's the kind of experience that the film version of *The Rise of Skywalker* works to create. "Abrams," writes Bean, "disregards exposition and instead relishes in each fleeting moment, forcing the viewer to keep up with the 'now' as opposed to whatever brought characters there from the past. ... Abrams didn't rely on footage that satisfied our need for plot continuity—instead, *The Rise of Skywalker* focused on the emotional drive of the main characters." Bean argues that the film represents a shift away from the traditional rules of storytelling, an attempt to "create art that is completely unfamiliar and unique to the medium," which ended up discomfiting most film critics and many fans.[37] For Bean, Abrams's focus on "emotional drive" in the construction of his film points to the future of cinema. What it also points to is the recognition that filmmaking may be most philosophical in those moments when it leads its viewers away from logic and toward an empathic identification with its characters. Film, unlike traditional philosophical thought, harnesses the power not only of thinking but also of feeling.

2

From Lucas to Lucasfilm

The Power of Myth

When George Lucas talks about what he hoped to achieve in creating *Star Wars*, he speaks not about philosophy, but about mythology. In a 1999 interview with Bill Moyers, Lucas said, "When I did *Star Wars*, I consciously set about to recreate myths and the classic mythological motifs. And I wanted to use those motifs to deal with issues that existed today."[1] For the first *Star Wars* film, "today" meant the late 1970s and the disillusionment that gripped the United States in the aftermath of the Vietnam War and Watergate; indeed, the Emperor was originally conceived not as a dark wizard in black robes, but rather as a bureaucrat named Cos Dashit.[2] *Star Wars*, Lucas would say much later on, "was really about the Vietnam War, and that was the period where Nixon was trying to run for a [second] term, which got me to thinking historically about how do democracies get turned into dictatorships? [Because] democracies aren't overthrown; they're given away."[3] Lucas had originally been slated to direct *Apocalypse Now* and worked on its development with screenwriter John Milius at the same time that he was developing *Star Wars*. In fact, Lucas even went so far as to scout locations in the Philippines for *Apocalypse Now* with his producing partner, Gary Kurtz.

The Vietnam War was the first televised war, its images beamed into living rooms in the United States each night during the evening news hour. One of the most chilling moments in *Dispatches*, Michael Herr's landmark book of war reporting about Vietnam, which was published in 1977, occurs when a captain tells him, "Come on, we'll take you out to play Cowboys and Indians," an acknowledgment of the power of popular Hollywood films to shape the US cultural imagination. Conceiving of themselves as "cowboys" enabled the soldiers dropping napalm to think of themselves as the good guys in a Hollywood Western. "I think," wrote Herr late in the book, "that Vietnam was what we had instead of happy childhoods."[4] Herr would later collaborate on the screenplay for *Apocalypse Now*, writing Martin Sheen's world-weary voice-over.

Herr's comment suggests there was a dark side to Lucas's approach to *Star Wars* as a fairy tale, or rather, perhaps, that Lucas was intent on drawing on the dark side of fairy tales that we tend to forget if all we've seen is Disney's classic movie adaptations. (In "Aschenputtel," the story by the Brothers Grimm that became Disney's *Cinderella*, the wicked stepsisters cut off parts of their feet in order to fit into a golden slipper and end up being blinded by doves.) Creating a space fantasy instead of a black comedy about Vietnam (the original concept for *Apocalypse Now*) enabled Lucas to translate the moral ambiguities of events like the My Lai Massacre into more abstract, mythologized terms, while asserting that individuals can retain a sense of agency even in the face of the dehumanizing forces at work in the United States' approach to the Cold War. "What these films deal with," Lucas told Moyers, "is the fact that we all have good and evil inside of us and that we can choose which way we want the balance to go."[5] This idea lies behind the narrative arcs of the characters who undergo change in the *Star Wars* saga: Anakin Skywalker, Han Solo, Luke Skywalker, Lando Calrissian, Kylo Ren, and Rey.

Once he began the process of imagining a "galaxy far, far away," however, Lucas began to explore many different but interrelated ideas. *Star Wars* "was made up of many themes," he told Moyers, "not just a single theme." Among the ideas that fascinated him was "our relationship to machines," which can be "fearful" but only because "they're an extension of the human, not mean in themselves." The film would also allow Lucas to explore "issues of friendship and your obligation to your fellow man and to other people that are around you," as well as the idea "that you have control over your destiny." These are philosophical issues, but Lucas chose to explore them through the lens of mythology and the techniques of storytelling that can be traced back in the Western tradition at least to Plato's depiction of Socrates, whose famous cautionary tale about the dangers of reliance on writing in the dialogue *Phaedrus* begins with a story about the god Theuth, drawn from the annals of Egyptian mythology.

When Lucas tells Moyers that *Star Wars* is in part about exploring the idea that "you may have a great destiny" and that "if you decide not to walk down that path, your life might not be as satisfying as if you wake up and listen to your inner feelings," it's clear that another crucial context for understanding the genesis of *Star Wars* is Lucas's own upbringing and early adulthood. With its depiction of fraught relations between fathers and sons, and between mentors and protégés, *Star Wars* is a mythologized version of Lucas's own experience of rejecting the path chosen for him by his "first mentor," his father, George Walton Lucas, Sr., who wanted him "to go into the stationery business and run an office equipment store":

> He built it up for me and for me to take over, and he was pretty much devastated when I refused to get involved in it ... I got really

mad at him and just basically said, "You know, I'll never work at a job where I have to do the same thing over and over again every day." And he just didn't want to hear that.[6]

Lucas had attended the University of Southern California's (USC's) film school, but he calls Francis Ford Coppola, whom he met on the Warner Brothers lot in 1967, his primary mentor as a filmmaker.[7] At USC Lucas had been drawn to the technical side of film production: "When I was in college, I took a creative writing class, but I really didn't like it. My real thing was art, drawing, visuals. ... I was bored by scripts, and most of the films I did were abstract visual tone poems or documentaries—those were the things I really loved."[8] It was Coppola who had urged Lucas to work on his writing: "You're never going to be a good director unless you learn how to write," Coppola told Lucas. "Go and write, kid."[9] The two founded the independent studio American Zoetrope in San Francisco in 1969, which would go on to produce not only Coppola's post-*Godfather* films (starting with *The Godfather II* [1974], *The Conversation* [1974], and *Apocalypse Now* [1979]), but also Lucas's pre-*Star Wars* films, *THX 1138* (1971) and *American Graffiti* (1973).

The commercial failure of *THX 1138*, however, caused Warner Brothers to withdraw its loan to Zoetrope, which was saved only by Coppola's triumph in *The Godfather*. Lucas had begun working on the script for *American Graffiti* while finishing up *THX 1138*, in part as a response to Coppola's challenge to him to "make a happier kind of film."[10] It was during the preproduction for *American Graffiti* that Lucasfilm was born. In *Empire Building: The Remarkable Real Life Story of Star Wars*, Garry Jenkins describes the company's modest birth at a home office in Mill Valley, California:

> At the advice of his lawyer, Tom Pollock, Lucas created a company to hire out his services for tax purposes. With Gary Kurtz and his

secretary, Dorothy "Bunny" Alsup, he kicked around a number of ideas for a corporate name. "We were trying to come up with a generic name. It was going to be Mill Valley Films at one point," recalled Kurtz.

Another idea had been the English-sounding Lucasfilm Ltd. "He was a bit leery of it. He thought it was kind of an ego thing," said Kurtz. "But we thought we'd just call it that for the incorporation and worry about it later."[11]

Later never came, and Lucasfilm would survive as an entity even after its creator was no longer a part of it.

The deal that Lucas and Kurtz had struck with Universal Studios to make *American Graffiti* had included a second film, "a Flash Gordon thing." In April 1973, frustrated by the initial response of Universal executive Ned Tanen to the first cut of *American Graffiti* and short of cash while the accountants worked on the film's budget, Lucas started writing outlines for the "Flash Gordon thing." Lucas told Moyers that to make "progress" you need to work with "people that are more skilled in a particular area than you are."[12] In the areas of scriptwriting, directing, and producing, Lucas learned the ropes by working with Coppola and Gary Kurtz. (Years later, Lucas would play that kind of mentoring role for Dave Filoni, when the two worked together on *Star Wars: The Clone Wars*, which premiered in 2008.) On a lark, Lucas had tried to secure the rights to Flash Gordon from King Features in 1971, but (Lucas said later) "they wanted Federico Fellini to direct it, and they wanted 80 percent of the gross."[13]

Failing to get those rights was perhaps the best thing that ever happened to Lucas, because he was forced "to do something more original ... to do something totally new."[14] The idea that originality means doing something "totally new" is perhaps the result of Anglo-European Romanticism's conception of originality, and literary scholars have argued that we should think of originality as a process of revision rather than creation from whole cloth, of retelling old stories in new and innovative ways. This conception of originality as revision and retelling undergirded Lucas's approach to the idea of *Star Wars*, as he turned back to the stories and films that had inspired him when he was young. "He spent much of each day," writes Jenkins, "soaking up a diverse collection of influences. As well as rewatching the beloved Flash Gordon adventures of his childhood he read science fiction's old and new masters, from Edgar Rice Burroughs to Frank Herbert's *Dune* and E. E. 'Doc' Smith's Lensman stories."[15] From the beginning, he and Kurtz believed that they were creating a modern fairy tale: "A long time ago in a galaxy far, far away was our version of once upon a time," Kurtz later reflected.[16] Being "totally new" meant steeping oneself in the past, so Lucas read not only modern classics of fantasy by C. S. Lewis and J. R. R. Tolkien, but also *Grimm's Fairy Tales*; works of Indian and Islamic religion and mythology; anthropologist James George Frazer's classic comparative text *The Golden Bough: A Study in Comparative Religion* (1890); and Joseph Campbell's work on mythology in *The Hero with a Thousand Faces* (1949).[17]

It was Campbell who would become the mentor that Lucas needed for *Star Wars*. Lucas credits his friendship with Campbell with "exposing [him] to a lot of things that made me very interested in a lot more of the cosmic questions and the mystery." In *The Hero with a Thousand Faces*, Campbell delineates the contours of a story that he finds recurring throughout storytelling traditions across the world, using the portmanteau word "monomyth," which he found in James Joyce's *Finnegans Wake*:

> The standard path of the mythological adventure of the hero is a magnification of the formula represented in the rites of passage: *separation—initiation—return*: which might be named the nuclear unit of the monomyth.

> A hero ventures forth from the world of common day into a region of supernatural wonder: fabulous forces are there encountered and a decisive victory is won: the hero comes back from this mysterious adventure with the power to bestow boons on his fellow man. (italics in original)[18]

The original trilogy, which recounts Luke Skywalker's rise from a farm boy on a desert planet at the outskirts of the galaxy to a warrior able to defeat Darth Vader, follows this narrative trajectory. From a certain point of view—the view, say, of the dark side of the Force, the prequel trilogy charts this trajectory as well, as it dramatizes the transformation of Anakin Skywalker into a dark-sider second only to the Emperor himself.

Cosmopolitanism and Multidisciplinarity

From Campbell, Lucas developed an interest in "ideas that seem to cut across most cultures," a perspective that is apparent as soon as Obi-Wan and Luke walk into the cantina on Tatooine in *A New Hope*, but that deepens and becomes more nuanced as the saga develops. From late 1997 to early 1999, the Smithsonian Institution's National Air and Space Museum presented an exhibition called *Star Wars: The Magic of Myth*, which was "inspired by Joseph Campbell's story of the 'hero's journey' presented in *The Hero With a Thousand Faces*, and by comments on the *Star Wars* films in the book and video series *The Power of Myth*."[19] In the exhibition's companion volume, curator Mary Henderson describes the first *Star Wars* trilogy as "one of the great myths of our time" and notes that "a myth does not exist in a vacuum; rather, it captures the spirit and concerns of the particular time and place out of which it has sprung—yet it manages to do so in a timeless fashion."[20] Henderson suggests that "this apparent contradiction is possible because at heart, we are all asking the same questions. Certainly the mixture of elements—the universal in conjunction with the specific, the story rooted within a particular culture combined with the timeless tale for all humankind—is another magical aspect of myth."[21] The conjunction of the universal and the specific that Henderson describes is another way of describing the perspective that I call "cosmopolitan."

The narratives that comprise the *Star Wars* saga dramatize the virtues of cultural cosmopolitanism, but Lucasfilm itself represents a cosmopolitan approach to the production of knowledge. If cosmopolitanism is based on the idea of conversations across cultural boundaries, then a cosmopolitan approach to knowledge would be based on the idea of conversations across disciplinary boundaries. In the world of scholarship, the approach I'm describing would be *multidisciplinary* rather than *interdisciplinary*: scholars would be rooted in particular disciplines, but would engage in significant conversations and collaborations with practitioners of other disciplines. In the world of artistic creation, most of the performing arts draw on a variety of disciplines including writing, acting, dancing, music, and image creation through costume and set design. To this list, filmmaking adds cinematography and special effects. Thinking and conversing across boundaries not only creates cosmopolitan citizens of the world but also leads to inspiration and innovation.

From Aristotle to Averroës to Da Vinci to Steve Jobs, groundbreaking thinkers and technological innovators have practiced multidisciplinary approaches. Jobs told his biographer Walter Isaacson: "I always thought of myself as a humanities person as a kid, but I liked electronics. Then I read something that one of my heroes, Edwin Land of Polaroid, said about the importance of people who could stand at the intersection of humanities and sciences, and I decided that's what I wanted to do."²² Jobs brought an artistic, design-oriented sensibility to the production of technological innovation; the special-effects pioneers at Lucasfilm used technological innovation to enable Lucas to achieve the artistic design that would prove crucial to the success of the first *Star Wars* trilogy.

In *Industrial Light and Magic: The Art of Special Effects* (1986), Thomas G. Smith, who served as the general manager of Industrial Light and Magic (ILM) for five years, describes the deterioration of Hollywood's special-effects expertise by the time Lucas sought to make *Star Wars*. Smith notes that in the early 1920s, film studios had "built complete production facilities, providing practically every service for themselves within studio walls. ... Every studio budget form had a section devoted to 'tricks' (as effects were then called), and most films used them." These so-called tricks "could help cut the budget on set construction, reduce the number of extras needed in a crowd scene, and eliminate the need to go to distant locations." Valuable as they were, special-effects artists rarely received credit for the work, "for it was felt by the studios that the audience should not be told that tricks were used." In the 1950s, audiences' tastes were beginning to change: "Audiences had gotten used to seeing real places in newsreels and were no longer content to have the idealized versions portrayed by the studio artists." Shooting on location became the fashion, and the studios closed their special-effects departments. According to Smith, "between 1960 and 1970, an entire generation of craftsmen were lost in the motion picture industry. So it was that when *Star Wars* was in production in the mid-1970s produced in 1977, George Lucas had to set up his own shop."²³ He hired a group of young technicians that included John Dykstra, Patricia Rose Duignan, and Richard Edlund, to work on the film and dubbed the group "Industrial Light and Magic."

In *Industrial Light & Magic: Into the Digital Realm* (1996), Duignan and Mark Cotta Vaz, a senior writer for the journal *Cinefex*, describe the can-do spirit of the ILM team:

> Lucas emulated the studio effects departments of old by forming Industrial Light and Magic. The original ILMers themselves were perceived by many as an insurgent group, young (the average age was late twenties) and eager but unschooled in Hollywood ways. ... With the resourcefulness of film *noir* gumshoes, those first ILMers searched Hollywoodland for the tools—notably abandoned VistaVision format cameras and printers—with which to create a revolution in special effects.[24]

The standard sizes for film in the 1970s were 35 mm and 65 mm. Edlund describes VistaVision as "a large format 35 mm system that feeds film through the camera horizontally rather than vertically, so you end up with an image twice the size of normal 35." He chose VistaVision over 65 mm "because 35 mm film stock is easier to work with and the equipment is far less cumbersome." But the existing cameras needed to be modified to create the high framerates that were necessary to achieve the effects Lucas wanted.[25]

"What separated this generation most from previous ones," writes Smith, "was that they knew the power of computer technology and how to use it."[26] Dykstra, for example, would spearhead the creation of a computer-controlled motion control system for cameras that became known as "Dykstraflex": "We took archaic cameras, built before we were even born, and we created hybrids of them by bolting different parts together."[27] Built before the advent of personal computers, the Dykstraflex system enabled its operator to use a computer to control seven axes of motion and, according to Vaz and Duignan, "replaced the old method of flying a model on wires past a camera, with blue-screen photography, and programmable repeatable motion-control track camera systems." In his account of the making of *Star Wars* for the BFI Film Classics series, Will Brooker explains what the system could do in terms that fans can understand. Calling the designers at ILM "a cross between Chewbacca and the Jawas" in their ability to "piec[e] together ideas from other people's junk and [test] the limits of newly constructed equipment," Brooker writes that "the Dykstraflex could follow a precise trajectory towards, for instance, a miniature TIE fighter, and then repeat the exact movement again to capture the path of an approaching X-Wing. The two shots would then be superimposed with other layers into a composite dogfight."[28] Dykstra and his colleagues Jerry Jeffress and Al Miller would win an Academy Award in 1978 for their work on the system.

Although the ILM team would disband after completing work on *Star Wars*, the success of the film meant that Lucas was able to reconstitute ILM as a permanent enterprise once work on *The Empire Strikes Back* began. Lucas relocated ILM and other parts of Lucasfilm to Marin County just north of San Francisco, away from the cacophony of Hollywood, and set up the ILM workshop in San Rafael "not far from the old downtown business strip where Lucas had filmed some of *American Graffiti* in 1973."[29] Dykstra, however, would not rejoin the group, having clashed with Lucas after the director returned from principal shooting to find ILM way behind schedule. Lucas exerted more direct control over ILM, imposing a discipline that wasn't Dykstra's style.

The early history of ILM offers a case study in the difficulties that can accompany both cosmopolitan conversation and multidisciplinary approaches. There turned out to be a generational divide between Lucas and Dykstra and his team, and Lucas was uncomfortable with the looseness of Dykstra's approach, which seemed to privilege technological advances over the timely generation of usable footage.

Lucasfilm: The Next Generation

The generational divide that marked Lucasfilm's creation of Industrial Light and Magic would eventually come to mark Lucasfilm itself, when Lucas made the decision to sell his company, paving the way for the company to become the province of a new generation of filmmakers.

In October 2012, the Walt Disney Company acquired Lucasfilm and its subsidiaries (including ILM) for $2.2 billion in cash and $1.855 billion in Disney stock. During a recorded announcement, Disney chairman Robert Iger praised Lucas as

> a true visionary and an innovative, epic storyteller, who has defined modern filmmaking with unforgettable characters and amazing stories. ... We're thrilled that George has entrusted the future of his extraordinary legacy to the Walt Disney Company and recognize what an honor it is. We truly understand the responsibility that comes with being the caretakers of such iconic characters that are beloved by hundreds of millions all over the world.

During his portion of the announcement video, Lucas said, "I've been a big fan of Disney all my life" and noted that the two companies were a perfect match because Lucasfilm is "like a mini-Disney" with "the same kind of operations." Lucas revealed that he'd been thinking about retiring for the previous four years and had invited Kathleen Kennedy, with whom he'd worked for forty years, to become cochairman of Lucasfilm in anticipation of her taking over the company and the *Star Wars* franchise. He chose Kennedy because he wanted to have the franchise move forward but needed to have "somebody I trusted who could take that franchise and make it work the way I intended it to." Lucas noted that he and Kennedy had been working with writers on future *Star Wars* films and had "a plan for VII, VIII, and IX, which is the end of the trilogy, and other films also."[30]

The announcement, which took place while the New York Stock Exchange was closed because of Hurricane Sandy, was something of a surprise, and the *New York Times* wrote that during "a hastily convened conference call with investors late Tuesday, Mr. Iger said Disney planned to revive the *Star Wars* franchise and release a seventh feature film in the series in 2015, with new films coming every two or three years thereafter." Iger reassured investors that Lucas would serve as a consultant on the film projects and said that Disney had received a detailed treatment for the next three *Star Wars* films as part of the acquisition.[31] During the video announcement, Iger noted that "the *Star Wars* universe now has more than 17,000 characters, inhabiting several thousand planets, and spanning 20,000 years, and this gives Disney infinite inspiration and opportunities to continue the epic *Star Wars* saga."

Disney would soon decide, however, that it was wiser for the creative talents at Lucasfilm not to be bound by the stories that had been told as part of the authorized "Expanded Universe." In 2014, an article on the *Star Wars* website noted that "while Lucasfilm always strived to keep the stories created for the EU consistent with our film and television content as well as internally consistent, Lucas always made it clear that he was not beholden to the EU." What fans referred to as the "G-Canon" included the six *Star Wars* feature films and the first six seasons of the television series *Star Wars: The Clone Wars* (2008–2014), with which Lucas was heavily involved. According to the website, "These stories are the immovable objects of *Star Wars* history, the characters and events to which all other tales must align." Moving forward, a new Lucasfilm Story Group would "oversee and coordinate all *Star Wars* creative development," across films, television series, books, comic books, games, and what Kennedy called "new formats that are just emerging." The website made it clear that the sequel trilogy "will not tell the same story told in the post-*Return of* the Jedi Expanded Universe." The EU stories would, however, remain in print, recategorized as "*Star Wars* Legends."

The writers and artists who created books, comics, and games for the Expanded Universe worked in careful coordination with each other and with Lucasfilm, in part through the efforts of Leeland Chee, who created and maintained a database of *Star Wars* facts referred to, appropriately, as "the Holocron," after a term (short for "holographic chronicle") invented by author Tom Veitch for his *Dark Empire* series of comic books.[32] Chee revealed that with the decision to make three new *Star Wars* movies to continue the story of the Skywalkers, one particular plot point within the Expanded Universe became problematic. In an interview with SyFy, Chee explained:

> For me it came down to simply that we had killed Chewbacca in the Legends—a big moon had fallen on him. Part of that [original decision] was Chewbacca, because he can't speak and just speaks in growls, he was a challenging character to write for in novels. Publishing had decided they needed to kill somebody, and it was Chewbacca.
>
> But if you have the opportunity to bring back Chewbacca into a live action film, you're not gonna deprive fans of that … There's no way that I'd want to do an Episode VII that didn't have Chewbacca in it and have to explain that Chewbacca had a moon fall on his head. And if we were going to overturn a monumental decision like that, everything else was really just minor in comparison.[33]

As a practical point, Chewbacca's character could provide the same kind of continuity between stories as the droids C-3PO and R2-D2: because he could be played by any actor with the requisite stature to wear the costume, the stories wouldn't have to account for any visible aging.

But if the sequel trilogy wasn't going to be an adaptation of the stories told in existing novels, it also wasn't going to be bound by the treatments that Disney had acquired from Lucas. In an interview with director James Cameron, Lucas said that his version of the sequel trilogy would have focused on the "microbiotic world" of the midi-chlorians, which he introduced into the *Star Wars* universe with *The Phantom Menace*:

> There's this world of creatures that operate differently than we do. I call them the Whills. And the Whills are the ones who actually control the universe. They feed off the Force.
>
> Back in the day, I used to say ultimately what this means is we were just cars, vehicles, for the Whills to travel around in. ... We're vessels for them. And the conduit is the midi-chlorians. The midi-chlorians are the ones that communicate with the Whills. The Whills, in a general sense, they are the Force.[34]

A trilogy based on that idea would have been very different from the two trilogies that had come before it, and Lucas (who found it harder to let go of *Star Wars* than he perhaps anticipated) blamed Disney (in an interview with Charlie Rose in 2015) for the direction in which it chose to take the franchise: "They wanted to do a retro movie. I don't like that. Every movie, I worked very hard to make them ... completely different—different planets, different spaceships to make it new." In a fit of pique, for which he later apologized, Lucas likened what he had done in selling the *Star Wars* films to Disney to selling his kids to "white slavers." The way in which Lucas described his feelings about not being involved with the production of *The Force Awakens* makes it clear how hard it was for Lucas to let go:

> They decided they didn't want to use those stories; they decided they were going to go do their own thing. ... They weren't that keen

to have me involved anyway, but at the same time I said, if I get there, I'm just going to cause trouble, because they are not going to do what I want them to do, and I don't have the control to do that anymore, so all I'll do is to muck everything up. So I said okay, I will go my way, and I will let them go their way.

And it really does come down to a simple rule of life, which is, when you break up with somebody, the first rule is: no phone calls. The second rule, you don't go over to their house and drive by to see what they're doing. The third one is you don't show up at their coffee shop or other things. You just say, no, go on, history; I'm moving forward, because every time you do—and we all learn this from experience—every time you do something like that you're opening the wound again, and it just makes it harder for you. You have to put it behind you, and it's a very, very, very hard thing to do. But you have to just cut it off and say, OK, end of ball game, I got to move on.

Lucas describes *Star Wars* as the story of a family—a "soap opera" more than a "space opera"—and the terms in which he describes leaving it to his heirs are very much couched in the metaphors of family.[35]

But the passing of *Star Wars* from Lucas's Lucasfilm to Disney's Lucasfilm is hardly a case of King Lear ill-advisedly leaving his kingdom and his fate in the hands of his "thankless" children. For one thing, as a result of the deal, Lucas has far more resources and freedom to do what he wants than the old king did. And the creative talents who have inherited Lucas's kingdom—directors like J. J. Abrams, Rian Johnson, Dave Filoni, Jon Favreau, Deborah Chow, Bryce Dallas Howard, Rick Famuyiwa, Patty Jenkins, and Taika Waititi—cherish it and are immensely grateful to Lucas for having conceived and nurtured it, even if they have found the task of developing it further more than a little daunting. Rian Johnson, the director of *The Last Jedi*, said in an interview, "I grew up not just loving *Star Wars*, I went to the film school I went to because I read a book about George Lucas and saw he went there."[36] Dave Filoni, who worked with Lucas on the *Clone Wars* animated series before moving on to *Rebels* and then *The Mandalorian*, says, "I felt privileged to be a part of telling the story; I felt grateful that I got to do it with George."[37] Howard, who directed the fourth episode of *The Mandalorian*'s first season and the eleventh episode of the second, says,

> I've always been in awe of *Star Wars* and the magic of that. What George has always done is bring collaborators in and see where you might go and take this. He really understood that the characters are meant to expand in ways that George might not even predict, and he's always been inclusive in that way. He's always wanted to push the story in directions that include other storytellers.[38]

Famuyiwa, who directed three episodes during *The Mandalorian*'s first two seasons, suggests that "what was always cool about *Star Wars* was that it was a galaxy, and therefore as a kid growing up, I always felt that there were stories in that galaxy that I could be a part of telling, even if it was just me and my friends, or me by myself with my action figures."[39] Favreau, who serves as the showrunner for *The Mandalorian* and two of its spin-offs, reveals, "*Star Wars* was a big influence on me: it came out in 1977, and I was born in '66, so I was right at the right age for that thing to hit. ... My tastes formed around George Lucas's *Star Wars*."[40]

If conceiving the first *Star Wars* film was George Lucas's greatest moment of inspiration, perhaps (in retrospect) the second greatest was the decision to let it go, to pass the torch to filmmakers for whom *Star Wars* was formative influence. Reviewing *The Last Jedi* for the *New York Times*, Manohla Dargis described Lucas's prequel trilogy as "pretty much a drag outside of some fleet light-saber duels and the arresting black-and-red patterning that distinguishes one villain" and argued the passing of the baton was a very good thing for the franchise:

> What has already made the new trilogy more successful is that its directors, J.J. Abrams ("The Force Awakens") and Mr. Johnson, are technically adept, commercially savvy *Star Wars* true believers who came of age in the post-Lucas blockbuster era. Each has had to navigate the intricacies of Mr. Lucas's sprawling fiction while handling the deep imprint created by Darth Vader's heavy-breathing menace, R2-D2's amusing beeps, Mr. Ford's insouciance, Mr. Hamill's earnestness, and Ms. Fisher's smarts and latter-day screwball charm. Unlike Mr. Lucas, though, Mr. Abrams and Mr. Johnson don't feel burdened by that legacy; they're into it, charged up, despite the pressures of such an industrial enterprise. They're resolving their cinematic father issues with a sense of fun.[41]

A December 2015 article in *Esquire* described Abrams as "the scion of the very movies he is now making," contending: "He is not just reanimating *Star Wars*. He is what *Star Wars* begot."[42]

More than anyone else, Abrams, who directed both Episodes VII and IX, served as the initial face of what we might call "Next-Gen Lucasfilm" (see Figure 4). Abrams, however, was at first reluctant to accept Kennedy's offer to direct Episode VII, even though he had been a *Star Wars* fan since the age of eleven—perhaps *because* he had been a *Star Wars* fan since the age of eleven. He told Kennedy that he had too many commitments, given his leading role in the rebooting of the *Star Trek* franchise, and he also preferred to turn his attention to original projects. But, the story goes, Kennedy persisted and hooked him by asking a simple question: "Who *is* Luke Skywalker?" Kennedy told *Entertainment Weekly*: "He said, 'Oh my God, I just got the chills. I'm in.' … I mean, it really was almost that quickly." Jettisoning the Expanded Universe meant that to all intents and purposes, the new trilogy would *be* an original project. At the time he signed on, Abrams recalled, the team of writers that Kennedy had assembled, which included Michael Arndt, Lawrence Kasdan, and Simon Kinberg,

> had just been hypothesizing and throwing out a bunch of what-ifs, but there was no story in place. It was, without doubt, a formidable assignment. There were so many options and so many paths that could be taken. Even when we were in debate—and sometimes it was frustrating and heated—it was always thrilling, because it seemed almost everywhere you looked there was something potentially extraordinary, which felt very much like the DNA of *Star Wars* itself.[43]

Figure 4 George Lucas and J. J. Abrams at the premiere of *The Force Awakens* in 2015. Photo credit: Frazer Harrison. Getty Images.

Perhaps because he came from the collaborative creative practice of filmmaking rather than, like *Harry Potter* author J. K. Rowling, from the solitary practice of novel writing, Lucas always seemed willing to let others play in the universe he had created, within certain limits. And, when it came time to create the prequel trilogy, he was willing to draw on ideas that others had contributed to the development of the *Star Wars* universe. For example, the name of the Empire's capital planet, "Coruscant," which became canonical when it was used in *The Phantom Menace*, actually first appeared in the first Expanded Universe novel, Timothy Zahn's *Heir to the Empire* (1991). In the rough draft of the script for *Return of the Jedi*, the planet is called "Had Abbadon."[44] Lucas would later say, "I had a million different names for the home planet of the Empire, but Coruscant came out of publishing."[45] Robert Iger was right when he described the "17,000 characters, inhabiting several thousand planets, and spanning 20,000 years" of the Expanded Universe as a source of "inspiration": even after the restriction of the *Star Wars* canon in 2014, characters and other ideas from the Expanded Universe have continued to appear in new *Star Wars* stories. The announcement on the official *Star Wars* website about the change in the canonical status of the Expanded Universe reassured fans that

> creators of new *Star Wars* entertainment have full access to the rich content of the Expanded Universe. For example, elements of the EU are included in *Star Wars Rebels*. The Inquisitor, the Imperial Security Bureau, and Sienar Fleet Systems are story elements in the new animated series, and all these ideas find their origins in roleplaying game material published in the 1980s.

Rebels (2014–2018) would later make prominent use of the blue-skinned Grand Admiral Thrawn, the central antagonist of Timothy Zahn's trilogy of novels, which began the Expanded Universe. *The*

Force Awakens drew on the Expanded Universe idea that Han and Leia were married and that a child of theirs would turn to the dark side. Ron Howard's film *Solo* is particularly full of "Easter egg" references to names and places from the Expanded Universe.[46] "Legends," in fact, seems like an appropriate name for this "rich content," as new *Star Wars* authors and directors draw on it as a body of lore in much the same way that Lucas himself drew on the lore that he discovered in the mythologies analyzed by Joseph Campbell.

In fact, for Next-Gen Lucasfilm directors Dave Filoni, J. J. Abrams, and Rian Johnson, growing up in the late 1970s and 1980s, the original *Star Wars* trilogy itself felt like a set of mythological stories, because the films were not yet readily available for home viewing. Filoni remembers that "back then ... you didn't have VHS or DVDs or any way to watch the movies over and over again. So we had the records, and the records were a big deal: *The Story of Star Wars* or *The Story of the Empire Strikes Back*, and we'd listen to those records over and over again. And we had the soundtracks."[47] Abrams reports that for him "the weirdest moment" during the production of *The Force Awakens* "was the first time I sat down with John Williams to show him about a half an hour of the movie. I can't describe the feeling. All I will say is, just to state the facts of it: I am about to show John Williams 30 minutes of a *Star Wars* movie that he has not seen that I directed." Abrams describes Williams's music as

> the DVD or Blu-ray of my childhood because we didn't, of course, have VHS tapes of movies to watch when we wanted to. So I would buy John Williams soundtracks, often for movies I had not seen yet, and I would lie on the floor in my room with my headphones on listening to the soundtracks which would essentially tell me the story of the movie that I didn't know. And I'd look at the photographs on the back of the album and I tried

to read what I could about the movie—but really, I would just listen to these soundtracks.[48]

In *The Art of Star Wars: The Last Jedi*, Rian Johnson reminds us that *A New Hope* was not released on the home video formats until 1982, and even then, at $79.99 it was priced for purchase by video stores rather than home users (see Figure 5):

> "I remember when we got the VHS for *Star Wars* from the video store," Johnson said. "We had our friends over, and we would watch it for twelve hours straight, over and over, until we had to give it back. There'd be like a three-month waiting list to get it. …
>
> I had the records. I had the storybooks. I had the holiday album. I had anything I could get that had to do with *Star Wars*. But one thing we didn't have was the movie. Largely, it was talking with your friends about the movie, pooling information and memories of it. And so it was a very strange and mythological experience of *Star Wars*. It mythologized the films in a very powerful way because, like God's absence, the actual object of your worship was not there. … So you and your friends end up studying the sacred texts and philosophizing about it. I hadn't really thought of it that way before, but that might be part of the reason why, in a way that can be hard to explain, *Star Wars* feels like such a powerful myth of our childhoods. Maybe it's because we couldn't see the actual movies.[49]

For these filmmakers, then, not only the "Legends" material that once comprised the Expanded Universe, but also the *Star Wars* films themselves play a role analogous to the one that Joseph Campbell's monomyth had played for Lucas, providing both an aura of mythology and a wellspring of stories from which to draw.

Part of the reason for the success of *The Mandalorian*, which unified a fan base that was divided by differing responses to the sequel

Figure 5 VHS Rental Edition of *Star Wars*. Rian Johnson: "I remember when we got the VHS for *Star Wars* from the video store. We had our friends over, and we would watch it for twelve hours straight, over and over, until we had to give it back. There'd be like a three-month waiting list to get it." Photo credit: Cyrus R. K. Patell. Collection of the author.

trilogy, was that it not only drew inspiration from the traditions that had inspired the first *Star Wars* films (such as the Western and the samurai film) but also paid homage to the Lucas's work through recreations of elements from the original films—some small, like the use of an ice cream maker that became a famous prop in *The*

Empire Strikes Back; some large, like the recreation of Jabba's throne room. In addition, Jon Favreau ad Dave Filoni incorporated fan-favorite characters from the original films (most notably Boba Fett), from the animated television series *Clone Wars* and *Rebels*, and even from novels such as Chuck Wendig's *Aftermath* into *The Mandalorian*.[50] Favreau and Filoni's approach to the series was to see it as a collaboration among directors and writers who were fans of Lucas's films and to acknowledge implicitly that *Star Wars* has always been a transmedia phenomenon.[51] Director Robert Rodriguez's creation of a home video featuring his sons in Boba Fett and stormtrooper Halloween costumes and handheld *Star Wars* action figures to dramatize his ideas for the arrival of Boba Fett in chapter 14 of *The Mandalorian* exemplifies this approach to filmmaking—as does Filoni's response: "Wait a minute: were those just action figures I saw? ... No, you don't understand: that makes it the coolest animatic ever."[52]

The first two trilogies were the product of a reluctant auteur—George Lucas—who recognized that filmmaking was ultimately a deeply collaborative enterprise and therefore created a corporation—Lucasfilm—and a subsidiary—Industrial Light and Magic—to help him realize his cinematic vision, a vision so palpable and capacious that it created legions of fans, including some who would go on to participate as filmmakers in the extension of that imaginative space into a "shared universe." The story of Lucasfilm is the story of how that vision gave birth to a corporate person that can be productively viewed as both "filmmaker and philosopher."

The idea of the corporate person became a flashpoint in US politics in 2010, when the Supreme Court decision *Citizens United v. Federal Election Commission* struck down limits on corporate expenditures in federal elections, overruling *Austin v. Michigan Chamber of Commerce* (1990), because (as Justice Anthony Kennedy put it writing for the majority) *Austin* "interferes with the 'open marketplace' of ideas protected by the First Amendment."[53] Corporate legal scholar Kent Greenfield argues that

> when the Supreme Court decided in *Citizens United v. Federal Election Commission* that corporations have a First Amendment right to spend unlimited amounts to influence elections, the decision quickly joined the rogues' gallery of despised Supreme Court rulings. As many as 80 percent of Americans believed the decision was wrong, and President Obama scolded the justices to their stony faces during a subsequent State of the Union address. Constitutional amendments to overturn the decision, and indeed take away all constitutional rights of all corporations, gathered steam.

In Greenfield's view, the answer to curbing the abuse of the electoral process by corporations is not to overturn the legal doctrine of corporate personhood, but rather to ensure that corporations actually become more like people "through a set of governance reforms that adjusts corporate decision making in ways that bring it closer to the good decision making of humans." Acknowledging that "the social and institutional purpose of the corporation ... is to make money over time," he argues that "many corporations have other reasons to exist as well" and offers the example of the *New York Times*, which "exists to make money, but it also has the purpose of producing the principal newspaper of record in the United States. The people who make up the *New York Times* corporation have organized themselves around an idea that is more than just making money."[54]

Lucasfilm is just such a corporation. Its goal is to make money to be sure, but it also exists to nurture and grow the shared universe that George Lucas created. The foreword that Lucas's anointed successor, Kathleen Kennedy, wrote for a volume dedicated to highlighting the importance of women in the *Star Wars* stories makes reference to the various products that Lucasfilm sells, but it also adopts a tone that suggests that making money isn't the most important part of the enterprise:

> In *Star Wars*, we are fortunate to have such a broad platform from which to tell our stories. In addition to films, there are animated series, novels, comics, games, and more. It's a testament to George's vision that what he began as a story to inspire, we continue to embrace as a beacon of empowerment and hope.[55]

That platform turns out to be a platform not only for storytelling, but for philosophizing as well.

3

Reversal and Recognition, Exile and Return

"No. *I* am your father."

The twist that comes in the climactic confrontation between Luke Skywalker and Darth Vader in *The Empire Strikes Back* is a marvelous example of the combination of reversal and recognition that Aristotle described as the high point of tragedy in his treatise the *Poetics*. When I first saw *The Empire Strikes Back* on the day of its premiere, which happened to be the day after my first-year college exams were finished, I suddenly understood, in a visceral way, the feeling that Aristotle was trying to describe when he used the terms "pity and fear" to describe the idea of *katharsis*. I'd studied the *Poetics* and puzzled over the descriptions of *katharsis* in both high school and college, but it was only while watching *The Empire Strikes Back* that I truly experienced the emotion. I'd come close one summer some years before during a staged version of *Oedipus Rex* on the steps in front of Columbia University's Low Library. When the actor playing the tragic king came back on stage with red ribbons billowing from the eyeholes of the white tragic mask he was wearing, I'd felt a frisson of dread, but the experience of watching Vader's revelation was far more powerful for me because I was invested in Luke and Vader in a way that I hadn't been for Sophocles's characters.

My two sons never had that moment of reversal and recognition. For the older, it was because of Lego. For the younger, it was because of the older. Let me explain.

We were visiting friends in New Haven one afternoon in the summer of 2003 when my older son was not quite three years old, and we were cycling through television channels looking for a baseball game. "Who is that black man?" my son asked, as an image of Darth Vader filled the screen. I decided on the spot that Vader would be too scary for him, so I said, "Nobody important," and changed the channel. He wasn't happy, but he went back to playing with his friend's Lego set—his first encounter with the plastic bricks. A few days later, my wife bought him his own little Lego set—Knights of Morcia, I believe—and thus began the Lego era in our household, which eventuated in our possessing literally tens of thousands of pieces. My son soon became interested in the Lego website, and I would look at it with him. He learned how to use the trackpad, and one afternoon, he saw a picture of Darth Vader on the site with a caption that read "The Story of Anakin Skywalker." Before I could stop him, he had clicked through, and four minutes later he'd basically been exposed to the key scenes in the Star Wars saga from *A New Hope* through *Attack of the Clones*. There was no dialogue, and the story, which was told in three parts with flashbacks and other temporal jump cuts, was enigmatic, but I was pretty sure he came away with one key piece of information: that the "black man" was Anakin Skywalker—which meant, of course, that he would always know that Vader was Luke's father (see Figure 6). When it came time to watch *The Empire Strikes Back*, there'd be no reversal and no recognition. His brother was born the next year and of course became privy to his older sibling's *Star Wars* knowledge. It

Figure 6 Luke surrendering himself to his father Darth Vader in the Lego short film *The Story of Anakin Skywalker*. No reversal and recognition for my kids! *The Story of Anakin Skywalker* (2002), directed by James Hutchinson. Photo credit: Lego/Lucasfilm.

was a point of some bitterness for the older one that I made him wait until he was seven to watch *Revenge of the Sith*, but the younger one (who saw it soon after) was only three.[1]

I later realized, however, that it didn't matter about the reversal and recognition. That was an experience that relatively few people would ever have, and in fact it was Lucas's contention that fans should eventually watch the movie in narrative order. Watching the films in that way means that the moment of reversal and recognition is still a moment of reversal and recognition for the characters, but no longer for the audience. In fact, that viewing order transforms the viewer's experience not only of *The Empire Strikes Back* but also of the entire original trilogy: the audience that has seen *Revenge of the Sith* first meets Luke and Leia with a sense of dramatic irony, because that audience knows that Vader is their father and that they are brother and sister. It's still the logic that drives *Oedipus* insofar as Sophocles's original audiences were familiar with Oedipus's backstory and spent the play waiting for him to discover it as well.

The secrecy surrounding the filming of the moment of recognition is by now legendary, so at first it puzzled me that there was comparatively little secrecy about the plot of *Revenge of the Sith*, the third movie in the saga, but the sixth to be released. *Revenge* came out in the United States on May 19, 2005, but the novelization was published on April 2 and the video game based on the film was released on May 4. What I began to realize is that secrecy about the plot was not an issue for this film, because Lucas was now explicitly following the logic of tragedy: the prequel trilogy was dramatizing the downfall of a hero, the transformation of the supremely gifted Anakin Skywalker—believed by some to be the "Chosen One" of Jedi legend—into the archvillain Darth Vader. Reflecting later on what he sought to achieve in the prequel trilogy, Lucas commented about how the original trilogy had failed to get across a portion of the "backstory" that he felt was crucial to an understanding of the larger story that he wanted to tell:

> It wasn't until *Jedi* came out that I realized I'd lost the tragedy of Darth Vader. In *Star Wars*, it's set up as "What is that guy? Is he a monster? Is it a robot?" They didn't know what he was. Over the three films his story dissipated. He was the chosen one of the prophecy, yet the irony was lost that it was the son bringing back to the father. It wasn't clear.
>
> I felt the story of Anakin Skywalker had enough pathos and enough of a story to enrich the prequels: how Anakin became a Jedi; how he learned to use the Force; the dark side of the Force; the light side of the Force, and midi-chlorians; this is where Obi-Wan came from; this is what their relationship was; how Anakin turned into Darth Vader.

For Lucas, the story of the prequels was: "How does this nice little kind kid, who has good intentions, is just like us, go wrong and become Darth Vader?"[2]

For the audiences who had seen the original trilogy, Anakin's fate was set, in much the same way that Oedipus's fate was set. Robert Fagles describes what classical audiences expected from the plots of tragic plays:

> Though the details of these traditional stories varied considerably from one teller of the tale to another (and especially from one city to another), and though the dramatist could (and often did) invent new variations, the main outlines of the best-known stories were fairly stable—Oedipus always kills his father and marries his mother, Eteocles and Polynices must kill each other. The dramatist who used his material derived a double benefit from the audience's knowledge of the stories: he could either lull them into expecting the familiar—and so increase the shock effect of some radical innovation in the story—or, renouncing surprise, he could pose the ignorant pronouncement of his characters against the audience's knowledge of their future and so produce dramatic irony.[3]

In the case of *Revenge of the Sith*, the question of how the story will unfold has less to do with plot than with an element of tragedy that Aristotle downplayed in his *Poetics*: spectacle, in this case the cutting-edge special effects and elaborate starship battles and lightsaber fights that all lead to the climactic duel between Obi-Wan and Anakin, which Anakin would lose. But just how would that duel actually unfold on the screen? And how would it feel to experience that already-iconic moment in a movie theater with a wide screen and thunderous sound? That was the element of surprise for the initial audiences of *Revenge of the Sith*, and it turned on spectacle.

I've used *Star Wars* to illustrate Aristotle's *Poetics* in undergraduate lectures, as a way of getting across what I believe to be one of Lucas's goals in creating the *Star Wars* saga: to create a mass entertainment that was the late twentieth century's equivalent for the Athenian tragedy of the late fifth century BCE. Fagles writes that during the festival of Dionysus in classical Athens, at which the god "was honored by performances, in the theater, of dithyrambs (lyric hymns sung and danced by a chorus of fifty), tragedies, and comedies," the audience "was, by our standards, immense; the theater building of the late fifth century, to judge from its ruins, could seat between fourteen and fifteen thousand spectators. They sat in rows that rise one above the other on the rocky southeastern slope of the Acropolis." These festivals, however, were not only religious celebrations, but also "an aspect of the city's political life," and their organization reflected the city's democratic principles: the dramatic competition's prizes were awarded by "ten judges, elected on the opening day by lot and sworn to impartiality." The orphans of warriors slain in battle were honored at these festivals, as were foreign leaders. The first three performances on each day were always tragedies, which evoked a mythic past but also the city's present. "These myths were the only national memory of the remote past," writes Fagles. "The stuff from which the tragic poet made his plays was not contemporary reality but myth. And yet it did reflect contemporary reality, did so perhaps in terms more authoritative because they were not colored by the partisan emotions of the time, terms which were in fact so authoritative that they remain meaningful for us even today."[4] Sophocles's *Oedipus* tells us a mythical story, but it also portrays a city suffering from a plague, and its first audiences had just experienced the trauma of a plague. Lucas's first *Star Wars* film may have invoked the mythic archetypes he studied in the work of Joseph Campbell, but as we have seen, it is clearly also "about" the moment in which it was conceived, marked inexorably by the cultural traumas of the Vietnam War and the Watergate scandal.

Despite the fact that it is really an incomplete set of lecture notes rather than a polished manuscript, Aristotle's *Poetics* has set the terms of debate for discussions of tragedy, whether classical, Shakespearean, or modern, and we can use it to understand the narrative dynamics of the Skywalker saga. It's important to remember that Aristotle was studying what was for him already a set of classic texts: the great age of Athenian drama was the fifth century BCE, and Aristotle wrote his study at least a century later. Aristotle, writes Jonathan Barnes, was "a thoroughgoing 'empiricist' in two senses of that slippery term. First, he held that the notions or concepts in terms of which we seek to grasp and explain reality are all ultimately derived from perception; ... Secondly, he thought that all science or knowledge is ultimately grounded on perceptual observations." Aristotle adopted the same method in attempting to understand how tragedy worked that he used when approaching the natural sciences: "As a biologist," writes Barnes, "Aristotle's primary research tool was sense-perception, his own or that of others; as an ontologist, Aristotle's primary substances were ordinary perceptible object."[5] Anthony Kenny argues that Aristotle's "considered opinion is that a poet is a craftsman, as befits the name of his trade; for *poiesis* in Greek is literally 'making'. Consequently, the advice that he offers is concrete and technical, about the choice of characters to represent and the internal structure to give to the plot."[6]

The goal of the *Poetics* is to bring to light the *tekhne* underlying the greatest tragedies. Although the term is generally defined as "art," "craft," or "skill," Malcolm Heath argues that "Aristotle defines *tekhne* as a productive capacity informed by an understanding of its intrinsic rationale (cf. *Nicomachean Ethics*, I 140a2of.)." and notes that, for Aristotle, understanding of *tekhne* is not necessarily something that even successful dramatists have: in section 54 of the *Poetics*, Aristotle "suggests that early dramatists discovered the best stories to use in tragedy by chance rather than by tekhne (54a9-12); trial and error established a repertoire of first-rate tragic stories, but the dramatists would not have been able to explain why those stories were best (as Aristotle thinks he can)."[7]

Let us remember that Aristotle defined tragedy as "an imitation of an action that is admirable, complete and possesses magnitude; in language made pleasurable, each of its species separated in different parts; performed by actors, not through narration; effecting through pity and fear the purification of such emotions." "Purification" is the term that translator Malcolm Heath uses to approximate *katharsis*, a term that appears only this one time in the text of the *Poetics* that survives. Heath points out that the term also appears in the *Politics*, during "a discussion of various uses of music," but that "there Aristotle says that he need give only a brief account, since he has discussed it in more detail in his *Poetics* (1341b38-40)."[8] Aristotle notes that comedy and epic are also forms of imitation: comedy "aims to imitate people worse than contemporaries," while tragedy imitates those who are "better"; epic resembles tragedy in its portrayal of "admirable people," but where tragedy "tries so far as possible to keep within a single day, or not to exceed it by much," epic "is unrestricted in time."[9] Epic thus does have an advantage over tragedy:

> Epic has an important distinctive resource for extending its length. In tragedy it is not possible to imitate many parts of the action being carried on simultaneously, but only the one on stage involving the actors. But in epic, because it is narrative, it is possible to treat many parts being carried on simultaneously; and these (provided that they are germane) make the poem more impressive. So epic has this advantage in achieving grandeur, variety of interest for the hearer and diversity of episodes; similarity quickly palls, and may cause tragedies to fail.[10]

But what might look like a liability for tragedy turns out to be a strength in the hands of the greatest dramatists: the necessity to pick and choose events carefully for inclusion in a play, to depict moments that rise to a certain level of "magnitude," leads to action that is more "concentrated" and therefore "more pleasant." In my reading of the *Poetics*, there is a link between this concentration and the achievement of the tragic effect of *katharsis* and the evocation of pity and terror. If the genres were to be ranked, tragedy seems, for Aristotle, to come out ahead of epic: "Anyone who understands what is good and bad in tragedy also understands about epic, since anything that epic poetry has is also present in tragedy, but what is present in tragedy is not all in epic poetry."[11]

One way of understanding how these ideas help us think about *Star Wars* is to see that Lucas is using both the archetypes that he discovered in Campbell and the cinematic archetypes with which he grew up to create a set of mythological stories that provided him and his successors at Lucasfilm with the kinds of imaginative resources that the ancient Greek dramatists had. To tell the story of Anakin Skywalker and his children, Lucas needed to create a backstory that involved an Old Republic and an ancient rivalry between the Jedi and the Sith, only some of which would be explored in the prequel trilogy. (Those stories would be explored by a host of licensed collaborators in the "Expanded Universe" of books, comics, and video games that was fully inaugurated with Timothy Zahn's bestselling *Heir to the Empire* in 1991 and that was given the status of "Legends" in the post-Disney era.) In choosing to start with the story of how Luke, Leia, and Han destroy the first Death Star, Lucas begins in medias res, as both classical Greek epics and tragedies do, leaving it to the audience to fill in the gaps—or at least to imagine that those gaps could be filled in, as it hears Obi-Wan refer early in the film to "the Clone Wars" and the betrayal and murder of Luke's father. With the 1977 *Star Wars*, Lucas chose a story within the set of stories that he was imagining, and the story he chose is what Aristotle's *Poetics* describes as a "whole": it possesses a certain magnitude by virtue of being the rebellion's first great victory and having a clearly defined beginning, middle, and end.

Having a clearly defined beginning, middle, and end is a prerequisite for a well-constructed *plot*, which Aristotle regards as the most important element for a successful tragic drama, followed in declining order of importance by character, reasoning, diction, lyric poetry, and spectacle. Aristotle argues that "the most important devices by which tragedy sways emotion are parts of the plot, i.e. reversals and recognitions," and a "complex" plot will involve at least one of these and ideally both.[12] Aristotle defines a "reversal" (*peripeteia*) as "a change to the opposite in the actions being performed ... in accordance with probability or necessity."[13] Heath notes that this definition is notably vague and "is emphatically not to be equated with the tragic change of fortune: a change of fortune is a characteristic of all tragic plots, simple as well as complex, while reversal is distinctive to complex plots."[14] I like to think of reversal as what literary scholars call *situational irony*, which is a plot development that involves a disjunction between what either the characters or the viewer expects to happen and what actually does happen. "Recognition" (*anagnorisis*) is, for Aristotle, "a change from ignorance to knowledge, disclosing either a close relationship or enmity, on the part of people marked out for good or bad fortune. Recognition is best when it occurs simultaneously with a reversal, like the one in the Oedipus."[15] For Aristotle, a tragedy is "complex" when it "depend[s] entirely on reversal and recognition."[16]

In *A New Hope*, Luke has been told by Obi-Wan that "a young Jedi named Darth Vader, who was a pupil of mine until he turned to evil, helped the Empire hunt down and destroy the Jedi Knights. He betrayed and murdered your father."[17] After Vader cuts off Luke's right hand during their lightsaber confrontation in *The Empire Strikes Back*, he says, "Obi-Wan never told you what happened to your father." Luke, in anguish, responds with the knowledge that he has been given: "He told me enough. He told me you killed him." When Vader reveals the truth, Luke responds with agonized disbelief: "That's not true. That's impossible!" What Vader has told him is the last thing that Luke—or the audience at the film's premiere—expected to hear. That audience included the film's cast. Mark Hamill later recalled:

> When we were shooting the climactic scene with my confrontation with Darth Vader, Irvin Kershner, the director, pulled me aside one day. He said, "I'm going to tell you something now. I know it, George knows it, and when I tell you, you'll know it. And the reason I'm putting it to you this way is that, if it leaks, we'll know it was you. ... In the script that was printed for the crew and for David Prowse, who was playing Darth Vader, the climactic twist was: "You don't know the truth. Obi-Wan killed your father." And then it was just as you see in the movie: I go, "NOOOO." ... And when you think of it, it's a pretty good twist.

But the real twist was even better: "I was just stunned. ... What a great, great twist! And I had to keep it a secret for like—between filming it and it coming out. The first time it was screened, Harrison turned to me and said, 'You never told me that.'"[18]

Until that moment it would have made little sense to think about *A New Hope* in the light of Aristotle's theory of tragedy. With its mystical wizard and its daring rescue of a princess in distress, the first film clearly drew on elements of fantasy and chivalric romance, but to think about it in terms of tragedy would have required placing too much emphasis on the death of a supporting character, Obi-Wan Kenobi. Moreover, his demise lacks the teleological finality that we associate with tragedy, given that he seems to be able to reach out from beyond the veil of death to exhort Luke to escape on the *Millennium Falcon* and then to offer Luke crucial advice and encouragement as he tries to destroy the Death Star.

The Empire Strikes Back was itself an act of reversal and recognition: it transformed the first film from a whole into a part—a beginning—

while providing a middle with a downbeat cliffhanger that promised a third part—an end—in order to create a new whole, and it led viewers to recognize that *Star Wars* was something much more—much deeper and potentially darker—than the uplifting fantasy that had enthralled the world three years earlier. The rare sequel that outdid its predecessor, *Empire*, is, by popular consensus, still the greatest of the *Star Wars* films, in part because of the way it raised the thematic complexity of the series to a new level.

Some familiar characters are transformed into tragic figures in the prequel and sequel trilogies. We don't really get to know Qui-Gon Jinn well enough to think of him as truly tragic, but over the course of three films we get to know Obi-Wan Kenobi quite well. Even as we see Anakin Skywalker rise and then fall, so too do we see Obi-Wan rise from being a Padawan in the first film, to a Jedi Knight in the second, to a Jedi Master in the third. And the combat between Obi-Wan and Anakin becomes a battle between two tragic heroes that—I believe intentionally—reminds us of the fatal conflict between Eteocles and Polynices, the sons of Oedipus. Why else have Obi-Wan say, "You were my brother, Anakin. I loved you" after the fight is over? The prequel trilogy thus creates additional poignance and significance in the final meeting between Obi-Wan and his former Padawan in *A New Hope*. Likewise, Han Solo is transformed into a tragic hero in *The Force Awakens*, playing a role analogous to the role Obi-Wan played in *A New Hope*: he is mentor to a future Jedi and sacrifices himself near the end of the story. And what could be more classically tragic than the fact that he is killed by his own son? We are reminded, perhaps, of the final lines of Sophocles's *Oedipus*: "Therefore one should never say a mortal man / is prosperous while he still waits to look upon his final day, / until he passes life's last limit having suffered no distress."[19]

The third film in the original trilogy, *Return of the Jedi*, adds a further level of complexity with the revelation that Leia is actually Luke's sister and Darth Vader's daughter, transforming the trilogy into a family saga in which a son, aided by a daughter, finds a way to redeem a father. The story of the Skywalkers thus resembles the kinds of mythic stories about royal and noble families that animate Greek tragedies and epics. In his discussion of the best kinds of tragic plot, Aristotle stipulates that the ideal tragic hero should be someone who "is one of those people who are held in great esteem and enjoy great good fortune, like Oedipus, Thyestes, and distinguished men from that kind of family" and that the plot must trace the protagonist's passage from "from good fortune to bad fortune—and this must be due not to depravity but to a serious error on the part of someone of the kind specified (or better than that, rather than worse)." He notes that "at first poets used to pick out stories at random; but nowadays the best tragedies are constructed around a few households, e.g. about Alcmeon, Oedipus, Orestes, Meleager, Thyestes, Telephus and any others whose lot it has been to experience something terrible—or to perform some terrible action."[20] Luke invokes the Skywalker lineage when he reveals to Leia that she is his sister:

> **LEIA:** Luke, don't talk that way. You have a power I ... I don't understand and could never have.
> **LUKE:** You're wrong, Leia. You have that power too. In time you'll learn to use it as I have. The Force is strong in my family. My father has it ... I have it ... and ... my sister has it. (ellipses in original)

This discussion recasts Luke's seeming crush on Leia in *A New Hope* and the kiss between them in *Empire* as a narrative thread that in a classical Greek tragedy might have led to dire consequences. Here it serves to set in motion the idea that there is something powerful in the Skywalker bloodline.

This idea is taken up by Rian Johnson in *The Last Jedi* with both Snoke and Kylo Ren invoking the strong connection between the

Skywalkers and the Force. Snoke chides his apprentice: "The mighty Kylo Ren. When I found you, I saw what all masters live to see: raw, untamed power. And beyond that, something truly special—the potential of your bloodline. A new Vader. Now I fear I was mistaken." Kylo later describes himself as if he belonged to one of the legendary houses of Greek myth that furnished stories for ancient singers and dramatists, while chiding Rey for her apparently humble origins:

> We can rule together and bring a new order to the galaxy. ... Do you want to know the truth about your parents? ... They were filthy junk traders who sold you off for drinking money. They're dead in a pauper's grave in the Jakku desert. You have no place in this story. You come from nothing. You are nothing. But not to me.

In his hubris, Kylo believes that he and only he can give Rey's life significance, conveniently forgetting that his grandfather, Anakin Skywalker, began life as slave.

Although some critics and a few fans relished the idea of the democratization of the Force that a "Rey from Nowhere" might represent, *The Rise of Skywalker* reveals, in keeping with Aristotle's idea of magnitude, that there is more to the story of Rey's bloodline than Kylo was able to see at first after touching her mind in *The Last Jedi*. "Do you know why the Emperor wants you dead?" Kylo asks Rey during one of his encounters with her through their shared Force bond in *The Rise of Skywalker*. In a dialogue that is punctuated by moments of rage as Rey swings her lightsaber at Kylo, he tells her the truth he has learned: "I never lied to you. Your parents were no one. They chose to be. To keep you safe. ... They sold you to protect you. ... It was Palpatine who had your parents taken. He was looking for you. But they wouldn't say where you were, so he gave the order." Later, when Rey asks him, "Why did the Emperor come for me? Why did he want to kill a child?" Kylo reveals: "Because he saw what you would become. You don't just have power. You have *his* power. You're his granddaughter. You are a Palpatine."[21] In *The Skywalker Legacy* (2020), the behind-the-scenes documentary about the making of *The Rise of Skywalker* that accompanied the home video release of the film, co-screenwriter Chris Terrio recalls, "We knew there would be a *Heart of Darkness*-y structure to the movie, and that this would be about Rey's journey to the darkest place, both for the galaxy and for her." The problem was how to figure out "how the past would come into the story, how the present and future would interact with that past." Having Palpatine somehow survive his apparent demise in *Return of the Jedi* solved that problem: "Within about 30 seconds of discussing that idea, we just knew that it was the right idea, because we knew that this has always been a story of Skywalkers and Palpatines." Abrams adds, "It's a generational story. And the idea of the story of these grandchildren grappling with the same things that their predecessors had dealt with: it just felt poetic."[22]

In developing this idea further, Terrio and Abrams decided that the connection between Kylo and Rey should be deepened beyond what Rian Johnson had portrayed in *The Last Jedi*, and they turned to a concept—what Terrio calls "the mythic dyad"—that Joseph Campbell mentions while discussing the idea of marriage in an interview that appears in *The Hero's Journey* (1990).[23] In what is new information for the audience about the workings of the Force, Kylo reveals to Rey that he and she are "a dyad in the Force ... two that are one." Together they can have unprecedented power: "We'll kill him together and take the throne. You know what you need to do." *The Rise of Skywalker* thus reworks the idea of twinship from *Return of the Jedi*, raising the stakes to create a bond across lines of enmity between noble houses. Ben Solo turns out, like his grandfather, to be a tragic hero, committing unspeakable acts after his fall to the dark side, including the taboo act of parricide. He is, however, redeemed at the end by his parents through the power of love. His parents sacrifice themselves to set him on the path to redemption. In embracing the light once more, Ben Solo finally proves himself worthy of his uncle's lightsaber and completes his training as a Jedi by sacrificing himself for his Force twin, Rey.

Meanwhile, the sequel trilogy sets up Rey's turning to the dark side as one possible future, indeed one that has been revealed to her in a series of Force visions, culminating in *The Rise of Skywalker*'s depiction of a "Dark Rey" who wields a double-bladed Sith lightsaber. Where Oedipus is undone by his ignorance of his genealogy, Rey is preserved by her ignorance, learning the truth only when she has gained the confidence, the skills, and the relationships that enable her to regard family not as destiny but as choice. This revelation transforms the nine-film saga into the story of two families imbued with extraordinary powers—the Skywalkers and the Palpatines—ultimately representing two different worldviews, the Jedi and the Sith. The title of the final film, in retrospect, tells us which house ultimately prevails. It's an epic struggle worthy of Greek mythology.

Hamartia and Hubris

One of the enigmatic key terms in Aristotle's *Poetics* is "hamartia," which is popularly referred to as "the tragic flaw." Scholars, however, have offered differing interpretations of the term, some suggesting that it represents a moral flaw, others suggesting it should be regarded as an intellectual error that has magnified repercussions when it is committed by a character with the kind of magnitude that tragic drama typically depicts. Arguing that "Aristotle's attempt to prescribe the best kind of tragic plot is therefore not as narrowly prescriptive as it may seem at first sight," Heath suggests that the term "hamartia" includes both "errors made in ignorance or through misjudgment" and also "moral errors of a kind which do not imply wickedness."[24] Oedipus, for example, is often seen to be flawed because of his hubris, the overconfidence that leads him to believe that he can defy divine prophecy and also solve problems like the riddle of the Sphinx or the source of the plague that is besetting Thebes at the start of Sophocles's play. Without that confidence, Oedipus would not be heroic, but his overconfidence ultimately leads to his demise.

The Skywalker saga includes examples of both kinds of hamartia. Anakin Skywalker in the prequel trilogy is powerful in the Force but also passionate in his emotions and his attachments. He is understandably afraid to lose his mother in *The Phantom Menace* and then to lose his beloved, Padmé, in the next two films. Unable to save his mother in *Attack of the Clones*, he gives in to a rage that leads him to massacre the Tusken Raiders who have held her in captivity, his first step toward succumbing to the dark side. Afterward, he and Padmé have a conversation that reveals the extent of Anakin's hubris:

ANAKIN: Life seems so much simpler when you're fixing things. I'm good at fixing things. Always was. But I couldn't— Why'd she have to die? Why couldn't I save her? I know I could have!

PADMÉ: Sometimes there are things no one can fix. You're not all-powerful, Ani.

ANAKIN: Well, I should be! Someday I will be. I will be the most powerful Jedi ever! I promise you. I will even learn to stop people from dying.

Palpatine tells Anakin in *Revenge of the Sith* that "the dark side of the Force is a pathway to many abilities some consider to be unnatural." Anakin has had visions in which Padmé dies in childbirth. Believing that conquering death is possible but arbitrarily forbidden by the Jedi,

Anakin falls prey to Palpatine's suggestion that by following the Sith way he will be able to save his beloved. Although he tells Palpatine that "the Jedi are my family," he ultimately puts his love for Padmé above the Jedi and believes Palpatine's claim that embracing "the power of the dark side" will give him the "power to save Padmé." In an irony worthy of Greek tragedy, it is precisely Anakin's embrace of the dark side that leads Padmé to the fate that Anakin had sought to avoid. Anakin is flawed but not wicked: his turn to evil has its origins in good intentions, but these are corrupted by his hubris. (As the third film in its trilogy, *The Rise of Skywalker* deliberately echoes not only *Return of the Jedi*, but also *Revenge of the Sith*. The opening crawl of the final film declares: "The dead speak! The galaxy has heard a mysterious broadcast, a threat of REVENGE in the sinister voice of the late EMPEROR PALPATINE." Palpatine uses the same line about "unnatural" abilities to explain his return to Kylo Ren and tries to use the same logic about turning to the dark side to protect one's family with Rey. She, unlike Anakin, isn't convinced, in part because she doesn't share his hubris.)

The Last Jedi, in contrast, explores the other kind of hamartia: the intellectual error that has dire consequences because of the stature of the figure who makes the mistake. Luke Skywalker had learned in the original trilogy that there is still good in Darth Vader and that conviction led to Vader's redemption and the defeat of the Emperor. By the beginning of the sequel trilogy, however, we find that Luke's life has not turned out as expected. In *The Force Awakens*, Han tells Rey and Finn why Luke has disappeared: "He was training a new generation of Jedi. One boy, an apprentice, turned against him, destroyed it all. Luke felt responsible. He walked away from everything." We soon learn that this apprentice was not just any apprentice: it was Ben Solo, Han and Leia's son and Luke's nephew. We learn more about the circumstances of Luke's failure in *The Last*

Jedi, when he calls his former belief that he could train Ben to be a Jedi "hubris" and describes his nephew's fall to the dark side:

> I saw darkness. I'd sensed it building in him. I'd see it at moments during his training. But then I looked inside, and it was beyond what I ever imagined. Snoke had already turned his heart. He would bring destruction, and pain, and death—and the end of everything I love because of what he will become. And for the briefest moment of pure instinct, I thought I could stop it. It passed like a fleeting shadow. And I was left with shame—and with consequence. And the last thing I saw were the eyes of a frightened boy whose master had failed him.

It's an error that has massive consequences for the galaxy, driving Ben Solo into the arms of Snoke and the First Order to become Kylo Ren. Luke then loses hope and disappears to Ahch-To, where he comes to believe that "the legacy of the Jedi is failure, hypocrisy, hubris. At the height of their powers," he tells Rey, "they allowed Darth Sidious to rise, create the Empire, and wipe them out. It was a Jedi Master who was responsible for the training and creation of Darth Vader." For these reasons, Luke swears, "I will never train another generation of Jedi. I came to this island to die. It's time for the Jedi to end." In contrast to the self-imposed exiles of Obi-Wan and Yoda, which are about protecting hope for the future, Luke's exile is about abandoning the past and losing hope. It is Rey who reminds Luke that it was also a Jedi who saved Darth Vader: she takes up the mantle that Luke once wore, arguing about Kylo, as Luke once had about Vader, that there is still good in him, that the Ben Solo in him still survives. "You failed him by thinking his choice was made," she tells Luke: "It wasn't. There is still conflict in him. If he turned from the dark side, that could shift the tide. This could be how we win." And eventually, in the climactic moments of *The Rise of Skywalker*, Rey's belief is affirmed.

Luke does find redemption, in part through Rey's influence and in part through the influence of his master, Yoda, who reappears as a Force ghost to cure Luke of his despair. In *The Rise of Skywalker*, Luke returns the favor to Rey, when she is on the brink of despair after discovering her true lineage and battling Kylo Ren on the ruins of the second Death Star.

LUKE: What are you doing?
REY: I saw myself on the dark throne. I won't let it happen. I'm never leaving this place. I'm doing what you did.
LUKE: I was wrong. It was fear that kept me here.

Commenting on Luke's character arc in *The Skywalker Legacy* documentary, Mark Hamill says, "The theme of redemption is important not just in *Star Wars*, but in life. I mean, no one's perfect. Jedi make mistakes. I think it's comforting the idea that despite having done wrong, either intentionally or unintentionally, they're able to write those wrongs and be forgiven."[25] Before giving her Leia's lightsaber, Luke tells Rey what he once learned and has now learned again: "Confronting fear is the destiny of a Jedi. *Your* destiny. If you don't face Palpatine, it will mean the end of the Jedi. And the war will be lost." What Luke conveys to Rey is a way to avoid hamartia. It helps that she isn't burdened by hubris.

Revenge or Return

The title for the third *Star Wars* film was originally intended to be the title with which it was eventually released: *Return of the Jedi*. But during production the title was changed to *Revenge of the Jedi*. Producer Howard Kazanjian would later recall: "George came to me and he said, 'The title of Episode VI is *Return of the Jedi*.' And I said, 'I think it's a weak title.' He came back one or two days later and said, 'We're calling it *Revenge of the Jedi.*'"²⁶ But five months before the release of the film, despite the fact that considerable publicity had been done using the title *Revenge of the Jedi*, Lucas changed his mind and returned to the original title. His reason: "Jedi don't take revenge." It didn't matter to Lucas that a toy licenser like Kenner would have to destroy $250,000 worth of packaging. "Philosophically, it's correct," Lucas explained to his marketing people. "'Revenge' has a ring about it that I think isn't right for this movie. It's negative and Jedi don't seek revenge. A Jedi Knight can't understand that as a concept of behavior."²⁷

The title of the third film calls attention to an important fact about the narrative arc that Lucas creates in the original trilogy: over against the logic of tragedy evoked by the climactic scene of *The Empire Strikes Back*, Lucas superimposes the logic of exile and return, which is commonly associated with the genre of romance in Western literature and which lies at the heart of the monomyth that Campbell discusses in *The Hero with a Thousand Faces*. Early in *A New Hope*, when Obi-Wan presents Luke with his father's lightsaber, he describes it as "an elegant weapon for a more civilized day."²⁸ What we discover by the end of *Empire* is that the surviving members of the Jedi Order—Obi-Wan and Yoda—are in self-imposed exile. It turns out, however, to be exile with a purpose, devoted to guarding the seed from which the Jedi Order might once again return.

Exile-and-return narratives tell the story of the making of the hero, while tragedy tells the story of the unmaking of the hero. Often, however, the distinction between them isn't that hard and fast. I mentioned earlier that the genre to which we assign the story of Anakin Skywalker's transformation into Darth Vader depends on our point of view. It's a tragedy as far as most of us are concerned, because it represents a fall into the dark side. But Emperor Palpatine would see it precisely the other way around, though that is a perspective that the films don't really allow their audiences to have. Likewise, for Kylo Ren in *The Force Awakens*, the events of the original trilogy represent a tragic arc, in which a great man is defeated, his mission left uncompleted. "I will finish what you started," Ren says, staring at the burnt remnants of his grandfather's helmet. In *The Rise of Skywalker*, however, Kylo corrects his understanding of his grandfather's arc. In returning to his identity as Ben Solo, he does indeed help to finish what his grandfather started: returning balance to the Force. Ben Solo's story is yet another invocation of exile and return.

Even in the story of Oedipus—perhaps *the* epitome of classical tragedy—we find elements of exile and return. One way of understanding the story of Oedipus is that it is a tragedy precisely because its hero doesn't realize that he is part of an exile-and-return story. As a child, subject to a prophecy claiming that his destiny is to kill his father and marry his mother, Oedipus is sent away from his native Thebes, ostensibly to be left to die. He survives, however, and is raised in another royal court, where he eventually hears the prophecy. Trying to avoid his fate, an act of compassion for his adoptive parents that is also an act of arrogance, Oedipus exiles himself, but that exile turns out instead to be a return to his native land. Before he arrives there, he performs an act that looks like magic, ridding Thebes of a plague by answering the riddle of the sphinx. To use Campbell's terms, Oedipus wins a "decisive victory" and "comes back from this mysterious adventure with the power to bestow boons on his fellow man." And he is elected king, a happy outcome were it not for that little misadventure along the way, in which Oedipus (experiencing perhaps an ancient form of road rage) kills an older man who turns out to be not only the King of Thebes, but also his father.

Thinking about *Star Wars* through the lenses of Aristotle's *Poetics* and the narrative logic of exile and return helps us to understand why certain moments in the *Star Wars* saga provide narrative cruxes that resonate well after we are finished watching the films. If the exile-and-return paradigm is the story of the making of the hero, while the tragic paradigm is the story of the unmaking of the hero, then these narrative paradigms also ask us to think about what it means to be a hero. They ask us to think about the nature of free will and human agency, and about the nature of fate or destiny. The Sith, far more than the Jedi, speak about destiny as if it were somehow unavoidable, adopting the position of the gods and their oracles in the shared universe of Greek tragedy. "You are fulfilling your destiny, Anakin," says Palpatine after Mace Windu's death. "Become my apprentice. Learn to use the dark side of the Force." Vader tells Luke, "You can destroy the Emperor. He has foreseen this. It is your destiny. Join me, and together we can rule the galaxy as father and son. Come with me. It is the only way." Luke defies the idea of destiny at this moment and then again when he has defeated Vader in front of the Emperor. "Good!" Palpatine exults. "Your hate has made you powerful. Now, fulfill your destiny and take your father's place at my side!" Once again, Luke resists the Sith conception of destiny: seeing the analogy between his father and himself, he throws down his lightsaber and replies, "Never! I'll never turn to the dark side. You've failed, your Highness. I am a Jedi, like my father before me." The Jedi believe in the freedom to choose, to make your own destiny. In the shared universe of Greek tragedy, such a belief is hubris, a defiance of the gods, and it is punished. In the shared universe of *Star Wars*, such a belief is the road to redemption.

Luke's renunciation of violence here is emblematic of the Jedi philosophy. Despite their prowess with the lightsaber, the Jedi are pacifists and, for the most part, reluctant warriors. "Wars not make one great," Yoda tells Luke in *The Empire Strikes Back*.[29] Obi-Wan in *A New Hope* and Luke at the end of *Return of the Jedi* show us that part of being a warrior is knowing when you must put aside your weapon, because fighting and violence are not the answer. Luke helps the Resistance—and especially the "trigger happy flyboy" Poe Dameron—to learn this lesson at the end of *The Last Jedi*, when he buys the Resistance's survivors the time they need to escape so that they can continue the battle another day. In *The Rise of Skywalker*, Rey uses her training in the ways of the Force—and Luke's and Leia's lightsabers—defensively, reflecting the Emperor's own destructive powers back on him, as Mace Windu tried unsuccessfully to do in *Revenge of the Sith*.

The *Star Wars* universe offers a platform for a discussion of the conflict between the claims of free will and those of destiny, but it ultimately promotes a point of view that embraces the power of human agency. Using theories drawn from psychology and sociology, Lucasfilm's traveling exhibition *Star Wars: Identities* restages this discussion as a consideration of the relative effect that nature and nurture have on a person's development. The exhibition's curators take their cue from the fact that Lucas deliberately patterned the prequel trilogy after the original trilogy: Anakin and Luke both grow up on Tatooine and both come under the influence of the Jedi and the Sith. The choices they make, however, are radically different. According to the introduction to the exhibition:

> The notion of identity has fascinated us for a long time. Throughout the ages, poets, painters, anthropologists, and psychologists have all wrestled with what it means to be *someone*, to be *yourself*, to be *unique*.
>
> *Star Wars* is very much about identity. Luke Skywalker's journey is about finding out who he really is and then becoming that person. Anakin Skywalker struggles with the person he thinks he should be, or could be, until finally he gives in to the person he feels he has to be and becomes Darth Vader. They are father and son; they

hail from the same planet and have many of the same abilities. But where Luke continued to fight for good, Anakin turned to the dark side. To understand why, we have to take a long look at their individual identities.[30]

In his introduction to the volume, Lucas indicates that to make the "fantasy world" of *Star Wars* believable, the characters "need to be identifiable so that the audience can connect to them." As a result, "these larger-than-life characters come complete with friends, enemies, values, and beliefs."[31] They are, in other words, embedded within a network of social relations and ideologies. Visitors to the exhibition are guided through ten areas devoted to different factors that go into the making of an identity:

Origins: species, genes, parents, culture
Influences: mentors, friends, events
Choices: occupation, personality, values

The exhibition uses concepts drawn from identity theories to illuminate *Star Wars*, even as it uses models, props, and images from *Star Wars* to illustrate these concepts. At the start of the exhibition, the visitor is asked to choose an avatar from a range of species; at each station, the visitor is asked to make a choice concerning one of the factors listed above. At the end, visitors get to see the characters they have created.

What emerges is an illustration of the ways in which biology is not destiny, which is instead largely a product of the choices we make in the contexts of our social networks. *The Rise of Skywalker* makes this idea the foundation for its climax—and thus the climax of the saga—as Rey rejects her bloodline—Palpatine—in favor of the larger family that the events of the three films have enabled her to develop: her adoptive parents and mentors, Luke and Leia Skywalker; her friends

Finn, Poe, Chewbacca, and BB-8; and beyond them, the thousand generations of Jedi that live in her.

Poor Oedipus. How different his fate might have been had he been part of the shared universe that is *Star Wars* rather than the shared universe of Aeschylus, Sophocles, Euripides, and ancient Athens.

4

Melodrama

In October 2013, Disney Interactive Studios announced that it would be releasing a game called *Tiny Death Star*, which had been created by the US game developer Nimblebit, based on the company's successful game "Tiny Tower." Like its predecessor, "Tiny Death Star" was a business simulation game, in which players would manage the construction of the Death Star and its development into a commercial center. The Death Star businesses were run within the game by "galactic bitizens" [*sic*] using a currency called "Imperial Credits," which were earned by selling products or by trading "Imperial Bux," the game's link to the real world of the gamer. Imperial Bux were in-game purchases that gamers could make to enable them to complete construction projects or product orders more quickly, to unlock aspects of the game, or to upgrade elements within it. Bitizens were sorted into such categories as "Bounty Hunters," "Cantina Crew," "Droids, "Hutt's Henchmen," "Ladies of the Rebellion," "Men of the Rebellion," "Rebel Aliens," or "Troops." The game was buggy from the start and eventually pulled from the various app stores in October 2014.

What was notable about the game within the *Star Wars* universe, however, was its depiction of the everyday side of life on the Death Star that did not appear in the movies. Michael Reeves and Steve Perry's novel *Death Star* (2007), a part of Lucasfilm's Expanded Universe set of novels and now part of its noncanonical "Legends" series, also explores the intrigues that surround the construction of the Death Star, giving life to the base in a way that the films do not. In both *A New Hope* and *Return of the Jedi*, the Death Stars were depicted as military bases and legitimate, indeed necessary, targets for destruction by the Rebellion. In the first film, the destruction of the Death Star was clearly a form of self-defense: the Empire had located the Rebel Base and was seconds away from using the Death Star to obliterate it, as it had obliterated the planet Alderaan earlier in the film. In order to function, however, military bases need nonmilitary personnel such as service workers and (*Tiny Death Star* suggests) businesspeople. When the Death Stars were destroyed, these nonmilitary personnel were collateral damage. When audiences cheered the massive explosions of the Death Stars, they were also cheering death of these people. But the films actively prevent their audiences from even thinking along those lines by drawing on the logic and techniques of melodrama, which promotes a black-and-white Manichean view of the world, with a clear separation between good and evil.

This chapter examines the ways in which the *Star Wars* universe uses melodrama in part because melodrama is one of those techniques of persuasion that is not typically available to philosophy. If we are interested in thinking about what resources film has that philosophy does not, then melodrama might serve as a useful case study. Melodrama is a blunt tool that enables viewers to realize quickly who the "good guys" and "bad guys" are in the world of a film. Greenblatt's analysis of textual dynamics asks us to pay attention to structures of praise and blame in two genres where it is easy to detect those structures: panegyric and satire. Melodrama is another form in which it is easy to detect structures of praise and blame. But just as Greenblatt complicates his argument by telling us that these structures can be found in all literary texts and that we must pay attention to the interplay between them, so too does the *Star Wars* universe complicate its use of melodrama. *Star Wars* appears to set up a moral system that is black and white, only then to complicate it by allowing gray areas to appear when we think closely about what we have seen.

The term "melodrama" is derived from the late eighteenth-century French word *mélodrame*, but its roots lie, like those of tragedy, in Greece during the fifth century BCE. The etymology of the term is combination of the Greek μέλος (melos) meaning "song" or "strain" and the Greek δράμα (drama) meaning "theatrical plot." Medieval morality plays, with their clear allegorical depictions of good and evil, are also part of the genealogy of the form. In his influential study *The Melodramatic Imagination* (1976), the literary scholar Peter Brooks describes how the genre arose as a result of state monopolies on dramatic production in France:

> The genre's own derivation ... is from pantomime by way of an intermediate form with the oxymoronic name of *pantomime dialoguée*. The emergence of pantomime as an important theatrical form in the late eighteenth century has to do in large part with the monopoly accorded to the official, patented theatres: the Italiens, the Opéra, and especially, the Théâtre-Français. They alone had the right to play both the classical repertory and full-scale new productions. The secondary theatres—most of which grew out of the acrobatic acts of fairs—were supposed to content themselves with ballets, puppet shows, pantomimes. The pantomimes were accompanied by music from the beginning; they gradually began to become more elaborate and to incorporate pieces of dialogue, coming close to resembling melodrama before the term had come into general usage.[1]

The abolition of the patents during the Revolution allowed these forms, including *les mélodrames*, to proliferate and flourish.

In cinema studies, however, the term "melodrama" has been used in two different senses, one more limited and associated with women's films,[2] the other broader and associated with a number of genres including the Western and the crime film. "Melodrama is a loaded term in film studies," writes Scott Higgins in his study *Matinee Melodrama* (2016):

> On one hand, it has been associated with a specific studio-era genre typified by the emotionally and sexually charged domestic dramas directed by Douglas Sirk, Nicholas Ray, and Vincente Minnelli in the 1950s. On the other, in the sense invoked here, melodrama refers to a tradition of spectacular theater that predates cinema and, in important ways, runs counter to studio-era feature films.[3]

Commenting on melodramatic Hollywood films of the 1940s, Steve Neale argues that at the time these films were made, the terms "melodrama" and "melodramatic" "meant crime, guns and violence; they meant heroines in peril; they meant action, tension and suspense; and they meant villains [who] could masquerade as 'apparently harmless' fellows, thus thwarting the hero, evading justice, and sustaining suspense until the last minute."[4] Hollywood melodramas hailed from different genres, but they shared a set of characteristics, which Neale identifies as follows:

> (1) An unequivocal dramatic conflict between good and evil; (2) the eventual triumph of the former over the latter; (3) three principal character-types or functions: hero, heroine and villain; (4) a demonstrative and often hyperbolic aesthetic by means of which characters were typed, dramatic conflict was established and developed, and motive, emotion, and passion were laid bare; (5) an often highly episodic, formulaic, and action-packed plot, normally initiated and often driven by the villain. ... and (6) the generation

of what were called "situations." ... On the stage, situations sometimes took the form of tableaux. But they were always in any case "pictorial" in nature. And they existed for the purposes of dramatic display, and the revelation of dramatic developments, reversals, recognitions and confrontations and of the reactions of the characters to them.[5]

These are characteristics that the *Star Wars* films share as well.

Although having music is no longer a requirement for a piece to be dubbed "melodramatic," music can be a powerful device to create melodramatic effects. Lucas was well aware of how music, together with costume and scene design, can create the sorting into good and bad that is a primary function of melodrama. Mark Hamill remembers watching the filming of Darth Vader's first appearance in *A New Hope* and asking Lucas, "You know in the script, aren't you going to cut to two characters saying 'Who's that?' 'That's the Dark Lord of the Sith, and he's the ... ' You know, some exposition. And George just casually said, 'Yeah, no, he's all dressed in black, and we'll play some scary music. They'll know he's the bad guy.'"[6] The ready identification of Vader as a bad guy, along with "scary music" that recalls the melodramatic Flash Gordon serials of the 1930s that inspired Lucas, enables the scene to fulfill what Brooks describes as the imperative of *mélodrame*: "making the world morally legible, spelling out its ethical forces and imperatives in large and bold characters."[7] Discussing the use of melodrama in the Hollywood Western, Lusted argues that "stories of innocent victims, unable to defend themselves against unspeakable acts of villainy, are central to the Manichean (polarised moral) world of melodrama."[8]

Melodrama makes its way into *Star Wars* in part through the influence of the Western. Lucas's comments on the Western make it sound as if it appealed to him less because it was a part of US cinematic history than because it represented a particularly American form of the mythmaking that he had been thinking about as a result of reading Joseph Campbell. Lucas told James Cameron:

> [Our shared] mythology, the last step that it had taken was the Western. The Western had a real mythology—you don't shoot people in the back. You don't draw first. You always let the woman go first. ... Then [the genre] got very psychological, and the Western went out of favor. It was really that that led me to *Star Wars*."[9]

The character most inspired by the Western hero is, of course, Han Solo, the film's version of the Lone Ranger, complete with vest, gun in holster, and a sidekick who—like the Ranger's Tonto—is "other," in this case the towering Wookiee, Chewbacca. Appropriately, Luke and Obi-Wan meet Solo in a cantina that has the rough-and-tumble atmosphere of the archetypal saloon from a Hollywood Western. The scene famously ends with a shoot-out in which Han kills the nonhuman bounty hunter Greedo.

The death of Greedo is, however, the second act of violence that we've seen in the cantina. Obi-Wan has dismembered a thug who has threatened Luke, thrown the boy across the room, and then fired his gun at the old man. It all happens very quickly, and apparently, it's all pretty routine: after pausing a moment to show us the dismembered limb and the gun it was holding, the camera shows us Obi-Wan retracting his lightsaber, Luke looking on in amazement, and the cantina patrons returning to their business, seemingly unmoved by the proceedings. It's that kind of place.

The scene has been the cause of much controversy among *Star Wars* fans because Lucas revised it four times. In the 1977 theatrical release, it seems clear that Han shoots first, though only after he's been threatened by Greedo:

GREEDO: Jabba's through with you. He has no time for smugglers who drop their shipments at the first sign of an Imperial cruiser.

HAN: Even I get boarded sometimes. Do you think I had a choice?

Han Solo reaches for his gun under the table.

GREEDO: You can tell that to Jabba. He may only take your ship.

HAN: Over my dead body.

GREEDO: That's the idea. I've been looking forward to this for a long time.

HAN: Yes, I'll bet you have.

Suddenly, the slimy alien disappears in a blinding flash of light. Han pulls his smoking gun from beneath the table as the other patrons look on in bemused amazement. Han gets up and starts out of the cantina, flipping some coins as he leaves.

HAN: Sorry about the mess.

Greedo has clearly threatened Han with mortal peril, and most audiences would have accepted that even if he fired first, Han was acting in what amounts to self-defense.

Lucas decided that he wanted the self-defense part to be clearer, however, so when it came time to release the special editions, he altered the scene. In the 1997 revised version, Greedo shoots first, wildly, and Han jerks to the right (via digital manipulation), dodging the shot, and then shooting Greedo dead. Lucas revised the scene again for the 2004 DVD release, shortening the time between Greedo's and Han's shots, and in 2011, for the Blu-ray release, the interval is tightened even further, with ten frames cut so that the shots are nearly simultaneous, making Han a very lucky boy (see Figure 7). In the Blu-ray version, the scene now takes almost exactly

Figure 7 Stills of Han Solo shooting Greedo: original 1977 version and 2011 Blu-ray version. Han shot first—and then he didn't: Lucas has revised this scene several times, most recently for the 4K version streaming on Disney+. *Top:* The 1977 version, just after Han has shot the bounty hunter Greedo. The moment he pulls the trigger is signified by a flash of light and smoke in which Greedo is obscured. *Bottom:* The 2011 Blu-ray version. Laser bolts have been added (see the circles), and Greedo's shot has already hit the wall while Han's is still on the way. Han's face has also been digitally altered. Photo credits: Lucasfilm Ltd. *Star Wars: Episode IV—A New Hope* directed by George Lucas © 1977 Walt Disney Pictures/Lucasfilm Ltd. All rights reserved. *Star Wars: Episode IV—A New Hope (Special Edition)* directed by George Lucas © 2011 Walt Disney Pictures/Lucasfilm Ltd. All rights reserved.

the same time as in the original release. A fifth version, however, accompanied the debut of the Disney+ streaming service, a change authorized by Lucas as he was preparing 4K-resolution versions of his films shortly before he sold Lucasfilm to Disney in 2012.[10] Now, just before firing, Greedo says something that, unlike the rest of his dialogue, is not subtitled: on the Internet it was quickly and widely reported that what he said was "Maclunkey."[11] On further reflection, it seems likely that what Greedo says is a Huttese phrase used in *The Phantom Menace* when the Dug podracer Sebulba threatens young Anakin before their race:

> **SEBULBA:** (subtitled) Neek me chowa, wermo, mo killee ma klounkee! (Next time we race, wermo, it will be the end of you!) Una noto wo shag, me wompity du pom pom. (If you weren't a slave, I'd squash you right now.) *SEBULBA turns away.*
>
> **ANAKIN:** (subtitled) Eh, chee bana do mullee ra. (Yeah, it'd be a pity if you had to pay for me.)[12]

Fans were outraged by the 1997 revision, weren't mollified by the subsequent changes that have Han and Greedo shooting almost simultaneously, and have been largely bewildered by the Disney+ revision.

Lucas has been asked about the controversial scene many times. In 2012, he told *The Hollywood Reporter*:

> The controversy over who shot first, Greedo or Han Solo, in *Episode IV*, what I did was try to clean up the confusion, but obviously it upset people because they wanted Solo [who seemed to be the one who shot first in the original] to be a cold-blooded killer, but he actually isn't. It had been done in all close-ups and it was confusing about who did what to whom. I put a little wider shot in there that made it clear that Greedo is the one who shot first, but everyone wanted to think that Han shot first, because they wanted to think that he actually just gunned him down.[13]

Three years later, he told the *Washington Post* that having Han shoot first "ran counter to 'Star Wars' principles":

> "Han Solo was going to marry Leia, and you look back and say, 'Should he be a cold-blooded killer?'" Lucas asks. "Because I was thinking mythologically—should he be a cowboy, should he be John Wayne? And I said, 'Yeah, he should be John Wayne.' And when you're John Wayne, you don't shoot people [first]—you let them have the first shot. It's a mythological reality that we hope our society pays attention to."[14]

In my opinion, Lucas has it wrong on two counts here. First, it isn't that fans want Han to be a cold-blooded killer, as he suggests in the first quote: for reasons that we'll discuss later on, the fans simply want the film that they saw in the theaters. Second, it isn't the case that the Western hero wouldn't shoot first. The whole point of the iconic shoot-out scene is that the quicker draw wins: the one who can get his gun out and shoot first. But even if one argues that Greedo didn't have a fair chance in the original film, the kind of provocation to violence that he offers fully justifies Solo's response—within the mythology of the Western that Lucas is evoking.

David Lusted argues that, with Owen Wister's novel *The Virginian* (1902), the logic of the Western hero changes from its depiction in the early nineteenth-century novels of James Fenimore Cooper:

> He becomes a hero who is prepared for violence and skilled in dealing with it, but only within the strict boundaries of defence of self or community. This code of honour rationalises and defends violent behaviour. It provides a morality that enables Westerns to honour the gunfighter whose actions against villainy may be unlawful, but embody a more meaningful justice.[15]

In *West of Everything*, Jane Tompkins argues to a great extent "the genre exists in order to provide a justification for violence. Violence needs justification because our society puts it under interdict—morally and legally, at any rate." She detects a pattern in the novel *Shane* that

> reproduces itself in a thousand Western novels and movies. Its pattern never varies. The hero, provoked by insults, first verbal, then physical, resists the urge to retaliate, proving his moral superiority to those who are taunting him. It is never the hero who taunts his adversary; if he does, it's only after he's been pushed "too far." And this, of course, is what always happens. The villains, whoever they may be, finally commit an act so atrocious that the hero must retaliate in kind. He wants to, and we want him to, and, if there's a crowd of innocent bystanders, they want him to, too. At this juncture, the point where provocation has gone too far, retaliatory violence becomes not simply justifiable but imperative: now, we are made to feel, not to transgress the interdict against violence would be the transgression.

Tompkins argues that such scenes of violence at the culmination of the plot provide a "satisfying sense of release for the audience"; in fact, she claims, "The entire purpose of the pattern ... is to get the audience to the point where it can't wait till the hero lets loose with his six-shooters."[16] It's this mythology that the depiction of Han in the cantina is evoking, and within that mythological pattern, it's okay for Han to behave as he did in the first version of the scene.

The anthology film *Solo* alludes to the controversy when it depicts a similar confrontation between a young Han and an antagonist, his former mentor Beckett, who is clearly about to shoot him. The scene is constructed as if it is a shoot-out from a Western. Beckett, speaking with what he believes to be dramatic irony (he knows what he's about to do but doesn't think Han suspects), tells Han, "I hope you're paying attention, because I'm about to tell you the most imp—" As he is speaking these words, the camera shows us Beckett tightening his finger on the trigger of his gun—and then Han shoots him. Dying, Beckett tells Han, "You made the smart move, kid. For once. I would've killed you." In addition to having Han's victim vindicate Han's action, the film also makes it clear that there's nothing cold-blooded about its hero, as he ends up performing an act of altruism that ultimately aids the Rebellion that he has no idea that he's going to join. (But we know.)

In seeking to clarify the defensive nature of Han's action in the cantina scene, Lucas's revisions actually constitute an approach to melodrama that is less sophisticated than in the original version. Although the *Star Wars* films seem at first glance to create a Manichean worldview in which existence is a constant battle between the light side and the dark side of the force, personified in the enmity between the Jedi and the Sith, the films actually complicate the ostensibly black-and-white moral structures that seem to be set into place through the use of the melodramatic techniques. The films' use of verbal humor acts as a deflationary counterweight to melodramatic hyperbole. In *A New Hope* much of this verbal humor arises from Han Solo (with whom we tend to laugh) and C-3PO (toward whom we direct an affectionately ironic perspective). But there is one moment of high drama—when Obi-Wan is trying to disarm the tractor beam so that the *Millennium Falcon* can escape—where the tension is heightened through the use of verbal comedy, which arises in this case from some banal conversation between stormtroopers:

INT. DEATH STAR—POWER TRENCH

Suddenly, behind Ben a detachment of stormtroopers marches to the power trench. Ben remains in the shadows as they move to within a few feet of him.

OFFICER: Give me regular reports, please.
FIRST TROOPER: Right.

All but two of the stormtroopers leave.

FIRST TROOPER: Do you know what's going on?
SECOND TROOPER: Maybe it's another drill.

Ben moves around the tractor beam, watching the stormtroopers as they turn their backs to him and chat. Ben gestures with his hand toward them, as the troops think they hear something in the other hallway. With the help of the Force, Ben deftly slips past the troopers and into the main hallway.

FIRST TROOPER: Have you seen the new BT-sixteen?
SECOND TROOPER: Yeah, some of the other guys were telling me about it. They say it's, it's quite a thing to … What was that?
FIRST TROOPER: That's nothing. Top gassing. Don't worry about it.[17]

This brief exchange makes us realize that there are real people—just "guys"—inside those skull-like helmets. Another moment uses humor to humanize the stormtroopers: when a group of four stormtroopers breaks into the control room where C-3PO and R2-D2 have been hiding, the fourth one hits his head on the door walking in. Lucas not only left in the shot, but also accentuated the moment by adding a sound effect so that we hear the helmet banging against the door (see Figure 8).

As the *Star Wars* universe has unfolded in subsequent films and other media, it has played much more with those gray areas that

Figure 8 Still of stormtrooper bumping his head on a door in *Star Wars* (1977). Stormtrooper hijinks: Lucas subtly humanizes the stormtroopers by letting us overhear a conversation about gear and by leaving in a shot in which the stormtrooper on the right in the still above hits his head on the door walking in. In fact, Lucas accentuated the moment by adding a sound effect so that we hear the helmet banging against the door. Photo credit: Lucasfilm. *Star Wars: Episode IV—A New Hope* directed by George Lucas © 1977 Walt Disney Pictures/Lucasfilm Ltd. All rights reserved.

classic melodrama seeks to obscure. The blue-skinned Grand Admiral Thrawn, a character by novelist Timothy Zahn in the trilogy that began the original Expanded Universe, was resurrected as a chief antagonist in the animated series *Star Wars: Rebels*, but the three Thrawn novels that Zahn has written to be part of the new canon offer readers a dramatization of life inside Palpatine's empire, before the rise of the Rebel Alliance; indeed, the epilogue of the third book uses a limited third-person narration to take us briefly into the mind of Palpatine himself. The protagonist of the game *Battlefront II*, Iden Versio, is a diehard Imperial officer: in the game's companion novel, *Battlefront II: Inferno Squad*, we learn that Versio has survived the destruction of the first Death Star, which she regards as a "terrorist act" that has caused the death of a million Imperial soldiers and citizens. (The game itself explores the revenge that Imperial forces take after the death of the Empire, leading Versio ultimately to join the Rebellion and, later, the Resistance.) The 2019 canonical comic series *TIE Fighter* presents the point of view of the Imperial pilots of Shadow Wing battling to restore peace to the galaxy. Referring to the rebels, one pilot says, "The point is they're the ones who started a war. Destroying that battle station was mass murder."[18] The pilots are made even more sympathetic for readers of the series *Han Solo: Imperial Cadet*, which portrays Han's time in the Imperial flight academy and introduces us to some of the pilots who will become part of Shadow Wing. Meanwhile, *Alphabet Squadron*, the companion novel to the *TIE Fighter* series, explores the difficulties that a defector from Shadow Wing has as she tries to adjust from the ordered regime of the Empire to the comparatively chaotic world of the rebellion. Imperial pilots who embrace the ideology of Empire are presented sympathetically in Claudia Gray's young adult novel *Journey to Star Wars: The Force Awakens: The Lost Stars* (2015). For the two protagonists, Thane Kyrell and Ciena Ree, joining the Imperial navy represents a chance to escape their backwater home planet, Jeluca, and do some good in the galaxy—at least at first. Finally, director Jon Favreau's live-action television series *The Mandalorian* is "set after the fall of the Empire and before the emergence of the First Order" and follows "the travails of a lone gunfighter in the outer reaches of the galaxy far from the authority of the New Republic."[19] At the 2019 "Star Wars Celebration" convention, Favreau described the title character as "a gunfighter, a bounty hunter, a citizen of the underworld on the outer reaches of the galaxy." Pedro Pascal, who plays the Mandalorian, was inspired by Clint Eastwood's antiheroic Man with No Name (as was Jeremy Bulloch the actor who played the fan-favorite Mandalorian bounty hunter Boba Fett in *Return of the Jedi*).[20] According to Carl Weathers, who plays the head of a guild of bounty hunters, "the Mando" is a character "who does what needs to be done."[21]

These representations complicate the original trilogy's deployment of the melodramatic imagination. The first *Star Wars* film makes use of archetypes and cinematic devices associated with Hollywood melodrama, and the Western in particular, which enable its audiences to get wholeheartedly behind Luke, Han, Leia, Chewie, and the Rebellion, and to cheer out loud when the Death Star and all its denizens are destroyed. But it also gives us the tools to pause, if we are so inclined, to think a little more deeply about what separates the good guys from the bad guys.

5

Individualism

If *Star Wars* drew significantly on the kinds of globally shared mythological traditions that Campbell explored in *The Hero with a Thousand Faces*, it also drew on the tradition of liberal individualism within both US political thought and US popular culture. In the catalog accompanying the National Air and Space Museum's exhibition "*Star Wars*: The Magic of Myth," Mary Henderson locates a large part of the appeal of Lucas's films in the fact that they portray a hero who "enter[s] the wilderness outside the technologically controlled world in order to discover the human animal inside the social machine. The hero can then assert his individualism instead of becoming a servant to the machine."[1] In this chapter, I will consider the ways in which the *Star Wars* shared universe dramatizes ideas drawn from both philosophical liberalism and the cultural mythology of rugged individualism—and demonstrates the need to shift the assumptions that undergird them.

Liberal Individualism and the Culture of Narcissism

The original *Star Wars* trilogy overlaps chronologically with a set of classic texts by US political theorists about the nature, function, and viability of liberal individualism. The first *Star Wars* film was published in 1977, six years after John Rawls's now-classic meditation on individualism, *A Theory of Justice*, as well as the legendary seminar co-taught at Harvard by Robert Nozick and Michael Walzer called "Capitalism and Socialism." Walzer recalls:

> In 1971, Nozick and I taught a course together called "Capitalism and Socialism," which was a semester-long argument out of which came his *Anarchy, State, and Utopia* and my *Spheres [of Justice]*. Rawls, Nozick, Nagel, and Dworkin were, I suppose, the leaders of the return of philosophers to "public affairs." For me, there was no return; I had never been interested in anything else.

Roughly speaking, and using labels that made both thinkers uncomfortable, Nozick personified the "libertarian" response to Rawls, while Walzer personified the "communitarian response." Walzer notes ruefully that "the Rawls/Nozick debate was, I think, pretty much over even before their deaths. In the philosophical world, Rawls and the Rawlsians won decisively; in the political world, I am afraid, the Nozickians won."[2] *Anarchy, State, and Utopia* was published in 1974 during the interval between *American Graffiti* and *Star Wars*; *Spheres of Justice* was published in 1983, the same year as *Return of the Jedi*.

I will not rehearse the arguments that are made by each of these three iconic philosophical texts, nor am I suggesting that Lucas read any of them. What I am suggesting is that all of them—Rawls, Nozick, Walzer, and Lucas—were responding in their different ways to a set of problems about the relationship between the individual and the state that became pressing during the 1960s. Although it is only in the prequel trilogy that Lucas depicts galactic politics in detail, he had US politics in mind as he wrote the first drafts for the first film, particularly his dissatisfaction with the Nixon administration. On one of his yellow pads, he scribbled:

The empire is like America ten years from now, after Nixonian gangsters assassinated the Emperor and were elevated to power in a rigged election; created civil disorder by instigating race riots aiding rebel groups and allowing the crime rate to rise to the point where a "total control" police state was welcomed by the people. Then the people were exploited with high taxes, utility and transport costs.[3]

Years later, Lucas told an interviewer that "while the psychological basis of *Star Wars* is mythological, the political and social bases are historical."[4]

The psychological turn in the Hollywood Western that Lucas cites and the consequent decline in the genre's popularity coincided with the crisis of confidence in US individualism that Christopher Lasch famously analyzed in his best-selling book *The Culture of Narcissism* (1979), published two years after the release of the first *Star Wars* film. Lasch argued that "the logic of individualism" had degenerated into "the extreme of a war of all against all, the pursuit of happiness to the dead end of a narcissistic preoccupation with the self." According to Lasch, "the culture of competitive individualism" was "a way of life that is dying," destroyed by its own internal contradictions and posing a serious danger to Americans' ability to create community.[5] Influenced by his reading of Lasch's book, President Jimmy Carter declared on national television on July 15, 1979, that the United States was suffering from a "crisis in confidence ... that strikes at the very heart and soul and spirit of our national will. We can see this crisis in the growing doubt about the meaning of our own lives and in the loss of a unity of purpose for our Nation." The speech, which was originally intended to have addressed the energy crisis that ensued after OPEC's oil embargo, came to be known as the "malaise" speech, although Carter never actually used the term. Carter concluded that "little by little we can and we must rebuild our confidence. We can spend until we empty our treasuries, and we may summon all the wonders of science. But we can succeed only if we tap our greatest resources—America's people, America's values, and America's confidence."[6]

Although US voters would ultimately shoot the messenger in the next election and elect Ronald Reagan to the presidency, Carter was right that Americans were eager to rebuild their confidence. *Star Wars* had offered them the opportunity to do just that by reinvigorating their faith in the idea that individuals matter. It probably didn't hurt that in its depiction of a plucky band of rebels taking on an oppressive imperial government with massive military resources, the film resonated with the cultural mythologies that had arisen around the War of Independence against Great Britain and with the protests against the war in Vietnam. In the documentary *Empire of Dreams*, the legendary CBS News anchorman Walter Cronkite comments, "George Lucas's *Star Wars* lifted us out of our sort of depression of the Seventies," while journalist Bill Moyers observes:

> Timing is everything in art. You bring *Star Wars* out too early, and it's *Buck Rogers*. You bring it out too late, and it doesn't fit our imagination. You bring it out just as the war in Vietnam is ending, when America feels uncertain of itself, when the old stories have died, and you bring it out at that time, and suddenly it's a new game. Also, it's a lot of fun. It's a lot of fun to watch *Star Wars*.[7]

Watching Luke Skywalker develop from a greenhorn into a rebel who can take down the Empire's most advanced and deadliest piece of tech provided a sense of wish fulfillment for a country mired in what seemed to be an increasingly deadly arms race with a totalitarian power.

Political theorists typically believe that liberal individualism is underwritten by ontological individualism, the belief that the individual has an a priori and primary reality and that society is a derived, second-order construct. The political theorist Steven Lukes writes that "according to this conception, individuals are pictured abstractly as given, with given interests, wants, purposes, needs, etc.; while society and the state are pictured as sets of actual or possible social arrangements which respond more or less adequately to those individuals' requirements." What is important to notice about this description is the importance of abstraction: ontological individualism presents what Lukes describes as "an abstract conception of the individual who is seen as merely the bearer" of "fixed and invariant human psychological features," which "determine his behaviour, and specify his interests, needs and rights."[8] If Rawls's theory of justice is built on a foundation of ontological individualism, it also depends on the ability of the individual to make use of reason and to be able to exert choice within a certain set of constraints. As the original trilogy progresses, Luke finds that he must make choices in the face of various constraints: what Vader calls his "destiny" on the one hand and what Obi-Wan and Yoda believe to be Luke's role in the reconstitution of the Jedi Order on the other.

From the start, however, Luke's individualism is tempered by a set of communitarian ideas about the nature of personal identity that he learns from Obi-Wan and Yoda. It is Obi-Wan Kenobi who begins to initiate Luke into the mysteries of the Force, telling him: "The Force is what gives a Jedi his power. It's an energy field created by all living things. It surrounds us, penetrates us. It binds the galaxy together."[9] The cynical Han Solo doesn't believe in the Force, telling Luke aboard the *Millennium Falcon*:

> Kid, I've flown from one side of this galaxy to the other. I've seen a lot of strange stuff, but I've never seen anything to make me believe there's one all-powerful force controlling everything. There's no

mystical energy field that controls my destiny. It's all a lot of simple tricks and nonsense.[10]

Reflecting back on what was at stake in the idea of the Force, Lucas told James Cameron that it was "about symbiotic relationships," adding,

> I think, personally, one of the core values we should have in the world, and kids should be taught, is ecology, to understand that we all are connected. Forget the mystical whatever. It's just very plain. We're all connected. What you do to somebody here, it affects somebody there, there, there, there. It comes back to you. You have to understand that you're a part of a very big picture.[11]

This point of view is expressed by Yoda in *The Empire Strikes Back*, when he tells Luke that "life creates" the Force, "makes it grow. Its energy surrounds us and binds us. ... You must feel the Force around you. Here, between you, me—the tree, the rock—everywhere. Yes—even between the land and the ship."[12]

This view of connectedness aligns *Star Wars* with aspects of the communitarian critique of US individualism during the 1970s and 1980s, which included not only Walzer and Lasch, but also such thinkers as Robert Bellah, Alasdair MacIntyre, and Michael Sandel. *Habits of the Heart: Individualism and Commitment in American Life* (1985), cowritten by Bellah, Richard Madsen, William M. Sullivan, Ann Swidler, and Steven M. Tipton, provides documentary evidence of the extent to which what they call "mythic individualism" continued to influence the ways in which social, political, and moral issues were discussed in the United States during the era in which *Star Wars* came into being. In particular, the book demonstrates that individualism essentially creates a vocabulary that limits the ways in which Americans think and speak about their communally oriented goals. The book's authors state that they seek "to deepen our understanding of the resources our tradition provides—and fails to provide—for enabling us to think about the kinds of moral problems we are currently facing as Americans."[13]

Habits of the Hearts begins by introducing the reader to four different individuals who are offered as representative character types: a corporate manager, a "concerned citizen," a therapist, and an activist. Claiming that these individuals "represent American voices familiar to us all," Bellah et al. also suggest that, if the four were to meet, there would be "sharp disagreements" among them and that these disagreements "would be versions of controversies that regularly arise in public and private moral discourse in the United States." Yet, among these four individuals, the authors discern "more than a little consensus about the relationship between the individual and society, between private and public good," a consensus that can be attributed to the fact that "they all to some degree share a common moral vocabulary," which Bellah et al. "propose to call the 'first language' of American individualism in contrast to alternative 'second languages,' which most of us also have."[14] Clarifying this terminology, Bellah et al. state that they use the term "language"

> to refer to modes of moral discourse that include distinct vocabularies and characteristic patterns of moral reasoning. We use first language to refer to the individualistic mode that is the dominant American form of discourse about moral, social, and political matters. We use the term second languages to refer to other forms, primarily biblical and republican, that provide at least part of the moral discourse of most Americans.[15]

According to the analysis presented in *Habits of Heart*, these second languages are vestigial, fragmentary, and relatively unarticulated.

Bellah et al. claim that, when Americans use "the moral discourse they share, what we call the first language of individualism, they have difficulty articulating the richness of their commitments."[16] According to Fredric Jameson, this inability to articulate communal feelings results from the fact that "the first language or discourse of individualism ... powerfully deflects and deforms everything that passes through it; like a system of cartographic projection, it translates the content offered it into the style and specificity of its own volumes and contours, with the Wittgensteinian consequence that whatever it cannot express falls outside of social reality." Jameson views *Habits of the Heart* as "a kind of 'language experiment' in which, minimally, [the authors] seek to make us aware of the asphyxiating confines and limits of the language into which we are locked; at their most ambitious, they seem themselves to strain to produce a new language capable of bursting the seams of the older one and making new realities and new possibilities appear."[17] What *Habits of the Heart* ultimately demonstrates, however, is the strength of those seams. Not only are its authors unwilling to break completely with the ideology of individualism (much to Jameson's chagrin), but they also leave us with profound doubts about the possibility of renovating that ideology. Although Bellah et al. believe that many of those whom they have interviewed are unwittingly engaged in the search for "a moral language that will transcend their radical individualism," they also confess toward the end of the book that "on the basis of our interviews, and from what we can observe more generally in our society today, it is not clear that many Americans are prepared to consider a significant change in the way we have been living."[18]

In *The Good Society* (1991), the follow-up to *Habits of the Heart*, Bellah et al. write that twentieth-century Americans "live through institutions," although they are loath ever to admit it. Continuing the line of argumentation begun in their earlier study, Bellah et al.

contend, "the individualistic assumptions of our culture lead us to believe that we can live as we choose, using the big institutions—the agencies of the state, the companies or organizations we work for, the schools we attend—for our own ends, without being fundamentally influenced by them." Like Michael Sandel, they find Americans to be constrained by a conception of identity that seems to make no provision for a communally constituted self, which prevents them from fully understanding the role that institutions play in both their personal lives and the life of their country. According to Bellah et al., Americans tend to follow the classic liberal view that "institutions ought to be as far as possible neutral mechanisms for individuals to use to attain their separate ends," fearing "that institutions that are not properly limited and neutral may be oppressive. This belief leads us to think of institutions as efficient or inefficient mechanisms, like the Department of Motor Vehicles, that we learn to use for our own purposes, or as malevolent 'bureaucracies' that may crush us under their impersonal wheels." The aim of *The Good Society* is to make the dynamics of institutional life more comprehensible and more acceptable to its readers, to give them a sense that they can bring about institutional change. The alternative, to imagine institutions as "autonomous systems operating according to their own mysterious internal logic, to be fine-tuned only by experts," is, in their view, "to opt for some kind of modern gnosticism that sees the world as controlled by the powers of darkness." Such a view "encourages us to look only to our private survival."[19]

That gnostic world controlled by powers of darkness is the world that the Empire has established in the first *Star Wars* trilogy. According to Lucas, "The endgame for the Sith was to bring the world into a very selfish, self-centered, greedy, evil place, as opposed to a compassionate place."[20] Just recognizing the existence of the Force, however, isn't enough: you need to adopt the right attitude toward it. Obi-Wan Kenobi's view of the Force provides the kind of moral language that Bellah et al. find lacking in US discourse during the 1970s. After Luke's first experience with the training remote aboard the *Millennium Falcon* leads him to say "I did feel something," Obi-Wan commends him: "You've taken your first step into a larger world," a line that is repeated during Rey's vision at Maz Kanata's castle in *The Force Awakens*.[21] After using his nascent Force abilities to destroy the Death Star, Luke will take his next steps into that larger world under the tutelage of Yoda in *The Empire Strikes Back*. The Sith are materialists in both the popular and philosophical senses of the term, but Yoda is a philosophical idealist: "Luminous beings are we," he says, pinching Luke's shoulder and adding, "not this crude matter."[22]

In the spring of 1980, less than a year after Carter's "crisis of confidence" speech and half a year before Reagan's election, that kind of sentiment was something that Americans seemed desperate to believe.

Rugged Individualism

Part of Reagan's appeal was his invocation of a tradition of rugged individualism, the cultural myth of the heroic loner, which has long been associated with the settling of the frontier in North America and in Hollywood with the genre of the Western. In the nineteenth century, rugged individualism became a way of articulating the distinctiveness of American experience as a result of westward settlement across the North American continent, and it is an expression within US popular culture of the logic of ontological individualism. This cultural mythology was codified when the young historian Frederick Jackson Turner gave a speech called "The Significance of the Frontier in American History" to the American Historical

Association during the 1893 Chicago Exposition. Later published as an essay that would be widely cited by scholars, the speech presented what became known as the "frontier thesis": Turner argued that "American social development has been continually beginning over again on the frontier" and that "this perennial rebirth, this fluidity of American life, this expansion westward with its new opportunities, its continuous touch with the simplicity of primitive society, furnish the forces dominating the American character." Among the "traits called out because of the existence of the frontier" were what Turner described as "that coarseness and strength combined with acuteness and inquisitiveness; that practical, inventive turn of mind, quick to find expedients; that masterful grasp of material things, lacking in the artistic but powerful to effect great ends; that restless, nervous energy; that dominant individualism, working for good and for evil, and withal that buoyancy and exuberance which comes with freedom."[23] Turner's hypothesis planted the seeds of the celebrated "myth-and-symbol" school of American Studies. The influence of the hypothesis stemmed from its ability to account for the prevalence of ontological individualism within US political philosophy and for the pervasiveness of individualism within US cultural mythology.

The cultural mythology of the rugged individualist idealized the acquisitive pursuit of dominion over both lands and peoples during the Westward expansion of the United States, which persists in debased form within the "middle American individualism" that the sociologist Herbert J. Gans investigated during the 1980s. Paradoxically, it was the banality of the popular individualism pursued by twentieth-century consumers that keeps the myth of rugged individualism alive, as a form of wish fulfillment for the "Middle Americans" whose most pressing concerns are pragmatically oriented toward material well-being. But rugged individualism also has material effects, and the oppressive masculinity of its ethos (apparent even in Lucas's remark that in the Western, "You always let the woman go first") is linked to the continued lack of equality for women in US culture.

Star Wars draws on this cultural mythology and on an iconic scene within the Hollywood Western: the gunfight between two antagonists. Moments of single combat punctuate the *Star Wars* films, and indeed each trilogy builds toward moments of single combat: Luke Skywalker versus Darth Vader in *Return of the Jedi*, Obi-Wan Kenobi versus Anakin Skywalker in *Revenge of the Sith*, and Rey versus Kylo Ren and then the Emperor in *The Rise of Skywalker*. George Lucas describes the logic behind the death of Yoda early in *Return of the Jedi* this way:

> As you're building to the climax of an endeavor such as this, you want the situation to get more and more desperate and you want the hero to lose whatever crutches he or she has helping along the way. One of the challenges here is that Luke should be completely on his own. He has to face the Emperor one on one.[24]

Abrams and screenwriter Chris Terrio revise this idea in *The Rise of Skywalker*, but in a way that is in keeping with Lucas's ethos. Early in the film, Rey plans to go on a mission to find the mysterious Sith planet Exegol and the resurrected Emperor. Poe tells her, "We're going with you." She responds: "I need to go alone." Finn chimes in: "Yeah, alone, with friends. ... We go together." And that's what happens. It's a lighthearted moment, but it foreshadows the climax of the film: although physically alone when she faces Palpatine, Rey has the spiritual support of "a thousand generations" of Jedi, who call to her through the Force and give her the strength to prevail.

The idea of being "alone, with friends" actually builds on concepts that Lucas himself began to develop in the original trilogy. In the same way, however, that he was seeking to update the global mythologies that Campbell investigated, Lucas also sought to update the mythology of rugged individualism. The aptly named Han Solo is the closest approximation in the film to the classic loner of Hollywood Westerns. Even the presence of his sidekick Chewbacca fits the mold: the Lone Ranger, as we've noted, had Tonto. The film, however, embeds its lone ranger into a group and makes him only one of the influences on the character who most closely approximates Campbell's "hero with a thousand faces," Luke Skywalker. In the first film, the others are Obi-Wan Kenobi and Leia Organa. The prominence of Leia within the film acts as a rejoinder to the masculinist bias of the Western and the rugged individualism that it embodies.

Princess Jedi

When he was little, my older son liked to play dress-up. His favorite two genres were princesses and Jedi Knights. ("Don't swing your lightsaber in the house!" either my wife or I would shout.) Very often he combined the two into "Princess Jedi" (see Figure 9).

Around the time he saw *Revenge of the Sith*, he started telling stories about Jedi, and he'd ask me to do the same as we walked to school each morning. He was particularly taken with the female Jedi Luminara Unduli, Barriss Offee, and—above all—the Twi'lek Aayla Secura, all of whom loomed large in the Expanded Universe. Once he discovered Princess Leia Organa, he decided that she too must have been a Jedi—in fact, the head of the Jedi Order.

He was ahead of the curve.

In the foreword to *Star Wars: Women of the Galaxy*, Kathleen Kennedy writes about the importance of women to *Star Wars* from 1977 to the present:

With that first film, and the cultural phenomenon that followed, George Lucas introduced the world to Princess Leia, a character who stood apart from most female leads of the day. With strength, courage, a quick wit and grit, she could easily hold her own against the predominantly male cast.[25]

If the virtue of masculinity was one of the unspoken tenets of the myths of rugged individualism on which Lucas drew in creating *Star*

Figure 9 Princess Jedi. Even in 2005, my son always knew that Leia was supposed to be a Jedi. Photo credit: Cyrus R. K. Patell.

Wars, his creation of Leia Organa represents an important revision. Lucas would later emphasize her role as a "senator," imagining that

> she graduated from college. She's a very smart person, very much in control. And she's a good shot. And the two guys were—one was naïve and didn't know anything, had no knowledge. The other one thought he knew everything, but he didn't know anything, either. She is the one that knew everything. She was the one that was driving the whole story.[26]

In *Return of the Jedi*, Lucas decided to make the leader of the Rebellion a woman named Mon Mothma. When it came time to depict Leia and Luke's mother Padmé Amidala in the prequel trilogy, he took the same approach: "She had Qui-Gon Jinn as her kind of Ben Kenobi. But she was the wisest of the group. She was the real heroine of all those pieces."[27] Meanwhile, the Padawan Ahsoka Tano emerged as a popular character in both the *Clone Wars* television series and its successor *Rebels*, the latter of which also featured two strong female lead characters, the Twi'lek captain Hera Syndulla and the Mandalorian Sabine Wren. In *Rogue One*, we learn that Syndulla has become a general in the Rebellion, while Wren becomes the leader of the Mandalorians, wielding their legendary symbol of power, the Darksaber.

In choosing to give Princess Leia a leading role in the action by making her smart and good with a blaster, Lucas was also revising the formula that Joseph Campbell presented in *The Hero with a Thousand Faces*. In her study *The Heroine's Journey*, Maureen Murdock recounts a 1981 conversation with Campbell about the role that women played in his paradigm:

> I knew that the stages of the heroine's journey incorporated aspects of the journey of the hero, but I felt that the focus of female spiritual

development was to heal the internal split between woman and her feminine nature. I wanted to hear Campbell's views. I was surprised when he responded that women don't need to make the journey. "In the whole mythological tradition the woman is there. All she has to do is to realize that she's the place that people are trying to get to. When a woman realizes what her wonderful character is, she's not going to get messed up with the notion of being pseudo-male."

Dissatisfied with this conception, Murdock sought to find a new paradigm, arguing that

> women do have a quest at this time in our culture. It is the quest to fully embrace their feminine nature, learning how to value themselves as women and to heal the deep wound of the feminine. It is a very important inner journey toward being a fully integrated, balanced, and whole human being. ... It is a journey that seldom receives validation from the outside world; in fact the outer world often sabotages and interferes with it.[28]

Star Wars dramatizes Lucas's dissatisfaction with this aspect of Campbell's model, its refusal to chart a hero's journey for women. The original trilogy depicts a woman who is able to be a leader of both men and women and a co-adventurer along with the man she loves. In *Return of the Jedi*, it is Han Solo who plays the role of damsel in distress and Leia who seeks to rescue him. When her plan fails and she is reduced to an object of male desire literally chained to her oppressor, Jabba the Hutt, she uses those very chains to strangle the Hutt and escape her oppression.

Kennedy was determined to build on this legacy of strong women characters in the sequel trilogy. After the release of *The Force Awakens*, co-screenwriter Michael Arndt said in an interview with the Writers'

Guild of America that Kennedy had approached him in May 2012 and asked him to write the entire sequel trilogy. He demurred, calling the project "just too crazy and daunting." But when she told him that it would be "an origin of a female Jedi," he said, "I'm in. I can't say no to that. I have to do it." After passing muster with George Lucas—the "test" involved "spend[ing] a lot of time talking about samurai movies" at Skywalker Ranch—Arndt was on board, eventually cowriting the screenplay with Lawrence Kasdan and J. J. Abrams, with Simon Kinberg serving as a consultant.

In *The Force Awakens*, Rey starts out as a quintessential individualist: an orphan, fending for herself on a harsh desert planet, who finds that she has powers that she never suspected. The film makes a joke at Finn's expense when he tries to take her hand while they are escaping the First Order: "What are you doing?" she asks. "I know how to run without you holding my hand!" She knows how to fly too, which is a skill that Finn lacks. By the time she sets out to find the Sith planet Exegol in *The Rise of Skywalker*, Rey has been trained by both Luke and Leia and studied the ancient Jedi manuscripts that Luke intended to burn. As a result, she has acquired Jedi skills, including unprecedented Force-assisted acrobatic jumping and Force healing, which outstrip anything that the films have depicted before.

In making Rey the new hope for the light side—and possibly the most powerful Jedi ever—the new trilogy picks up on an idea that Lucas toyed with when revising the second draft of his script for *Star Wars* in 1975. In *Star Wars Art: Ralph McQuarrie*, Lucas is quoted as saying, "At one point, I was going to have a girl at the center of the story. Luke Skywalker might never have been; he might have been a heroine" (I, 72). Gary Kurtz adds, "In a couple of paintings that Ralph did when we were just getting ready to shoot, Luke was a girl. For some of those longer shots, it didn't matter because the important thing was the atmosphere rather than any of the actual detail" (I, 75).

Several of McQuarrie's sketches depict Luke as a girl, including a logo sketch that depicts a bearded Han Solo with a lightsaber and a female Luke (with a blaster). By midsummer of 1975, however, McQuarrie's sketches show Leia much as we come to know her in the film.

> I wanted Leia to be tough, and I wanted her to be young. I didn't want to exploit the fact that she was a girl. She could just as easily have been a prince rather than a princess. I didn't want to make her this sexy, typical princess kind of thing where everybody was watching her shape more than they were listening to who she was. (I, 91)

The character that Lucas is describing here is Leia, but it also sounds a lot like Daisy Ridley's Rey.

Strong women appear throughout the sequel trilogy. In *The Force Awakens*, Rey is aided by both a wise old male figure in Han Solo and a wise old female figure in Maz Kanata, herself a rugged individualist who can hold her own in a fight, as her brief appearance in *The Last Jedi* demonstrates. At the climax of *The Force Awakens*, despite being untutored in the use of a lightsaber, Rey is able to channel her growing Force powers enough to defeat Kylo Ren and inflict a saber burn on his face. The sequel trilogy also presents an older Leia who is now a "General" and the leader of the Resistance; in the *Last Jedi* she demonstrates Force powers that enable her to survive the destruction of the bridge of her flagship. *The Last Jedi* adds additional strong female characters in Paige Tico; her sister, Rose; and General Amlyn Holdo. Both Paige and Holdo sacrifice themselves heroically for the Resistance, while Rose saves Finn from certain death near the film's climax. Meanwhile, the dark side is bolstered in the sequel trilogy by the addition of the silver-armored Captain Phasma, played by the towering Gwendolyn Christie, a *Game of Thrones* favorite; additional aspects of Phasma's story were explored in both a novel that presented her backstory and a comic series that depicted her actions between *The Force Awakens* and *The Last Jedi*. *The Rise of Skywalker* adds the warrior Jannah (played by Naomi Ackie), an expert with a crossbow, and a space pirate named Zorii Bliss (played by Keri Russell), who adopts a Mandalorian's devotion to her helmet and has expert piloting and shooting skills.

All of this suggests that one way of understanding the progression from original trilogy to prequel trilogy to sequel trilogy is to see a gradual expansion of the depiction of women's power. The Skywalker saga as a whole offers a powerful rejoinder to both the masculinist bias of Campbell's presentation of the monomyth and the association between liberal individualism and patriarchy. Sadly, even at this late date, that rejoinder puts it well ahead of the curve of US culture and has irritated those fans who are invested in the traditional masculinist vision of rugged individualism, which they believe was expressed by the original trilogy. As we will see, there have been many conversations prompted by the *Star Wars* universe (and particularly the sequel trilogy) that replicate—and are perhaps inspired by—the breakdown in civility that has characterized public discourses with the rise of masculinist authoritarian populisms around the world at the start of the twenty-first century.

6

Technophobia

Why must Luke Skywalker turn off his computer in order to destroy the Death Star at the climax *A New Hope*?

We know the answer to this question within the narrative framework that George Lucas establishes for us during the film. Darth Vader tells us why: scoffing at an Imperial general's contention that the battle station known as the Death Star is "the ultimate power in the universe," Vader proclaims, "Don't be too proud of this technological terror you've constructed. The ability to destroy a planet is insignificant next to the power of the Force."[1] But why create this narrative logic at all? What larger ideological contexts lie behind it? What set of cultural hopes and anxieties could underlie the mythology of the Jedi and their relationship to the Force?

I suggest that a crucial component of the cultural logic that animates not only the *Star Wars* films but also the various *Star Trek* series, and a host of other popular late twentieth-century representations of advanced technology is, in fact, technophobia—the fear of technology. These representations are symptomatic of deep anxieties about the erosion of individual agency that have a long history in Western culture but seem to have become intensified by the rapidity of technological change in the late twentieth century.

Consider these examples which followed in the wake of the first *Star Wars* film.

Steven Spielberg's *E.T. The Extraterrestrial* (1982) plays on our fears of technology: in the tense final half hour of the film, we assume that the men in the hazmat suits seeking to find E.T. are up to no good. The *Terminator* series of films, which began in 1984, depict the attempts of an artificial intelligence named Skynet to wipe out humanity. The *Transformers* television series (1984–1987) and subsequent blockbuster films (starting with *Transformers* in 2007) feature giant robots from outer space, many of which are out to destroy humankind. The fourth season of the Marvel television series *Agents of S.H.I.E.L.D.* pits its heroes against a malevolent AI, described as a "life-model-decoy" or LMD. Incredulous that anyone would create such a thing, one agent asks another, "Haven't these people seen any movies from the '80s? The robots always attack."

But it wasn't just the 1980s, and it wasn't just robots. For example, *Titanic* (1997) may be a sentimental and tragic love story, but it has a deep undercurrent of technophobia running within it: it is, after all, a story about a technological disaster caused by scientific hubris, the "unsinkable" ship that fails to live up to its billing. The *Lord of the Rings* films (2001–2014) are, at least in part, about the dangers of industrialization (think of Saruman's tearing down forests to manufacture his Uruk-hai warriors and their weapons) and dramatize the struggle to acquire and wield what amounts to a manufactured superweapon: the "one ring to rule them all." In *Spider-Man* (2002) and *Spider-Man 2* (2004), Peter Parker develops his strange new powers after being bitten by a genetically engineered super-spider (updated from the radioactive spider that appeared in the original comic book), while the Green Goblin and Doc Ock are the results of new military technology gone awry. *Avatar* (2009) is about the misuse of technology by a greedy corporation intent on strip-mining a planet full of natural marvels. And in *Star Trek*—one of the most successful science-fiction series of all time—we find a similar undercurrent of technophobia. Many episodes of the original *Star Trek* television series pitted Captain Kirk and his comrades against machines that sought to restrict the freedom and autonomy of human beings. Although the original *Star Trek* series (1966–1969) did celebrate the technological advances that were making space travel a reality in the 1960s, the show frequently dramatized the need for technology to remain under human control, a theme that marks all of the subsequent *Star Trek* films and television series. These films and television series are merely the tip of the iceberg: the deep-seated fear that humanity will be unable to control the technologies that it creates is an abiding theme in the history of motion pictures.

Moreover, *A New Hope* was one of a number of films released in the late 1970s and early 1980s that promoted a mythology of rugged individualism based on single combat in which technology is seen as a necessary evil at best: it must either remain firmly under human control or be avoided altogether. To cite only two examples, in 1985's *Rocky IV*, our hero Rocky Balboa's regimen of chopping down trees, hauling dogsleds, and carrying logs in the snow of Krasnogorsk outside Moscow enables him to defeat a Soviet boxer trained with the latest sports technology. In the 1987 film *Predator*, Arnold Schwarzenegger's commando must battle an extraterrestrial hunter of human beings who is equipped with incredibly advanced weaponry and tracking systems. So how does Schwarzenegger's character defeat this alien and its superhuman technology? By covering himself in mud, building traps made with wooden stakes, and using a bow and arrow.

Something similar occurs in the climactic battle of *Return of the Jedi*. Mark Hamill remembers that Lucas "loved the idea of medieval technology taking down advanced technology with catapults and trip-wires and all that sort of thing."[2] Lucas himself commented:

> The Wookiee planet that I created for *Star Wars* was eventually turned into the Ewok planet in *Jedi*. I basically cut the Wookiees in half and called them Ewoks! I didn't make Endor a Wookiee planet because Chewbacca was sophisticated technologically and I wanted the characters involved in the battle to be primitive.[3]

Low tech is the mark of the true individualist. We like it that the *Millennium Falcon* is ramshackle and every now and then needs Han to pound his fist on its panels in order to work more or less properly.

It seems counterintuitive: how can the 1977 *Star Wars*, a movie that led to a revolution in special-effects technology, possibly be an example of the fear of technology? Technophobia is often a response to—and therefore is often accompanied by—its opposite, technophilia, the love of technology. As Isaac Asimov has pointed out, "any technological advance, however fundamental, has the double aspect of good/harm and, in response is viewed with a double aspect of love/fear." Asimov gives the examples of two early technological advances within primitive human cultures: the controlling of fire and the making of weapons. "Fire warms you, gives you light, cooks your food, smelts your ore—and out of control, burns and kills. Your knives and spears kill your animal enemies and your human foes and, out of your control, are used by your foes to kill you."[4] Technology can be celebrated, but only as long as it remains instrumental. The successful special-effects film itself might represent an example of the proper use of technology.

The Luddite Imagination

There's a name for this attitude toward technology: Luddism. The term comes from the Luddite Rebellion, which erupted in Nottinghamshire in 1811 when stocking-knitters broke into workshops and sabotaged the "wide-frame" machines that were threatening their livelihoods. It has come to signify an irrational hatred of technology and progress. But recently historians have argued that the Luddites were not opposed to machines and technology per se; what they opposed was the use of machines to establish a system of economic and social domination. After all, those who became Luddites had worked since the sixteenth century on relatively complex knitting machines, but the machines were used by a single individual, working out of a cottage or a small shop. In the early nineteenth century, however, these artisans saw their way of life threatened by the introduction of large-scale machines, housed in massive buildings, which automated a good deal of the weaving process. The weavers recognized that these machines threatened to transform what had been the product of artisans into something that could be mass-produced. The Luddites were protesting the beginnings of the exploitation of the working classes that would accompany the onset of industrialism.[5] In both the Luddite Rebellion and the rebellion that *Star Wars* depicts, we find an attempt to preserve and promote individual agency and to instill an attitude toward technology that harkens back to the conceptions of "art" or "skill" that are a part of the etymology of the term "technology," an attitude that preserves the dignity of the individual.

Technology is supposed to be about designing tools, machines, and techniques that can make us more skillful, that enhance our ability to act in the world. It is supposed to extend both individuality and agency. But does it? Are we compromised if we use a tool rather than our own two hands, if we require the assistance of technology to achieve our ends? Can we take full credit for our achievements if we need technological assistance? We probably would not consider someone who uses a computer-aided design program to create an image to be as true an artist as someone who uses pencil and paint. We do not allow athletes to take advantage of biotechnological advances such as steroids, for example. Indeed, this example suggests a further fear that we might be damaging ourselves as we use technology. Is it possible that reliance on technology erodes our ability to be self-reliant, to be independent and autonomous? Does it compromise our very identity?

Plato thought so. He may well be one of the earliest recorded human technophobes in Western culture. He was wary of the changes arising from a revolution in communications technology—namely, the invention of writing. In the *Phaedrus*, Plato recounts how Socrates argues that writing is a tool that diminishes us: it weakens our memories and makes us think we know more than we do. It is a crutch for the mind. It is, says Socrates, "but a reminiscence of what we know." Moreover, written texts cannot defend themselves, respond to questions, or clarify their arguments; they are imprecise and static. What is better than the written text, according to Socrates, is oral speech, because it is dynamic. For these reasons, reliance on technology is dangerous and unwise in Plato's *Phaedrus*.

In John Milton's epic poem, *Paradise Lost* (1674), it is dangerous and even immoral. In Book 6 of the poem, the apostate angel Lucifer proves his unworthiness by violating the traditional rules of combat during the war in heaven between his force of Rebel Angels and the forces of God, led by the archangels Michael and Gabriel. After suffering losses during the first day's fighting, Lucifer devises what Milton calls "devilish Engines": he builds cannons capable of simulating the wrath of God's thunder. The angel Raphael—who is recounting the story of the battle to Adam—describes Satan's invention as a "fraud." The cannons work at first:

> From those deep throated Engines belched, whose roar
> Embowelled with outrageous noise the air,
> And all her entrails tore, disgorging foul

> Their devilish glut, chained thunderbolts and hail
> Of iron globes; which, on the victor host
> Levelled, with such impetuous fury smote,
> That whom they hit, none on their feet might stand,
> Though standing else as rocks, but down they fell
> By thousands, Angel on Archangel rolled,
> The sooner for their Arms; unarmed, they might
> Have easily, as spirits, evaded swift
> By quick contraction or remove; but now
> Foul dissipation followed and forced rout;
> Nor served it to relax their serried files. (ll. 586–600)

Raphael describes this setback as an "indecent overthrow" (l. 602), and it does not last for long. Finding their weapons to be an impediment that prevents them from making tactical use of their abilities as "spirits," the angels perform a version of Luke Skywalker's decision to turn off his computer: they finally throw away "their arms" and "from their foundations loosening to and fro / They plucked the seated hills, with all their load" (ll. 643-4) and bury Satan and his allies "under the weight of mountains" (l. 652). To add insult to injury, the devils find that "their armour helped their harm, crushed in and bruised / Into their substance pent, which wrought them pain / Implacable, and many a dolorous groan" (ll. 656-8). In *Paradise Lost*, reliance on technology is the Devil's strategy.

Paradise Lost was published in 1667, but a similar conception of what kind of weaponry is morally permissible on a battlefield can be found more than 200 years later. In *The Social History of the Machine Gun* (1975), John Ellis argues that the machine gun, though invented in 1862, was not used widely until the First World War, because of an anti-machine mindset among the officer corps of Western Europe, which was drawn primarily from landed gentry rather than industrialists. Recognizing that "machines had brought with them industrialisation and the destruction of the traditional social order," these officers felt that they must hold the line on the battlefield: machines "must not be allowed to undermine the old certainties of the battlefield—the glorious charge and the opportunities for individual heroism."[6]

The Jedi embody the kind of individual heroism that these officers want to preserve and promote. The Jedi, of course, do not eschew technology altogether. No Jedi feels dressed without his or her lightsaber (see Figure 10). But these are personal and indeed handmade weapons. Each Jedi is an artisan who designs and fashions his or her own weapon. Indeed, construction of the lightsaber signifies the culmination of a Jedi's training: as Darth Vader himself tells Luke Skywalker in *Return of the Jedi*, "I see you have constructed a new lightsaber. Your skills are complete."[7] Their attitudes toward the

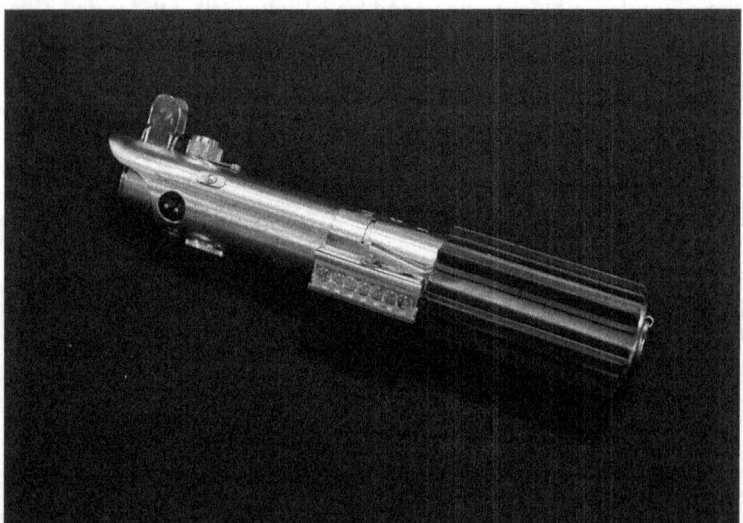

Figure 10 Luke Skywalker's first lightsaber. The prop that Mark Hamill used in the 1977 film. Photo credit: Mark Ralston. Getty Images.

lightsaber thus resemble the attitudes held by the original Luddites. The sequel trilogy places even greater emphasis on the significance of the lightsaber: it is Rey's finding of the lightsaber that Luke lost on Cloud City that sparks the vision that represents her "first step into a wider world"; it is Luke's shocking rejection of that same lightsaber that provides the first indication of the thematic dynamics at play in *The Last Jedi*; it is the use of Luke's and Leia's lightsabers by Kylo and Rey, respectively, that serves as the symbolic foundation for the resolution of *The Rise of Skywalker*; and the final moments of that film demonstrate that Rey has constructed her own lightsaber, signifying that *her* skills are complete.

In *The Human Condition* (1958), Hannah Arendt argues that "the task and potential greatness of mortals lie in their ability to produce things—works and deeds and words—which would deserve to be and, at least to a degree, are at home in everlastingness, so that through them mortals could find their place in a cosmos where everything is immortal except themselves."[8] The name that Arendt gives to the activity that produces "things" in this sense is "work," in contrast to "labor," which is what human beings do in order to subsist. "Labor" is therefore natural, while "work" in Arendt's conception "corresponds to the unnaturalness of human existence, which is not imbedded in, and whose mortality is not compensated by, the species' ever-recurring life cycle."[9] To describe the human being who works, Arendt uses the term *homo faber* (literally, "man the maker") in contrast to the human being who merely works, whom she designates *animal laborans*. Moreover, Arendt asserts, "No work can be produced without tools, and the birth of *homo faber* and the coming into being of a man-made world of things are actually coeval with the discovery of tools and instruments."[10]

Arendt was a critic of the way that modernity had developed in the West, in part because she believed it brought with it the devaluation of *homo faber* and the elevation of *animal laborans* because of a misunderstanding of the nature and significance of tools and technology. The development of the belief "that every tool and implement is primarily designed to make human life easier and human labor less painful" gave priority to the use that *animal laborans* could make of tools rather than *homo faber*, who gradually came to be seen "not as the maker of objects and the builder of the human artifice who incidentally invents tools, but considers himself primarily a toolmaker"—indeed, a maker of "tools to make tools"—who only incidentally also produces things."[11] Using the term "world" to represent what man creates that is durable, Arendt argues that modernity has led us to forget that "*homo faber*, the toolmaker, invented tools and implements in order to erect a world, not—at least, not primarily—to help the human life process." For Arendt, then, the pressing question "is not so much whether we are the masters or the slaves of our machines, but whether machines still serve the world and its things, or if, on the contrary, they and the automatic motion of their processes have begun to rule and even destroy world and things."[12] Arendt hints at the idea of technological determinism, the idea that a society's technologies have a profound impact on its modes of organization and its cultural values.

Arendt's discussion depicts the creation of tools as part of the process by which human beings attempt to achieve a higher purpose, to move beyond mere survival to the achievement of something durable that can outlast brief human lifespans. But the emphasis on toolmaking takes on a life of its own, and tools are regarded as an end rather than a means for *homo faber*, an end that provides means for *animal laborans* to labor more effectively. The higher purpose of toolmaking is thus lost. Arendt's fears are dramatized by the first *Star Wars* trilogy, in which the Empire constructs a Death Star and uses it to destroy a world—literally—before our eyes. In *The Force Awakens*,

J. J. Abrams depicts a further advance in Death Star technology: the First Order's Starkiller Base is able to destroy several planets at once—and from long range. *The Last Jedi* and *The Rise of Skywalker* show us the proliferation of Death Star technology, as its laser cannons are made portable.

In the first trilogy, the Empire is personified for the films' audiences by Darth Vader and his mechanized breathing. In *Return of the Jedi*, Obi-Wan adopts a view close to technological determinism when he suggests to Luke that Vader cannot be redeemed: "He is more machine now than man. Twisted and evil."[13] But as we've seen, even Vader has his doubts about the power of the machine, which he believes is far outstripped by "the power of the Force."[14] Vader's belief is proven to be correct at the end of the film, when Luke destroys the Death Star using the Force rather than his ship's computer to aim his missile. The Empire's decision to build a second Death Star shows that it hasn't learned from its mistake, and the trilogy's finale once again affirms the power of the Force—and all it stands for—over technology.

Arendt's account also offers us a way of thinking about the use of special effects in the *Star Wars* films. Lucas's goal in creating Industrial Light and Magic was not to create a special-effects shop and a technologically advanced set of filmmaking tools for their own sake: he was doing what was necessary to try to translate the images he had in his head onto the screen. His goal was to make a durable thing in Arendt's sense of the term, a work of cinematic art that would be a permanent part of human storytelling culture. Indeed, for Arendt, the true work of art is the highest example of human making: it has a "transcendence" that "distinguishes the great work of art from all other products of human hands" and legitimates "the conviction of *homo faber* that a man's products may be more and essentially greater than himself."[15]

The first *Star Wars* films made significant use of puppets, models, and advanced computer-controlled stop-motion techniques, but by the time Lucas came to make the prequel trilogy, digital special effects were sufficiently advanced to enable him to create scenes (like a meeting between Han Solo and Jabba the Hutt in the Mos Eisley spaceport) that he had not been able to film properly in the 1970s due to technological (and financial) limitations. Lucas took advantage of digital technology to revise the original trilogy, adding digital characters and vehicles to make both Mos Eisley and the Cloud City in *Empire* seem properly populated, and even completing and restoring the scene between Han and Jabba. Critics of Lucas's "special editions" of the original trilogy believed that he was making these changes just because he could, that the existence of the tool engendered a desire to use the tool in ways that, for some fans, had the effect of destroying the world of the original films with which they had fallen in love. Some fans preferred the less mimetically convincing puppet Yoda that was used in *The Phantom Menace* to the digital version that replaced it when the film was released on home video. If the special-effects film is an example of the right use of technology, then for these fans the overuse of digital special effects represented a decadent phase that led to the wrong use of technology.

The sequel trilogy would remedy that problem. Describing the genesis of *The Force Awakens*, screenwriter Lawrence Kasdan told *Vanity Fair*, "There was a feeling, even I think when George was still there, that we wanted to have more of a slightly retro feeling—more tactile and less CG-oriented."[16] The visual design team went to the Lucasfilm archives to consult the legendary production paintings that Ralph McQuarrie had created in 1975 for the first film.[17] Neal Scanlan, the special-effects artist who supervised creature effects for *The Force Awakens*, reported, "We tried to hold on to the same philosophy as they had in 1977, where people ran out to hardware shops, bought a bunch of stuff and used their imaginations."[18] This attitude is a way of returning to the idea of *homo faber* and its emphasis on making something durable: the aesthetic of the films emphasizes a kind of palpability that Abrams and his colleagues do not believe that digital effects alone can achieve. Part of the immediate appeal of the *Mandalorian* television series was its return to practical effects that recall the look of the 1977 film, even as it used a revolutionary new 3D visualization technology called "Stagecraft," developed by ILM and first used on the film *Solo*. Stagecraft creates a more "realistic" filmmaking experience for actors, who act against virtual backgrounds rather than green screens.[19]

Arendt's account might also remind us of the genealogy of a kind of technology that is seen as the ultimate piece of toolmaking: the robot. The word first appeared in 1921 in the play *R.U.R.* by the Czech playwright Karel Čapek, and it was coined by Čapek's brother, Josef, from the Czech word *robota*, which means "forced labor" or "servitude." "R.U.R." stands for "Rossum's Universal Robots," and Čapek's allegorical play depicts a company whose founder, Rossum (from the Czech *rozum*, meaning "reason"), has discovered how to make artificial persons. His nephew realizes that by simplifying the process and stripping these persons of feelings and other unnecessary attributes, he can create the perfect worker: the robot. These robots are much in demand; eventually they are used as mercenaries with devastating results. And when the wife of the company's director secretly has one of the scientists enable the robots to transcend some of their limitations because she feels sorry for them, disaster ensues. The robots revolt, and in the end all human beings but one—a worker—are killed. The play ends when two robots—one male, one female—develop emotions: they will repopulate the earth with a new race of super beings.

The term "robot" is thus linked from its very inception to the idea that technology will destroy its creators if it is not treated responsibly. The play was a success and opened in London, where it sparked debates and commentary from prominent intellectuals including George Bernard Shaw. Critics quickly recognized that one of Čapek's key sources was Mary Shelley's novel *Frankenstein* (1818). Shelley subtitled her novel "The Modern Prometheus," recognizing that the Prometheus myth is all about technological progress, the transmission of fire technology from the gods to human beings. Shelley understood the connection between the Prometheus myth and her era's increasing faith in scientific and technological progress; her modern Prometheus is deluded by his mastery of technology into thinking he is a god.[20]

If fire is humankind's first tool, then the robot is the ultimate tool: the machine that can perform tasks that were once only the province of human beings. In *R.U.R.*, the company director's dream is a world in which robots have freed humankind from the necessity to labor, essentially undoing the curse of original sin: "There'll be no more poverty," he says. "Yes, people will be out of work, but by then there will be no work left to be done. Everything will be done by living machines. People will do only what they enjoy. They will live only to perfect themselves."[21] The various versions of Frankenstein suggest a less idealistic attitude: near the beginning of *The Bride of Frankenstein* (1935), Colin Clive's Frankenstein laments the failure of his experiment: "I did it. I created a man. And who knows in time I could have trained him to do my will. I could have bred a race." This Frankenstein does not seem interested in engendering another free and equal being; he seems, instead, bent on the creation of a race of robots that will do his bidding. The Frankenstein films further suggest the robotic nature of the monster in a way that Shelley did not by implanting bolts into the side of the monster's neck—pieces of machinery that have now become a permanent part of Frankenstein's pop iconography (see Figure 11).

Figure 11 Boris Karloff as the Monster in *The Bride of Frankenstein* (1935). The most iconic—and arguably the most horrific—aspect of Boris Karloff's portrayal of "the Monster" in James Whale's films *Frankenstein* (1931) and *The Bride of Frankenstein* (1935) is the two metal bolts in the sides of his neck, which emphasize the link between the creature and technology and make him a cyborg. Photo credit: Universal Pictures.

Not Robots, but Droids

Narratives about robots investigate what happens when the lines between the human and the machine begin to blur. From *Frankenstein* through *R.U.R.*, from *2001* to the *Terminator* and *Matrix* films, the creation of an intelligent machine is continually depicted as both a dream and a nightmare, the highest possible achievement of human technology, but potentially the achievement that will be the undoing of humanity. Even in the ostensibly enlightened future culture depicted by *Star Trek: The Next Generation* and *Star Trek: Voyager*, which feature an android commander and a holographic doctor, respectively, these nearly human machines experience glitches that frequently render them dangerous to their fellow crewmen.

If, as I've suggested, Stanley Kubrick's *2001: A Space Odyssey* shaped the immediate horizon of expectations for science-fiction films when Lucas was putting together the first *Star Wars* film, then Lucas's depiction of robots and artificial intelligence is one of the ways in which he challenges that horizon. Indeed, this portrayal marks a departure from his own science-fiction film *THX 1138* (1971), which featured robot police who were cold and mechanical. Lucas signaled the difference by calling the robots in *Star Wars* "droids" in order to avoid the negative connotations that have tended to accompany the word "robot" since its appearance in *R.U.R.* Indeed, in his foreword to Anthony Daniels's autobiography, *I Am C-3PO* (2019), J. J. Abrams argues that the presentation of the droids he "first met when [he] was ten years old" was crucial part of the film's effect on its first audiences. Describing the first scene aboard Leia's Blockade Runner ship, Abrams writes that "what happens next is what's most important. We fall in love"—with the droids: "Nearly the instant we meet stalwart droids C-3PO and R2-D2, we laugh. They become our way into a galaxy we're so desperate to be a part of."[22]

The droids C-3PO and R2-D2 are the only characters who appear in each of the nine films of the Skywalker saga, and the films use C-3PO, R2-D2, and the sequel trilogy's BB-8 and D-O as an ethical index: the good guys treat their advanced droids as sentient individuals worthy of respect and protection; the bad guys use their droids as interchangeable and disposable robots. Think about the treatment of droids by the Trade Federation in *The Phantom Menace* (1999), the

Empire in the original trilogy or *Rogue One* (2016), the neo-Imperial First Order and the shady characters Unkar Plutt and Teedo in the sequel trilogy, or the administrators of the Kessel spice mines in the anthology film *Solo* (2018). Then contrast that with the individual construction of lightsabers by the Jedi and later Luke, the fact that the good guys call their droids by nicknames ("Artoo," "Threepio"), or the real affection that Han Solo has for his ramshackle ship the *Millennium Falcon*. Indeed, in *Solo*, we learn that Han's personification of the *Falcon* isn't merely the sentimental personification that ship's captains have long used in referring to their ships with feminine pronouns. In fact, the Falcon's computer turns out to be an amalgam of two artificial intelligences, its original droid brain and the brain that has been salvaged from the freethinking droid L3, whom the film has depicted affectionately as Lando Calrissian's erstwhile—and female—buddy.[23] The droids are able to escape to the planet Tatooine with the Death Star plans because the Imperials aren't looking for droids: "An escape pod was jettisoned during the fighting, but no life-forms were aboard," an officer tells Darth Vader, who realizes that the plans must nonetheless be hidden in the pod. But the first words that we hear Threepio utter when we see him and Artoo on the planet indicate that he, at least, considers himself to be a "life-form": "How did we get into this mess? I really don't know how. We seem to be made to suffer. It's our lot in life."[24]

Interestingly, the droids did not exist in the first treatment for the 1977 film, which instead featured two Imperial bureaucrats modeled after the two farmers in Akira Kurosawa's *The Hidden Fortress* (1958): they were there for comic relief. Later, as he began to flesh out the universe that he had imagined, Lucas decided to focus on the droid as "the lowest person on the pecking order, basically like the farmers in *The Hidden Fortress*."[25] The low standing of the droids becomes clear quickly when our heroes walk into the Mos Eisley Cantina. Full of all kinds of exotic nonhumans, the Cantina seems like a cosmopolitan sort of place, but the bartender points to the droids and tells Luke Skywalker: "We don't serve their kind here. They'll have to wait outside. We don't want them here."[26] As the film progresses, we see just how unenlightened the bartender's attitude is, as the droids establish themselves as heroic characters who are crucial to the Rebellion's success—and to the film's.[27]

Ironically, after the release of the 1977 film, Lucasfilm's treatment of the actor who plays Threepio, Anthony Daniels, was not as enlightened as it might have been, perhaps due to the success of Daniels's performance, which convinced many viewers that the droid was a "real" robot. In his autobiography, Daniels writes that he was deliberately left out of all the publicity promoting the film:

> Apparently, whoever was responsible for the marketing of the film, felt it would detract from the believability of the robot, were it to be known that it was, in fact, a costume with a person inside. An actor, responsible for bringing the character to life—for every nuance of performance, every gesture, every reaction, each emotion. … I was pleased, if not amazed, that fans were so convinced by my depiction of a technology that is still far from becoming a reality. But would it really have harmed the box office to admit there was an actor inside the suit?[28]

Lucas himself, frustrated by the technical difficulties posed by Daniels's costume, only managed to compliment Daniels on his performances months after the film's premiere. Noting that he "wouldn't be writing here without the inspiration of George Lucas's inspiration," Daniels nevertheless notes that "sincerely grateful as I am, it's perhaps understandable that I would have preferred to feel that respect from the start."[29] In his foreword, Abrams makes sure not to replicate Lucas's mistake. "Why is it that we fall in love with Threepio the moment we meet him?" he asks. "My humbling experience on these films has given me the answer: It's because there's a man inside."[30] These anecdotes have the effect of reinforcing the idea of treating others with dignity and respect that is necessary—whether those "others" are droids or actors—but not always a natural impulse.

At the same time, the *Star Wars* films themselves also respect droids by allowing some droids to be "bad guys." The battle and destroyer droids fight on the side of the Separatists against the Jedi in the prequel trilogy and the canonical *Clone Wars* television series, and it is literally a dark version of BB-8 in *The Last Jedi*—BB-9E—who exposes Finn, Rose, and DJ to Captain Phasma and the First Order. In *The Empire Strikes Back*, one of the bounty hunters assembled by Darth Vader to track down Han Solo and Princess Leia is the droid IG-88, who would become a fan favorite in the Expanded Universe stories, leading to the inclusion of a similar bounty-hunting droid, IG-11, in the live-action television series *The Mandalorian* (2019–). The comic series *Doctor Aphra* goes so far as to include two psychotic killer droids who happened to be the same models as Threepio and Artoo. What the *Star Wars* saga does not depict, however, in contrast, say, to *Star Trek*, is a beloved droid character turning bad, either due to a programming malfunction or being hacked. The innate fear of the dangers of artificial intelligence that animates *R.U.R.*, *2001*, *Star Trek*, the *Terminator* and *Matrix* films, and the film and then the television series *Westworld* is not an abiding fear in the *Star Wars* saga.

Like the Luddites before them, what motivates the good guys in the *Star Wars* films is not the fear of technology per se—not even at its most advanced in the form of artificial intelligence—but rather, the fear that technology will be removed from their control and misused to enhance the agency of the few at the expense of the many. The *Star Wars* films suggest that human beings must develop a healthy relationship to the technologies they create by recognizing the responsibilities that accompany the creation of advanced technologies. Indeed, the depiction of the droids suggests that once we create artificial intelligences, we need to respect them as intelligences and not denigrate them as artificial. Treat droids like Artoo and Threepio with respect and dignity, and they will reciprocate.

Čapek's play *R.U.R.* reminds us that Mary Shelley's novel *Frankenstein* is a story about scientific advances and the creation of new technology, but readers might be forgiven for not thinking about this idea because the novel itself de-emphasizes it. Victor Frankenstein refuses to divulge the process by which he brings his creature to life lest hearers who miss the point of his history might be tempted to replicate his procedures. And the creature is presented as a human being rather than a machine. The first Hollywood film versions, James Whale's *Frankenstein* (1931) and *The Bride of Frankenstein* (1935), change the logic of Shelley's novel by taking us into Frankenstein's lab and emphasizing the process of creation (which involves lots of machines and the use of electricity generated by lightning). Arguably the most monstrous thing about the creature as played by Boris Karloff is the prominent presence of the two metal bolts in the side of his neck, which (as we've noted) signify a link to the idea of the robot. But they also connect the creature to a figure that looms large in the technophobic imagination: the cyborg.

Hybridity and the Cyborg

The cyborg is a hybrid of human and machine, a human being who has been augmented with machine parts so that he or she is no longer—fully, completely, only?—human. The cyborg represents a challenge to the idea of the liberal individual, either because it represents the erosion of individuality or because its augmented powers render ordinary human individuals comparatively inadequate. In fact, however, the cyborgs that any of us are likely to meet on any given day are neither grotesque nor threatening. My late aunt, for example, was a cyborg, because she had a machine implanted in her: a pacemaker. Such a cyborg does not make us uncomfortable. But what if people were to have chips implanted in their brains that could heighten their intelligence? We start to get squeamish. We start to worry about whether such people are altered in some fundamental way. Our understanding of human identity starts to seem unclear, even fragile.

The cyborg often appears in US popular culture as a monstrous hybrid, a figure that inspires fear. For example, the most fearsome enemy in *Star Trek: The Next Generation*, *Star Trek: Deep Space Nine* (1993–1999), and *Star Trek: Voyager* is the Borg, a race of voraciously imperialistic cyborgs who seek "to raise quality of life for all species" in the galaxy by establishing a "new order" in which all technologies, cultures, and species will be assimilated, becoming "one with the Borg." Each physical Borg unit may look like an individual humanoid, but in fact each is simply a cog in a giant machine, an expendable part of a greater whole. Assimilation into the collective intelligence that is the Borg means not only loss of humanity but also loss of individuality. Darth Vader at least has that: in contrast to what Obi-Wan believes, Vader retains his individuality, a fact that ultimately makes his redemption possible at the end of *Return of the Jedi*.

The Borg serve as an allegory for late twentieth-century fears about what technology does to us: it strips us of individuality; it mechanizes us; it makes us part of a hive mind. It should come as no surprise that the Borg were also the most popular villain among *Star Trek* fans. Indeed, in a bid to boost ratings for *Star Trek: Voyager*, a female Borg named Seven-of-Nine was added to the crew of the Starship Voyager, and many of the show's episodes during its final seasons revolved around the problems that arise during her resocialization into humanity. Similarly, the foe that dominated the final seasons of the third *Star Trek* series, *Star Trek: Deep Space Nine*, was the Dominion, a technologically advanced society of shape-shifters whose natural state is liquid rather than solid and whose idea of Nirvana is to merge into a collective state called "The Link," in which the concept of individuality is meaningless. In the second season of *Star Trek: Discovery*, a hive-mind AI called "Control" seeks to wipe out all sentient organic life and uses swarming networked nanobots to take over human hosts. The Borg, the Dominion, and Control tap into some of US culture's deepest fears, and late twentieth-century films such as the *Alien* series (1979–1997), *Starship Troopers* (1997), *The X-Files* (television series 1993–2002, 2016–2018; film 1998), and *The Matrix* (1999) employ the hive mind in a similar fashion, depicting it as an enemy to be combated.

These representations of the hive mind draw on the post-nuclear logic of the Cold War imagination. Often, they are latter-day manifestations of the fears dramatized in such science-fiction films of the 1950s as *The Thing* (1951), *Invaders from Mars* (1953), *Invasion of the Body Snatchers* (1956), and *The Blob* (1958). In *Them!* (1954), giant ants—like the Cold War itself a product of the nuclear age—are described as "chronic aggressors [who] make slave laborers out of their captives." A scientist in the movie shows a film about the ants and emphasizes the "industry, social organization, and savagery" of the ants, warning that "unless the queens are destroyed, man as the dominant species on this planet will probably be destroyed." To the audience within the film watching the documentary footage, the scientist is talking about ants, but to the 1950s audience watching *Them!*, he is quite clearly talking about communism. Indeed, near the end of the film, when the army is sent to Los Angeles to do battle with the ants, a reporter asks, "Has the cold war gotten hot?" making the allegory explicit. And in *The Blob*, individuals in a small town are assimilated by the voracious blob, which grows larger with each human meal and can only be defeated through a kind of literal cold war: it is frozen with a multitude of CO_2 fire extinguishers and then dropped into the ice of the Arctic.

The hive mind makes a few appearances in the *Star Wars* universe. In *The Phantom Menace*, the Trade Federation employs battle droids that are controlled and coordinated by a central computer aboard its fleet's flagship. This design proves to be a fatal flaw, because when young Anakin Skywalker manages to destroy the flagship using his single-pilot fighter, the droids who have invaded the planet Naboo, and seem to be winning the climactic battle, suddenly shut down. In *Attack of the Clones*, we learn that these droids are manufactured on the planet Geonosis by an insect-like species that turn out to have a hive intelligence, although that fact is only implied rather than openly stated in the film. The film reveals that the Geonosians are at work on what audiences who have seen the original trilogy will know to be the Death Star. The workings of the Geonosian hive mind are explored more fully in the novel *Catalyst*, which depicts the early stages of the superweapon's development.

Attack of the Clones also reveals the development of the Republic's clone army, which recalls the dynamics of a hive intelligence: the clones are identical, interchangeable, and programmed through brainwashing to follow commands. In *Revenge of the Sith*, the clones are revealed to have a particular piece of programming called Order 66 that, when activated, leads them to be convinced that the Jedi are traitors. After the coup against the Jedi, the droids are decommissioned and the clones take their place to become the first Imperial stormtroopers. In *Catalyst*, the analogy between the Geonosian hive and the servants of the Empire—whether stormtroopers or other workers—is made explicit: the lead scientist looks around the facility where he works and tells a coworker, "This place has become a hive." The coworker replies, "It's like this all over. The institute is conscripting candidates from university programs even before they graduate. So many people working on so many projects."[31] In the *Clone Wars* television series, it's revealed that the clones technically are cyborgs, because their hive programming is the result of a piece of hardware implanted into the bodies. The Clones who have defied Order 66 and become major characters in the series have discovered the existence of the chips and removed them, allowing them to be immune to Order 66's command to kill all Jedi. Although they do draw on the same cultural associations that motivate Cold War representations of the hive mind, the *Star Wars* depictions generally differ because they don't imagine the hive intelligence to be a primary threat: in all cases, the hive is subjugated to the control of someone outside the hive, and the communal mind is depicted as a tactical weakness.

The hive mind scares us because it is a mind that resembles a machine. It transforms individuals into interchangeable parts rather than unifying them into a collaborative enterprise in which each can maintain his or her individuality. It seems soulless, devoid of that prized quality individuality, a point driven home in *Star Wars* by analogy that the prequel films draw between the Separatist's droid army and the Republic's clones. Twentieth-century US popular culture often used the hive mind as a figure for communism. But depictions of the hive mind persist even with the waning of communism in Europe, and that is because there are other fears that find expression in depictions of the hive mind. First, hives are communities governed by queens. They are matriarchies, and thus represent a challenge to the patriarchal norms that undergird US popular culture. In *Star Trek: First Contact* (1996), we see that Captain Jean-Luc Picard's assimilation into the Borg collective is a form of rape, in which he is penetrated and feminized. The hive mind is thus a challenge to traditional—that is, rugged and male—individualism.

Second, the Borg's desire to "assimilate" other species invokes the depictions of the hive mind as a threat to individualism that can be found in nineteenth-century yellow peril fictions like P. W. Dooner's *Last Days of the Republic* (published in 1880, two years before the Chinese Exclusion Act), which depicted all Asians as insect-like automata who, if allowed to immigrate and participate in American democracy, would inevitably overrun the United States and assimilate its culture. During this period, the Chinese were described as completely alien because their culture was regarded as the antithesis of American individualism. Putting self-interest aside, the Chinese banded together and managed to undercut white labor by working harder and for lower wages; they were depicted as inhuman in their ability to subsist on starvation wages. According to a message sent by the California legislature to the US Congress in 1877, the "compensation" for Chinese labor "is so low in proportion to the necessities of life in California that the white laborer cannot compete with the Chinaman."[32] Indeed, although the original *Star Wars* trilogy seems at first to have an enlightened attitude toward race—one of the marks of the Empire's illegitimacy is its discrimination against nonhuman species—the Orientalist depiction of the Trade Federation's Neimoidians in *The Phantom Menace* draws on the latter-day yellow peril imagery that was present in the 1930s serials like *Flash Gordon* that inspired Lucas.

In short, technophobia often serves as a cultural metaphor for other sorts of anxieties. Pop representations of technophobia are often about more than simply the threat to individualism that technology is thought to pose: they are also about the fear that individuality and agency are somehow being threatened by social changes linked to class, race, ethnicity, and gender relations. In 1997, the year that the *Star Wars* trilogy was rereleased with great commercial success, Ted Kaczynski, the "Unabomber," was brought to trial. The *New York*

Times described Kaczynski as the "ultimate technophobe," and in his manifesto, "Industrial Society and Its Future," Kaczynski wrote that "modern man has the sense that change is imposed on him, whereas the 19th-century frontiersman had the sense that he created change himself, by his own choice." By destroying technological society, Kaczynski believed, humankind could regain that sense of control, living alone or in small groups and communing with "wild nature." But even as Kaczynski's manifesto attacks technology in the name of individualism, it also assails "leftists" and "feminists" because they are "anti-individualistic [and] pro-collectivist."[33] Kaczynski was an extremist to be sure, but what I am suggesting is that he presents a pathological version of a set of fears that seems to run deep within US culture. Often, fear of technology acts as a cover for fears about the changing dynamics of class, gender, sexuality, and race. When Americans think about workplace automation, the dominance of the "Big Five" tech companies, or genetic engineering with suspicion, it is the same suspicion with which they regard group-oriented ideas such as affirmative action, feminism, and socialism: all of these fears represent manifestations of anxiety about the erosion of individual agency. In short, what appear to be disparate phenomena are, in fact, manifestations of a single cluster of cultural anxieties, an ideological hive.

Cultural studies scholarship, however, has seen in the cyborg not a reason to fear but rather a way to challenge individualist modes of thinking. For the feminist theorist of technology Donna Haraway, the cyborg is important as a cultural icon precisely because it poses these kinds of challenges to the normative views about identity imposed by individualistic culture. She suggests that the cyborg may serve not only as a symbol of late twentieth-century conceptions of identity but also as a challenge to the political systems that engender and enforce them:

> From one perspective, a cyborg world is about the final imposition of a grid of control on the planet, about the final abstraction embodied in a Star Wars apocalypse waged in the name of defense. ... From another perspective, a cyborg world might be about lived social and bodily realities in which people are not afraid of their joint kinship with animals and machines, not afraid of permanently partial identities and contradictory standpoints.

For Haraway, the "political struggle is to see from both perspectives at once because each reveals both dominations and possibilities unimaginable from the other vantage point."[34]

I suggest that something like a dialogue between these two points of view is at work in the *Star Wars* films, though of course the saga as a whole encourages its viewers to adopt the second perspective. In the first film, Obi-Wan comments about Darth Vader that he has become more machine than man, but the overall arc of the film suggests that the mechanization of Vader is only an external manifestation of his decision to dehumanize himself by embracing the dark side of the Force. And Obi-Wan himself becomes something of a Victor Frankenstein-figure whose overstepping of boundaries leads ultimately to the creation of Darth Vader, a being in whom the human is nothing more than a ghost in the machine. It is, of course, Emperor Palpatine who is the final Frankenstein, as he takes the near-dead Anakin Skywalker and gives him new life as Darth Vader in a scene near the end of *Revenge of the Sith* that makes overt visual reference to imagery from Frankenstein films. Palpatine and Vader's Empire is a version of the first perspective that Haraway describes, as the two Sith lords seek to impose a grid of control not just on a world but on the entire galaxy.

The ideas of the hive mind and of networked intelligence that underlie the figure of the cyborg actually do play a role in the climactic moments of *The Rise of Skywalker* and thus the finale of the saga. The ancient temple in which the Emperor has been resurrected has the look of a hive, and he and Rey are surrounded by drone-like cultists whose features are completely obscured by their dark Sith robes. Palpatine urges Rey to kill him and take the Sith throne: "You will take the throne. It is your birthright to rule here. It is in your blood. Our blood. ... Kill me and my spirit will pass into you, as all the Sith live in me. You will be empress. We will be one." As the confrontation nears its end and a rejuvenated Palpatine seems to be on the verge of destroying her, Rey hears the voices of Jedi from the past, urging her to rise and face the Emperor. Palpatine taunts her: "You are nothing: a scavenger girl is no match for the power in me. I am all the Sith." He seems to mean that literally. She responds, "And I—am all the Jedi," but it's clear that she means it metaphorically. She has heard and been inspired by individual voices, each of which can be identified (and are—in the film's credits). She is an individual, who has found what she told Luke she needed in *The Last Jedi*: "my place in all this." She retains her individuality as part of a network of intelligence and spirit that draws on the Jedi past. Luke makes the distinction clear as he prepares her to face Palpatine: "A thousand generations live in you now. But this is your fight."

But just as *Star Wars* seems to set up the black-and-white logic of melodrama only to complicate it, so too does the saga feature a complicated attitude toward the blurring of boundaries between human beings and machines that cyborgs, hive minds, and networked intelligences represent. In addition to the sympathetic depiction of the droids, the saga also transforms not only Darth Vader but also his son and eventual redeemer, Luke Skywalker, into cyborgs. Vader, of course, comes closer than Luke Skywalker to embodying US pop culture's image of the cyborg as a monstrous hybrid, but at the climax of his duel with Vader, a point-of-view shot of Luke's cybernetic hand indicates that he is struck by the resemblance between his father and himself. In *Empire*, Vader wins their lightsaber duel by cutting off the hand with which Luke is holding his weapon; at the climax of *Return*, the tables are turned, and Luke has dismembered his father. The addition of a cybernetic implant has not made Luke into a monster, and the camerawork suggests that he realizes that the same is true of his father, despite his much more significant augmentation.

The signature piece of technology in the *Star Wars* universe is the lightsaber, the weapon of the Jedi knights. The first time we see one in the 1977 film, Obi-Wan describes it as "an elegant weapon for a more civilized day. For over a thousand generations the Jedi Knights were the guardians of peace and justice in the Old Republic. Before the dark times, before the Empire."[35] In the original trilogy, our knowledge of the nature of the weapon builds incrementally.[36] Han Solo disparages it as an "ancient weapon," that's "no match for a good blaster," and the officer who hands Luke and his lightsaber over to Vader in *Return of the Jedi* says, "He was armed only with this," as if the lightsaber were something either relatively trivial or completely unknown to him.[37] (Perhaps he'd never had occasion to see Vader use his.) We see the damage that it can do when Obi-Wan dismembers one of the patrons in the cantina who is threatening Luke early in *A New Hope*, and Obi-Wan later suggests to Luke that wielding the weapon successfully requires the ability to channel the Force.[38] Luke has learned enough about using a lightsaber to be able to wound Darth Vader in *Empire* before ultimately succumbing, and by the beginning of *Return* he has a new lightsaber, built to pay homage to Obi-Wan's, which he wields effectively during the escape from Jabba's palace. None other than Vader comments, late in *Return*, "I see you have constructed a new lightsaber. ... Your skills are complete. Indeed, you are powerful, as the Emperor has foreseen."[39] The saga as a whole culminates with the revelation in the final scene of *The Rise of Skywalker* that Rey too has built her own lightsaber, fashioned from the staff that she has carried throughout the sequel trilogy, thereby completing her journey to become a Jedi.

We are told nothing about the mechanics of the construction of lightsabers in the original trilogy. In fact, an article on lightsabers on the website *Den of Geek!* argues that "the enduring appeal of the lightsaber was enhanced by the sense of mystery surrounding them in the original trilogy. Fans had no idea how they were made, and—for the first two films—we only saw three of them (Luke's first one, Obi-Wan's, and Vader's)."[40] As the *Star Wars* universe expanded, however, more details about lightsabers emerged. In *Star Wars: The Complete Visual Dictionary (New Edition)*, we are shown a cross section of a lightsaber in a section called "Special Technology" and given this description (which seems to draw on physics that don't exist in our galaxy):

> Lightsabers tend to a follow a similar basic structure, although many are very individualized by their Jedi builders. While the pure energy blade has no mass, the electromagnetically generated arc wave creates a strong gyroscopic effect that makes the lightsaber a challenge to handle. Operating on the principle of tightly controlled arc-wave energy, it requires focusing elements made of kyber crystals. A lightsaber must be assembled by hand, as there is no exact formula for the crucial alignment of the irregular crystals. The slightest misalignment will cause the weapon to detonate on activation.[41]

An episode from the fifth season of *The Clone Wars* television series depicts Yoda leading a group of Jedi "younglings" to the Jedi Temple on the planet Ilum to participate in a ritual called "the Gathering" in which they will find the special crystal around which they will build their first lightsabers. The official canon now calls these crystals

"Kyber crystals," and starwars.com tells us that Ilum was not their only source:

> At the heart of every Jedi lightsaber is a kyber crystal found on several planets, most notably the icebound caves of Ilum. This crystal is attuned to the Force, and connected to a Jedi Knight on a deeply personal level. In this way, a lightsaber is an extension of a Jedi's Force awareness. Because Jedi let the Force guide their selection of the crystal, the vibration that the crystal creates in the lightsaber blade helps Jedi center themselves and find balance in the Force. In this way, a Jedi can center his or her attention beyond the distractions of combat. A lightsaber crystal is colorless until first attuned and connected to a Jedi—at which times it glows either blue or green, or in some rare instances, another shade. From that point on, it retains that hue.

The novel *Ahsoka* includes a chapter written from the point of view of the crystals on the planet Ilum: "All they had to do was be patient and grow."[42]

The Marvel comic series *Darth Vader* tells us how the Sith imbue their crystals with the red color that is their hallmark. "A red saber is no different than any other," Palpatine tells Vader, "except that it has been made to bleed." One of the first tasks that Palpatine sets Darth Vader is to acquire a crystal by killing one of the few remaining Jedi:

> The crystal from any Jedi's saber will do. As you know, the Kybers are alive, in their way. Like any living thing, they can feel pain …. Through the dark side, you must pour your pain into the crystal. And when, at least, the agony becomes more than it can stand … a beautiful crimson … the color of your rage.[43]

These accounts of the construction of lightsabers extend the idea that the weapon and its wielder exist in a symbiotic relation by transforming the saber itself into a kind of cyborg, a fusion of something living and something mechanical, once again playing with the boundary that discomfits so many technophobic works of popular culture.

The film *Rogue One* provides a further twist: it is kyber crystals, mined from the sacred planet Jeddha, that power the Empire's Death Star. In other words, the same crystals power both the Jedi's iconic weapon and the Empire's. Ultimately the depiction of technology that we find in the *Star Wars* universe resonates with Asimov's assertion about the interplay of good and harm in any technological advance that I cited at the beginning of this chapter: "Fire warms you, gives you light, cooks your food, smelts your ore—and out of control, burns and kills."[44] In other words, fire, like any technology, is neutral: whether it is used for good or ill depends on who is using it and what their intentions are. Like Asimov, *Star Wars* seems to argue against the idea of technological determinism, as expressed by scholars like Jerry Mander who wrote in *Four Arguments for the Elimination of Television* (1978), an influential book that was roughly contemporary with the first *Star Wars* film: "Americans have not grasped the fact that many technologies determine their own use, their own effects, and even the kind of people who control them. We have not yet learned to think of technology as having ideology built into its very form."[45] What technological determinism boils down to is this: if you build a Death Star, you're going to use a Death Star, and you're going to be defined by your Death Star.

Instead, *Star Wars* seems to suggest that technology is an amplifier of human agency and, therefore, should worry us for the same reason that we worry about the way that humans act: because each human being contains the potential for Light and the potential for Dark.

7

Cosmopolitanism

From Multiculturalism to Cosmopolitanism

By the time Luke, Obi-Wan, C3PO, and R2D2 walk into the Mos Eisley cantina in search of a pilot who can help them return the Death Star plans back to the Rebellion, we've already seen Tusken Raiders and Jawas, so we know that humans are not the only sentient beings in the *Star Wars* universe. But when the camera cuts to a nonhuman with a triangular head and glowing orange eyes surveying the scene, followed by three quick shots of various kinds of nonhuman characters, we realize that we are part of a profoundly multicultural—indeed, multispecies—galaxy.

The 1977 trailer for the film had promised "a spectacle light years ahead of its time," "an epic of heroes and villains and aliens from a thousand worlds." Of course, calling nonhumans "aliens"—derived etymologically from the Latin *alius* meaning "other"—indicates an anthropocentric point of view. As the films progress, we discover that such a point of view is one of the prejudices of the Empire, which happily subjugates all species but seems only to employ humans aboard its military vessels in the original trilogy and in the *Rebels* television series. (In Timothy Zahn's novel *Thrawn*, which depicts the rise of the title character—a blue-skinned, red-eyed Chiss from the galaxy's "Unknown Regions"—to the rank of Grand Admiral, we see the ways in which nonhumans are denigrated within the Empire. Thrawn thinks to himself at one point: "Disrespect for nonhumans might not be official policy, but it nonetheless quietly pervaded the navy. Thrawn would have to try twice as hard as anyone else, and succeed twice as often, just to stay even with them.")[1] And, as we've already noted, soon after Luke and the droids enter the cantina, we realize that the droids are treated as second-class citizens. For a US audience in 1977, the snarling bartender's refusal to serve the droids evokes the context of the Civil Rights movement of the 1960s. As I noted earlier, these lines are one of the ways in which *Star Wars* establishes the system of values that will operate in the course of the film and its successors.

The droids are one index to the system of values within the films: the "good guys" treat their sentient droids as persons. The same goes for the treatment of nonhumans. After all, one of the most important good guys is Chewbacca the Wookiee, who, like Artoo and Threepio, becomes a character beloved by fans and whose death in the Expanded Universe stories was one of the factors that led Disney to relegate those stories to the status of "Legends." The good guys, in other words, believe in what would soon be a word about which people in the United States would have strong opinions: multiculturalism.

The first *Star Wars* film was released just before the "culture wars" of the 1980s in the United States; by the time the prequel trilogy was completed, the wars were done and, at least institutionally in the United States, multiculturalism had triumphed. The culture wars had their roots in the Civil Rights Movement and the 1965 Hart-Celler Act, which reformed US immigration policy by removing the quota system based on national origins that had been in place since the 1920s and had been upheld in 1952 by the McCarran-Walter Act. The new system put in place worldwide per-country limits of 20,000 visas per year with an overall annual ceiling of 290,000 immigrant visas. These were divided between 170,000 for the Eastern Hemisphere and 120,000 for the Western Hemisphere, the first time that any limits had been placed on immigration from the Western Hemisphere.[2] Immigration policy continued to be a live issue in the years surrounding the first *Star Wars* films. Erika Lee notes that

> in 1976, the Immigration and Nationality Act of 1965 was amended. The new provisions extended to the Western Hemisphere the 20,000 per-country limit and a slightly modified version of the seven-category preference system. In 1978, immigration legislation was passed to combine the separate hemispheric ceilings into a worldwide ceiling of 290,000 with a single preference system.[3]

The combination of the new policies enacted by the Immigration and Nationality Act, sentiment against the Vietnam War, and the rise of the Black Power movement created a powerful tide of ambivalence about the idea of "America" in the late 1960s. The melting pot and assimilation became synonymous with racial and ethnic oppression, and "affirmative action" as a governmental mechanism for remedial antidiscrimination came into being. The immigration historian Reed Ueda argues that "unlike the political climate that absorbed immigrants of the early twentieth century according to individual identities, the reorganization of the political system based on ethnic identity led to the absorption of immigrants not as individuals but as members of official groups."[4] Four groups were deemed to be qualified for remediation on the basis of historical and ongoing discrimination: African Americans, Asian and Pacific Island Americans, Hispanic Americans, and Native Americans.

In 1972, the American Association of Colleges and Teacher Education published a policy statement entitled "No One Model

American: A Statement on Multicultural Education" that rejected the idea of the melting pot in favor of the promotion of "cultural pluralism":

> Multicultural education is education which values cultural pluralism. Multicultural education rejects the view that schools should seek to melt away cultural differences or the view that schools should merely tolerate cultural pluralism. Instead, multicultural education affirms that schools should be oriented toward the cultural enrichment of all children and youth through programs rooted to the preservation and extension of cultural alternatives. Multicultural education recognizes cultural diversity as a fact of life in American society, and it affirms that this cultural diversity is a valuable resource that should be preserved and extended. It affirms that major education institutions should strive to preserve and enhance cultural pluralism.

Declaring that "to endorse cultural pluralism is to endorse the principle that there is no one model American" and "to understand and appreciate the differences that exist among the nation's citizens," the statement connects multicultural education, not to the empowerment of groups, but rather to the tradition of liberal individualism by seeing "differences as a positive force in the continuing development of a society which professes a wholesome respect for the intrinsic worth of every individual." Describing "cultural pluralism" as "a basic quality of our culture" rather than "a temporary accommodation to placate racial and ethnic minorities," the statement advocates a four-pronged program designed to promote cultural pluralism "at every level":

> (1) the teaching of values which support cultural diversity and individual uniqueness; (2) the encouragement of the qualitative expansion of existing ethnic cultures and their incorporation into

the mainstream of American socioeconomic and political life; (3) the support of explorations in alternative and emerging life styles; and (4) the encouragement of multiculturalism, multilingualism, and multidialectism.[5]

These debates are part of the cultural backdrop of the original *Star Wars* trilogy, in which our heroes become part of a Rebellion that espouses pluralist values. Financial constraints likely prevented the scenes on Yavin IV in the first film from showing the truly multicultural nature of the Rebellion, but by the time of *Return of the Jedi*, the Rebel forces are depicted as multispecies, and the fleet is commanded by the amphibious nonhuman Admiral Ackbar, who resembles a bipedal fish. By the 1990s, the pluralist view of education seemed to have carried the day throughout the US secondary school education system. The American history syllabus adopted by the public school system in New York City in 1990 announced, "In the final analysis, all education should be multicultural education."[6]

The triumph of multiculturalism in the aftermath of these "culture wars" has had a beneficial effect on US educational policy and US public discourse more generally, though a significant backlash began to emerge after the election of Barack Obama. In promoting the value of cultural diversity, multiculturalism led to the recovery of neglected histories and artistic traditions, and it has fostered a greater sense of toleration (and even appreciation) for various kinds of difference. Along with the gains, however, there were costs, including increasingly rigid ideas about identity politics and a reluctance to offer critiques of practices across cultural boundaries. Arguing for the superiority of a cosmopolitan rather than a multiculturalist approach to culture and politics, Kwame Anthony Appiah argues that "multiculturalism often designates the disease it purports to cure," because its approach to the promotion of cultural diversity is often strongly inflected by a pluralism that, as the intellectual historian David Hollinger puts it, "respects inherited boundaries and locates individuals within one or another of a series of ethno-racial groups to be protected and preserved." Hollinger argues that

> pluralism differs from cosmopolitanism in the degree to which it endows with privilege particular groups, especially the communities that are well established at whatever time the ideal of pluralism is invoked. ... In its extreme form, this conservative form takes the form of a bargain: "You keep the acids of your modernity out of my culture, and I'll keep the acids of mine away from yours."[7]

Multiculturalism, as institutionalized in the United States, often pushes its commitment to pluralism so far that it results in a cultural impasse, bringing about a skittishness, a reluctance to speak across cultural boundaries. The logic goes something like this:

> I like my culture because it's mine. But I respect yours. I want you to respect mine. I prefer mine because it's mine. And I imagine that you prefer yours because it's yours. I really can't comment on yours because it's yours, and I don't belong to it. I cherish my long-standing practices and values; out of respect, I'll refrain from commenting on your long-standing values and practices. If I happen to find some of your long-standing values and practices distasteful or even repugnant, well, we'll just agree to disagree.

The problem with this strongly pluralist stance is that it doesn't allow us to address problems like genocide or slavery. Is it okay for a culture today to pursue either of these practices just because it's been a part of the culture for centuries? Aren't there some ideas that are simply bad ideas and that can't be ignored in the name of toleration? Multiculturalism can veer toward moral relativism, and that is a direction that cosmopolitan theory seeks to avoid. Cosmopolitanism is about figuring out whether certain ideas that human beings concoct are better than others. It gives us ways of respecting cultural boundaries but also of crossing them. The cosmopolitan experience is all about finding sameness across gulfs of difference, but it isn't about eradicating gaps in cultural experience: rather, it is about bridging them.

It's worth remembering that tolerance is derived from the Latin verb *toler*, which means "to bear" or "suffer." Toleration thus connotes a tinge of negativity. In contrast to strongly pluralist multiculturalists, cosmopolitans seek more than just the bearing or suffering of otherness: they seek to embrace otherness as a way of expanding awareness and knowledge. Nevertheless, tolerance is a sine qua non for both multiculturalism and cosmopolitanism, and it is a value that is practiced by those who follow the light side of the Force in *Star Wars*. But is the *Star Wars* universe tolerant in a meta sense? Can we imagine Lucasfilm portraying, for example, LGBTQIA+ characters in its stories in the future, given that the only relationships we've seen on screen before *The Rise of Skywalker* are heterosexual? Mark Hamill was asked this very question during a Q&A session at the Oxford Union. After noting that he had read online that J. J. Abrams "is very much open to that idea," Hamill said that fans have asked him:

> "Could Luke be gay?" And I'd say it's meant to be interpreted by you. If you think he's gay, of course he's gay. ... Judge Luke by his character, not by whom he loves.[8]

Only half-joking, Hamill jokes about the traumatic effect of discovering, as Luke does, that "the only girl you had a big crush on is your sister," before adding, more seriously:

> They're fantasies meant for children—children of all ages of course—but because they are that, they aren't meant to address adult sexuality specifically. But, I was saying that, it's a universe

of acceptance and unification. It's helping others less fortunate than yourself, it's acts of selflessness, of caring and sharing. To me that should tell you that if we can accept characters of every kind—of human and alien—what are the odds, c'mon? I mean … It's obviously a galaxy far, far away that's filled with inclusive tendencies.[9]

In fact, LGBTQIA+ characters *have* entered the canonical *Star Wars* universe, most prominently in the character of the self-described "rogue archeologist" Chelli Lona Aphra, introduced in the third issue of the *Darth Vader* comic series that ran for twenty-six issues from 2015 to 2016. Conceived by writer Kieron Gillen as a kind of "inverse Indiana Jones" (her moral flexibility gives her more in common with Jones's nemeses René Belloq and Irina Spalko), Dr. Aphra became the star of her own self-titled series in 2016, and starwars.com described her as a "fan favorite." Gillen describes Aphra as a "lesbian," noting, "I've never written her with any romantic interest in men." As far as Gillen is concerned, the *Star Wars* universe isn't bound by the same categories of identity that we take for granted:

> One of the things we wrote inside the first arc was that homophobia as we know it doesn't really exist in the *Star Wars* universe. No one raises their eyebrow, no one seems surprised when it happens. It's kind of just something that's there, so the way that they process sexuality has got to be different anyway, and how they choose to identify, as well.[10]

Writing in *Slate*, Alan Scherstuhl argued that Aphra's adventures "constitute the freshest, most surprising stretch of *Star Wars* storytelling since Lucas sold the franchise."[11] In fact, the most "progressive" thing about the comic series is that it doesn't make a big deal about Aphra's sexuality, which is treated as just one of her characteristics. The idea that same-sex relationships may well be a routine aspect of the *Star Wars* universe is suggested in passing by the young-adult novel *Ahsoka*, in which a young woman develops feelings for the former Padawan (feelings that aren't reciprocated, as it turns out).[12] A same-sex (though bi-species) relationship can be found in the television series *Star Wars: Resistance*, which is aimed at a younger audience. The two spare-parts dealers, Orca and Flix, hail from different species—the diminutive Orca is a Chadra-Fan and the birdlike Flix is, well, something else—but they are both coded male. During the press coverage for the show's second season, the executive producers confirmed what many fans suspected: "I think it's safe to say they're an item," executive producer Justin Ridge told the *Coffee with Kenobi* podcast. Fellow executive producer Brandon Auman added, "They're absolutely a gay couple, and we're proud of that."[13] Finally, the closing celebration of *The Rise of Skywalker* features a same-sex kiss between two women—Commander D'Acy and her wife Lieutenant Wrobie Tyce—a scene that was cut from the film when it was shown in Singapore and in the Middle East.[14]

The view that the *Star Wars* universe is one of "acceptance and unification"—and the particular way in which Hamill interprets those terms—is of course the perspective of the Rebellion and the Jedi. "From a certain point of view" (to quote Obi-Wan Kenobi), those are also the ideals that the Empire and the Sith pursue. Palpatine and Vader also seek the unification of the galaxy, but their idea of acceptance is different: rather than accepting the multiple points of view, they demand acceptance of their point of view in the name of "order." After defeating Luke in *The Empire Strikes Back*, Vader urges him, "Join me, and I will complete your training. With our combined strength, we can end this destructive conflict and bring order to the galaxy."[15] For the Sith, the democracy of the Republic meant inefficiency and disorder; their authoritarian system provides order and security for those who willingly submit to it. During the climactic duel between Obi-Wan and Anakin in *Revenge of the Sith*, Anakin declares, "I do not fear the dark side as you do. I have brought peace, justice, freedom, and security to my new Empire."

Obi-Wan's response to Anakin is that "only a Sith Lord deals in absolutes." When Obi-Wan tells Luke in *Return of the Jedi* that the account he provided of the death of Anakin Skywalker was true "from a certain point of view," Luke scoffs in disbelief. Obi-Wan, however, adds: "Luke, you're going to find that many of the truths we cling to depend greatly on our own point of view." Theorists of cosmopolitanism like Appiah argue that because, as fallible beings, we can never know for sure that beliefs are correct, we must always be testing our points of view. We must determine the relative worth of our ideas through *conversation*, which is the primary means through which cultural bridges are built. Appiah invokes "conversation in its older meaning of living together, [of] association" as well as in "its modern sense" of simply talking with one another.[16] The kinds of conversations that Appiah has in mind, however, are much more than simple chitchat or the exchange of pleasantries. They are dialogues in which we are willing to put our central beliefs on the line: we commit ourselves to conversations in which we are willing to have our minds changed about cherished beliefs and values. In Obi-Wan's view, the Sith are what Appiah would call "counter-cosmopolitans," his term for fundamentalists who believe that they possess the one true belief system and aren't interested in discussing alternatives or in engaging in cosmopolitan conversations.[17]

One way that cosmopolitan theory helps us to understand the philosophical components of the *Star Wars* films is to see them as staging precisely these kinds of conversations. In *The World According to Star Wars* (2016), the legal scholar Cass Sunstein reminds us that "unlike a political platform or a religious tract, Star Wars doesn't tell you what to think. It invites speculation. You can understand it in different, even contradictory ways." He goes on to make an argument about interpretation that is consonant with the model of reading that I derived earlier from Greenblatt, Jauss, and Fish:

> For open-textured works, acts of interpretation—including acts by those who are continuing the texts they themselves started—have a creative feature. They aren't just about excavation. They involve choice. True, any interpretation has to fit the material. You can't easily say that *Star Wars* is really about the evils of deficit spending, the problem of climate change, or the importance of increasing the minimum wage. But interpreters have a lot of room to understand it in a way that fits with their own deepest concerns.[18]

He then presents ("with apologies and a salute to Wallace Stevens") "thirteen ways of looking at *Star Wars*," including one that takes the point of view of the Empire: "Maybe the Jedi are the wrongdoers—baffled, stumbling, unable to maintain stability. Maybe Emperor Palpatine is the secret hero, after all. Maybe that's the dark heart of the *Star Wars* series. Maybe that's where its sympathies really reside." Asking whether that "argument seem[s] nuts," he notes that "at least since 2002, intelligent people have argued that it's right. ... *The Force Awakens* is all about the tension between order and chaos, and it's secretly in favor of the former. In that respect, it is following the first two trilogies." Having entertained the possibility, Sunstein concedes: "I agree, the idea that *Star Wars* favors the Empire is definitely nuts. (*The Force Awakens* does create some complications, but it would be a real stretch to contend that the New Order [*sic*] has things right.)."[19]

If it's true that seeing Palpatine as the secret hero of the *Star Wars* saga is "nuts," it is because the film has used the devices and archetypes that we've been discussing—tragedy, exile and return, melodrama, the monomyth of the hero, the ideology of liberal individualism—to nudge the conversation it stages about the relative merits of freedom versus order in the direction of the former. But the scholars who have made this argument are detecting something that likely is at work in the unconscious of the films, because it was at work in the mind of Lucas: a discomfort with the chaos that an emphasis on freedom brings and a yearning for some of the benefits that a more orderly approach confers. In his contribution on *Star Wars* to the BFI Film Classics Series, Will Brooker persuasively argues that the distinctions between the Empire and the Rebel Alliance are less clear than it might at first seem. He attributes this blurring of boundaries to Lucas's conflicting desires as a filmmaker:

> George Lucas's first ever movie was a stop-motion cine film of plates, stacking themselves up and then unstacking. He liked objects, and order, and control. He was, on one level, deeply invested in what the Empire looked like and represented, in its clean and shiny surfaces and its formal, rigid structure. But because he was trying to make a straightforward fable about good and evil, he had to let the Rebels' casual, careless improvisation into the structure he secretly admired, to disrupt it, and destroy it.[20]

As a filmmaker in the 1970s, Lucas saw himself as a freedom fighter, seeking to get out from under the corporate control of the studios, yet (as we've seen) he wasn't entirely comfortable with allowing the level of freedom that John Dykstra wanted to have at ILM. Lucas seems to have been aware of the contradiction, not only within himself, but in the trajectory of his career. Brooker reminds us that in the 2004 documentary *Empire of Dreams*, Lucas commented on the irony of his becoming a studio head:

> What I was trying to do was stay independent … but at the same time I was sort of fighting the corporate system which I didn't

like. And I'm not happy with the fact that corporations have taken over the film industry. But now I find myself being the head of a corporation. So there's a certain irony there, in that I've become the very thing that I was trying to, uh, avoid. Which is basically what part of *Star Wars* is about.[21]

Lucas no doubt has the story of Anakin Skywalker in mind here. When Obi-Wan cuts Anakin down on Mustafar after recognizing the full extent of Anakin's acceptance of the dark side near the end of *Revenge of the Sith*, he laments, "You were the Chosen One! It was said that you would, destroy the Sith, not join them. It was you who would bring balance to the Force, not leave it in Darkness."

Cultural Purity

Cosmopolitan conversation may be less about effecting change than about managing the changes that are inevitable in the life of a culture. Cosmopolitans understand that cultures are dynamic and always subject to change. Appiah's influential account of cosmopolitanism is based on the belief that it is the natural tendency of cultures to reinvent themselves. Cultures, in his account, never tend toward purity; they tend toward change, toward mixing and miscegenation, toward an "endless process of imitation and revision."[22] To keep a culture "pure" requires the vigilant policing often associated with fundamentalist regimes, xenophobic political parties, or (as it turns out) certain kinds of *Star Wars* fans. Appiah writes, "When people speak for an ideal of cultural purity, [for] sustaining the authentic culture of … the American family farm, I find myself drawn to contamination as the name for a counter-ideal."[23] In seeking to appropriate and negative term and give it a positive connotation,

Appiah is pointing out that what the cultural purists might regard as "contamination" is simply the way culture works. "Cultural purity is an oxymoron," Appiah writes. "The odds are that, culturally speaking, you already live a cosmopolitan life, enriched by literature, art, and film that come from many places, and that contains influences from many more."[24] In this view, *Star Wars*, with its plethora of influences from not only the history of cinema but the history of the world, is inherently cosmopolitan in its inception, execution, and impact.

The idea of cultural purity may help us understand some of the controversies that have erupted around the *Star Wars* universe as it developed after 1983: why some fans were vehemently opposed to the CGI revisions that Lucas had made to the original trilogy, first in the "Special Editions" released in 1997, then in the DVD release, and on into the Blu-ray and then the 4K version streaming on Disney+; or objected to the narrative arc of the prequel trilogy; or have objected to the sequel trilogy's (human) multiculturalism and its depiction of Luke Skywalker as a failed Jedi master.

For some members of the generation of fans from the 1970s and 1980s, the "authentic" versions of the *Star Wars* films are the versions they saw in the theaters, which are no longer available on video. In a piece entitled "Can We Ever Make Peace with the 'Star Wars' Special Editions?" and posted to the website Collider on the fortieth anniversary of the first *Star Wars* film, Matt Goldberg writes that "while the original versions of the original trilogy are out there if you're willing to find them, what's officially for sale are the Special Editions. They're like the movies you remember, except with regrettable added material and changes that no one likes." Goldberg concedes, however, that if you want to introduce your children to *Star Wars* and can only show them the Special Editions, it isn't a disaster: "The power of *Star Wars* can't be snuffed out by the Special Editions' changes, and just as these changes have engendered their fair share of detractors (myself included), we must also admit that none of us have abandoned *Star Wars* because of them." He concludes that he has now "begrudgingly come to terms with the Special Editions. It's taken a while, and they'll never sit completely right with me, but I also know that whenever *Star Wars* comes on TV, I'll watch it. That's the power of these movies, and while they may not be the perfect relics we once knew, the Force is still strong with them."

The idea that the original trilogy films are "perfect relics," however, is not the way that Lucasfilm thinks about them or about the larger project that is *Star Wars*. As Will Brooker notes in his 2002 study of *Star Wars* fandom, Lucasfilm is not making movies for the diehard fans:

> *Star Wars* is not a dead franchise, kept alive in cultural memory by the fan minority, but an industry, delivering product to a worldwide audience. The prequel trilogy is not aimed at the diehards who run websites, but at the cinemagoer who took his kids to see *The Phantom Menace* as a fun blockbuster and will never write a fan story about Obi-Wan Kenobi. To Lucasfilm, Ltd., *Star Wars* is not a cult text or a folk myth but an ongoing business, a series of trademarks and properties that need to be protected; their main relationship is not with the type of dedicated fan discussed here—who could all boycott the saga with very little effect on box office receipts—but with mainstream moviegoers and their children.

And as we've seen earlier, Kathleen Kennedy sees selling products as only a part of the mission of Lucasfilm, noting that what Lucas "began as a story to inspire, we continue to embrace as a beacon of empowerment and hope."[25] *Wired* writer Adam Rogers describes the responsibility that Kennedy and Lucasfilm have taken on in "building out a universe that someone [George Lucas] loved so much he made the rest of us love it too. It's like continuing the construction of a cathedral someone else designed, or being the commander of a generations-long starship mission. It is an honor, but I suspect also a burden."[26]

Lucas, for one, considered the films far from "perfect": in the documentary *Empire of Dreams*, Lucas reflects that with the rerelease of the trilogy in a "Special Edition" for the twentieth anniversary of the first *Star Wars* film he was able to include

> things that I couldn't afford to do at the time, things that I had to give up on because I just didn't have the time or money or the power to do it, I was able to go in and complete the films the way I intended them to be and have it be pretty much the way I want them to be.[27]

For Lucas, the films represent a living art form, and the comparatively poor technical quality of the first trilogy represented, in his view, not only a failure to realize his original vision fully, but also an impediment to enjoyment for new audiences. Describing the task that Lucas and ILM faced in creating the Special Editions, Mark Cotta Vaz wrote in the special-effects journal *Cinefex* that

> ILM digital tools would be employed to repair tell-tale optical effects, integrate computer generated creatures and cityscapes within existing footage, provide new cuts to both expand on and replicate sequences, and generally bring the film up to date for modern audiences accustomed to early flawless visual effects spectacle.

The goal was not to change the film in any substantive way: "No new characters and plotlines would be introduced; and ILM's digital spruce-up would have to reproduce the lower-tech aesthetic of that earlier filmmaking and effects era." The goal was rather to remove imperfections such as "tell-tale optical effects" that were artifacts of the rudimentary state of green-screen work when the films were first made.[28] In addition, in preparation for the project, Lucasfilm discovered that the existing prints of the films—particularly of the first film—had degraded or were damaged, so "the *New Hope* Special Edition project grew to include the restoration of the original negative," thus properly preserving the film for posterity and today's digital formats.[29] Patty Blau of ILM said later, "Being able to perfect these pictures generated a lot of excitement in-house, and it got us into the spirit and gestalt of that whole world, something to take with us into the work for the prequels."[30]

As Blau's comment suggests, for Lucas and Lucasfilm the work on the Special Editions was in some sense a dry-run for the work that would be required for the prequel trilogy, which Lucas had only decided to make once he came to believe that digital special-effects technology had progressed to the point where he wouldn't have to compromise his vision as he had with the original trilogy. Commenting on the release of the original trilogy on DVD in 2004 for which he made additional revisions (see Figure 12), Lucas spoke to the Associated Press about the nature of a filmmaker's creative process:

> To me, the special edition ones are the films I wanted to make. Anybody that makes films knows the film is never finished. It's abandoned or it's ripped out of your hands, and it's thrown into the marketplace, never finished. It's a very rare experience where you find a filmmaker who says, "That's exactly what I wanted. I got everything I needed. I made it just perfect. I'm going to put it out there." And even most artists, most painters, even composers would want to come back and redo their work now. They've got a new perspective on it, they've got more resources, they have better technology, and they can fix or finish the things that were never

done. ... I wanted to actually finish the film the way it was meant to be when I was originally doing it. At the beginning, people went, "Don't you like it?" I said, "Well, the film only came out to be 25 or 30 percent of what I wanted it to be." They said, "What are you talking about?" So finally, I stopped saying that, but if you read any interviews for about an eight- or nine-year period there, it was all about how disappointed I was and how unhappy I was and what a dismal experience it was. You know, it's too bad you need to get kind of half a job done and never get to finish it. So this was my chance to finish it.

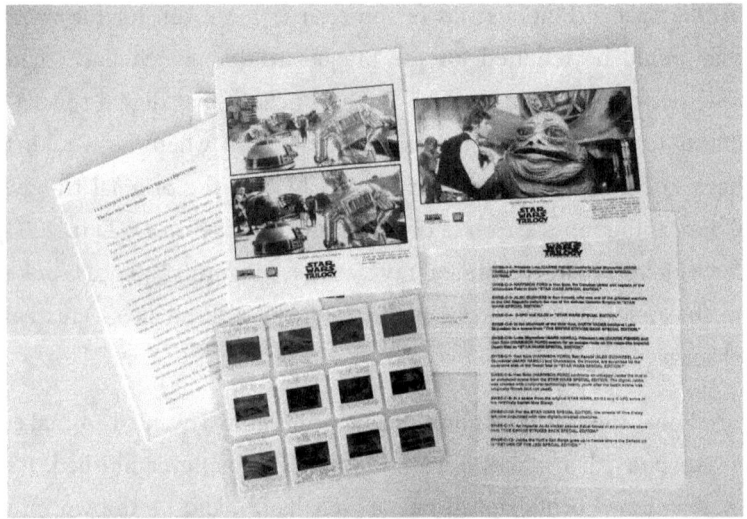

Figure 12 Press kit for the "Special Edition" rerelease of the original *Star Wars* trilogy. This press kit promoted the release of the Special Editions of the original trilogy, in which George Lucas used digital effects technology to bring scenes that he considered to be defective closer to his original vision. The caption for the still image featuring C-3PO tells us that "the streets of Mos Eisley are now populated with new digitally-created creatures," while the caption for the second still reveals that "the digital Jabba was created with computer technology twenty years after the basic scene was originally filmed (but not used)." Photo credit: Cyrus R. K. Patell. Collection of the author.

Asked whether he had ever considered putting restored versions of the original films on the discs along with the revised versions, Lucas replied:

> The special edition, that's the one I wanted out there. The other movie, it's on VHS, if anybody wants it. ... I'm not going to spend the, we're talking millions of dollars here, the money and the time to refurbish that, because to me, it doesn't really exist anymore. It's like this is the movie I wanted it to be, and I'm sorry you saw half a completed film and fell in love with it. But I want it to be the way I want it to be. I'm the one who has to take responsibility for it. I'm the one who has to have everybody throw rocks at me all the time, so at least if they're going to throw rocks at me, they're going to throw rocks at me for something I love rather than something I think is not very good, or at least something I think is not finished.

Explaining why he didn't pay too much attention to fan reactions when making choices that have to do with his films, Lucas described science-fiction and *Star Wars* fans as "very independent-thinking people. They all think outside the box."[31] Lucas perhaps underestimates the extent to which the particular innovation to which his *Star Wars* films have contributed—the creation of the "shared universe"—has changed the dynamic between the films and their fans, almost inviting the fans to consider themselves co-creators of the works. For Lucas, the bottom line is that *he* is the filmmaker: *Star Wars* fans, he said, "all have very strong ideas about what should happen, and they think it should be their way. Which is fine, except I'm making the movies, so I should have it my way."[32] From 1997, when he released the "Special Editions" of the original trilogy, to 2005, when *Revenge of the Sith* was released, Lucas returned to the auteurist mode with which he had begun his career. And then, seven years later, he let it go—or at least, he freed Lucasfilm from it.

It's thought that a part of the reason that Lucas decided to sell Lucasfilm to Disney twelve years later is that he simply grew tired of all of the criticism from fans who were unwilling to see *Star Wars* as he did, as an ongoing project subject to revision and change. As Brooker notes, criticism of the prequel trilogy from fans was just as harsh as criticism of the Special Editions. Some fans objected to the fact that *The Phantom Menace*, which featured a preteen Anakin Skywalker, was pointedly aimed at children, leaving them feeling left out. Consider, for example, this account by Andrea Alworth, a then-thirty-something British schoolteacher interviewed by Will Brooker for his study *Using the Force: Creativity, Community and Star Wars Fans* (2002):

> I saw *A New Hope* back when it was simply *Star Wars* in '77 and was hooked. I think it was the scene with Luke gazing at the setting suns that nailed me through the heart. As a young teenager, just beginning to explore the boundaries of my life and the possibilities ahead, I knew exactly what young Luke was thinking and feeling.

Noting that she had "read all the EU fiction and numerous fanfic stories, [had] collected some of the comics and trading cards, [and had] a smattering of SW paraphernalia lying about the house," Alworth told Brooker, "I care about the characters in the SW universe. In a way, I share a sense of fellowship with them," though she is careful to add, "I know the difference between fantasy and reality, and though the characters in SW will never be as precious to me as my 'real' friends, I still wish the best for them." She describes what she experienced when she encountered "that lonely farm boy on a planet in a galaxy far, far away" as "a bond." Alworth was one of those fans who was bitterly disappointed by *The Phantom Menace*.

> After my first viewing, I and two friends stood around in the parking lot talking for a long time about our impressions. All of

us are long-time SW fans, and all of us were disillusioned. Perhaps it is our age—having grown up before video games became so popular—but we all would have gladly traded about 5 minutes of pod race for some more intimate conversations between major characters that would have fostered more empathy on our part. And who was GL making the movie for, we wondered?[33]

The actor Simon Pegg, who would go on to have leading roles in the *Mission Impossible* franchise starring Tom Cruise and in J. J. Abrams's *Star Trek* reboots, was so disgusted by *The Phantom Menace* that he ended up creating a BAFTA-nominated British sitcom called *Spaced* that included criticisms of the film in almost every episode.[34] Despite the fact that he played the junk-dealer Unkar Plutt in *The Force Awakens*, Pegg would later become a vocal critic of the sequel trilogy as well, finding himself particularly dismayed by the way that Rian Johnson handled the question of Rey's lineage in *The Last Jedi* and suggesting that Abrams had wanted to go a different route. Disappointed fans like Pegg adopt a kind of atavistic approach in which they yearn for some lost original conception. Many fans who were highly critical of the prequel trilogy found themselves longing for the halcyon days when Lucas was in charge of Lucasfilm.[35]

Embracing Change

I have to confess that despite having fallen in love with *Star Wars* in 1977 and being among those who experienced the "I am your father" moment as an utter surprise, I find many of these controversies puzzling. But then, I would, because I have never been interested in the idea of cultural purity. My parents were boundary-crossers by virtue of their coming from Asia to the United States and eventually marrying one another. My father is a Parsee, born in Karachi, when Karachi was a part of India. My late mother was a Filipino. They had met at the International House at Columbia University, my father coming to study mathematical statistics, my mother to study literature and drama.

In matters of religion, however, they were fairly conventional. They weren't active believers, though we did attend dinners that were held to mark the Zoroastrian New Year (at least until those dinners were moved to Westchester), and we did celebrate Christmas, making it a point to attend the Christmas Eve services at Riverside Church, in New York, a few blocks up the street from where we lived. My mother sometimes liked to attend Easter services there as well. It was always assumed that I would have a religion and furthermore that I would become a Zoroastrian like my father. As my mother explained it, it was so that I could keep my options open. I could convert to Christianity, but not to Zoroastrianism, because Zoroastrianism didn't accept converts. But, when the time came during third grade for my *navjote* ceremony to be performed, we couldn't find a priest. We kept hearing excuses along the lines of, "I would do it, but my mother-in-law is very old-fashioned." The problem was that my mother was a Christian.

Finally, we managed to secure the services of a priest from Mumbai who was traveling in the United States and spending some time in New York. Four years later, we had to go to London to have my sister's ceremony done. And then, there were moments during the preparation for the ceremony when my aunt had to deputize for my mother, because Christians weren't allowed in certain areas of the Zoroastrian temple. Many years later, I realized that these experiences introduced me to the real-world dynamics of cosmopolitanism. My parents' marriage was an emblem of cosmopolitan cultural mixing, while the priests' belief in the importance of cultural purity served as an emblem of all the forces that are arrayed against cosmopolitanism.

My wife, a mixture of various European genealogies, has a similar attitude, and so our kids have grown up to consider the cosmopolitan point of view completely natural. Here's what they think about cultural purity: they're the kind of kids who used to build *Star Wars* Lego sets (or, when they were younger, have daddy finish what they'd started) and then immediately dismantle them and reassemble them into new formations that would help them tell the stories that they wanted to tell. For a while, they got into the customization of Lego minifigs, making use of decals, paints, markers, and a moldable substance called Sugru to customize them. No Krazy Glue for them (cf. *The Lego Movie*). Every now and then, they would have an atavistic moment in which they asked me to help them put a set back together the way it was at first—which inevitably proved to be impossible because the pieces were spread far and wide, some invariably lost, others customized. There's an allegory in that.

Despite all of my propaganda, my sons preferred the prequel trilogy because they were enthralled by the mythology of the Jedi. Only as they've grown older have they come to appreciate the original adventures of Luke, Han, Chewbacca, and Leia—and I suspect it's because they loved *The Force Awakens* and wanted to fill in the backstory.

The rerelease of the original trilogy in 1997 allowed a new generation of audiences to see the films in theaters and fall in love with them. Writing before the prequel trilogy was complete and well before the purchase of Lucasfilm by Disney ensured a future for the *Star Wars* universe, Brooker argued that "there will be at least one more Star Wars generation after his—the children who grow up with the prequel trilogy—and when Episode III is history they too will meet again and recognize one another, finding they can talk in an old language, unearthing their shared past and establishing new alliances." My kids belong to that generation. A similar dynamic is occurring with the sequel trilogy, and—if Lucasfilm is a careful steward of the universe it has inherited—it will occur again and again in the future.

With, perhaps, one exception: the *Star Wars* saga is a global phenomenon, but it has never caught on in China, despite the fact the action-oriented film series such as the *Avengers*, *Transformers*, and *The Fast and Furious* have been box office hits there. "One after another," the *New York Times* noted in early 2020,

> "Star Wars" movies have flopped in China, defying efforts to bring one of the most successful franchises in history into a market that has printed money for the heroes, monsters and robots of other films. The latest "Star Wars" movie, "The Rise of Skywalker," has followed the trend by grossing nearly a billion dollars worldwide and barely breaking $20 million in China.[36]

Most commentators agree that the reason is historical: when the first *Star Wars* film was released in 1977, China was just emerging from its Cultural Revolution period, and Western films were not being shown there. The first *Star Wars* film to be released in China was *The Phantom Menace* in 1999, and as Lisa Hanson pointed out in *Forbes* shortly after the release of *The Force Awakens*, "Many *Star Wars* franchise fans worldwide were children in the 1970s and 1980s, but in China today's primary movie-going audience was born between the years of 1985–1999. Therefore, the powerful nostalgia factor that the most recent Star Wars movie has going for it in North America is lost on most Asian movie viewers."

We might recall Bill Moyers's comment about how the timing of the first *Star Wars* film helped it capture the imaginations of US filmgoers in 1977:

Timing is everything in art. You bring *Star Wars* out too early, and it's *Buck Rogers*. You bring it out too late, and it doesn't fit our imagination. You bring it out just as the war in Vietnam is ending, when America feels uncertain of itself, when the old stories have died, and you bring it out at that time, and suddenly it's a new game.

The 1977 film created a horizon of expectations for *Star Wars* films, a horizon that was altered and deepened by the release of *The Empire Strikes Back* and *Return of the Jedi*. That horizon in turn shaped responses to the prequel and the sequel trilogies, not always, as we will see, in ways that have been supportive of Lucasfilm's efforts to tell new *Star Wars* stories. The horizon of expectations for Chinese viewers formed much later and much differently. Indeed, for Chinese audiences, "Star Wars" may well connote something old-fashioned and less appealing than say, *Hobbs & Shaw*, the 2019 spin-off of the *Fast and Furious* franchise. According to Ying Xiao, a professor of China studies and film at the University of Florida, the "somewhat abstruse, complicated jargons and plots" make it "quite difficult for a Chinese audience who was not raised along with sequels to comprehend, digest and appreciate the attraction."[37] One Chinese college student told the *South China Morning Post*, "If the new 'Star Wars' sequels were not named after 'Star Wars,' it would be better."[38]

Whether Lucasfilm can use new storylines to shift this horizon of expectations now that the Skywalker saga has reached its end remains to be seen. But the difference in the effects of *Star Wars* in the United States and China points to the power of the horizon of expectations as a theoretical concept when we seek to understand how the meanings of works of art and other cultural artifacts are shaped by historical contexts.

Toxic Fandom

I have argued that the *Star Wars* shared universe provides a platform for philosophy, an imaginative arena that can stage debates about the nature of humanity and its relationship to ideas such as agency, destiny, technology, heroism, gender, and difference. But that platform, though it's built around an imaginary galaxy far, far away, nevertheless also reflects some of the controversies in which our real world is mired. It should not surprise us, I think, that with the gradual erosion of civility in the United States, British, and European public discourse in the early decades of the twenty-first century that the dissatisfaction of certain fans with the choices made by Lucas and Lucasfilm from 1997 to 2020 became virulent. The *Star Wars* fans who believe that the original trilogy was about Luke Skywalker's rise from obscurity to inheritor of the Jedi mantle were dismayed to find him portrayed as something other than a master of the universe in the sequel trilogy. The sequel trilogy was made during a time when open sexism and xenophobia not only didn't rule out candidates for political office in the United States, but actually enabled them to get elected. It should not, therefore, have been surprising that a vocal minority of fans decided that *Star Wars* was and should be about the triumph of white masculinity and waged hate campaigns on social media against the stars of the sequel trilogy—most prominently, Daisy Ridley and Kelly Marie Tran—who didn't fit that profile. The criticisms extended to Kathleen Kennedy, the woman who took over Lucasfilm from George Lucas with his blessing.

The attacks on Lucasfilm generally and *The Last Jedi* in particular were reminiscent of the attacks on the Special Editions and the prequel trilogy, but due to the amplifying effects of social media, they became much more virulent: given the toxic masculinity that seems to be on display in these attacks, the now-shopworn metaphor "It's [blank] on steroids" seems strikingly appropriate. After the release of *The Phantom Menace*, some fans of the original trilogy lashed out at the vision that Lucas had adopted for his new trilogy. In an interview with BBC Newsnight in 1999, Lucas dismissed the idea that there was something racist about Ahmed Best's portrayal of Jar Jar Binks:

> The movie is pretty neutral. It *is* in outer space. How in the world can you take an orange amphibian and say that he's a Jamaican? I mean even the idea that you can take his ears and call them dreadlocks is kind of a strange stretch, as far as I'm concerned. It's completely absurd.

Lucas argued that "what that came out of ultimately was, there is a group of fans from the films that don't like comic sidekicks":

> They want the films to be tough and like *Terminator* ... real guy movies. And they get very, very upset—and very opinionated—about anything that has anything to do with being child-like. The movies are for children, but they don't want to admit that. Or a comic sidekick, because they don't want comedy in these movies. In the first film, they absolutely hated Artoo and Threepio. Now Jar Jar's getting accused of the same thing.[39]

Ahmed Best was so distraught about the virulent criticism that both his character and he received that he considered suicide. Best told *Wired* magazine in 2017, "I had death threats through the internet." Best says, "I had people come to me and say, 'You destroyed my childhood.' That's difficult for a 25-year-old to hear." Lucas had, in fact, called Best during the summer of 1999 to reassure him:

> "George said, 'This happened with the Ewoks. It happened with Chewbacca. It happened with Lando Calrissian,'" Best recalled. "He was used to this. He knew what was going to happen."

Twenty years from now, Lucas said, things were going to be very different, and people were going to see this character in a new way. Best just needed to focus on the future.[40]

In fact, on the twentieth anniversary of the release of *The Phantom Menace*, the movie's merits were being reevaluated. At a panel celebrating the anniversary at the "Star Wars Celebration" convention in Chicago, Lucas sent a video message declaring that *The Phantom Menace* was "one of my favorite movies" and that Jar Jar was his favorite character. When Ahmed Best walked onstage to be interviewed in front of the crowd, he received a standing ovation.

"Why are some *Star Wars* fans so toxic," asked Luke Holland in the *Guardian* during the summer of 2018, calling out "a poisonous tributary of fanboyism that appears again and again." What should be a golden era for *Star Wars* fans given Disney and Lucasfilm's ambitious plans for the shared universe turned out to be vexed. Holland writes that what makes "Star Wars fandom a drag in 2018" is

> other Star Wars fans. Or, more specifically, that small yet splenetic subsection of so-called "fans" who take to the internet like the Wicked Witch from the West's flying monkeys to troll the actors, directors and producers with bizarre, pathetic, racist, sexist and homophobic whingebaggery about the "injustices" that have been inflicted upon them. Truly, it's embarrassing to share a passion with these people.[41]

Esquire writer Matt Miller called 2018 "the year *Star Wars* fans finally ruined *Star Wars*." Establishing his bona fides by confessing that he cried when Han Solo met his demise in *The Force Awakens*, Miller writes, "In 2018, I've gotten literal death threats, been called homophobic slurs, even called racist (toward *Star Wars* fans?) about a family movie that defined my childhood. And this isn't a problem limited to my experience—oh no—my online harassment has paled in comparison to others (specifically the female stars of the two new films)." Miller lamented that "*The Last Jedi* inspired the worst impulses of a far-right movement that's taking hold of the internet and extending its influence into the real world." Noting that as he wrote there was still "a year until Episode 9," he called on "true fans to take control of this narrative—to formulate eloquent, and loud, and respectable opinions about what *Star Wars* has and should always mean. That's our only hope."[42] One sign of hope was the reception that Kelly Marie Tran received at "Star Wars Celebration" (see Figure 13), which Clarisse Loughrey described in the *Independent* as "a battle won":

> Kelly Marie Tran, who had faced months of racist and sexist abuse online following her role as Rose Tico in 2017's *The Last Jedi*, was given a rapturous reception on taking the stage at Chicago's Wintrust Arena. At the world's biggest Star Wars convention, attended only by the most dedicated of fans, she was embraced with an open and loving heart. "Kelly! Kelly! Kelly!" they chanted, rising to a standing ovation. She cried. I cried. It seemed like most of the auditorium cried.[43]

Afterward an interviewer for Yahoo Entertainment pointed out to Tran that "besides the actual trailer and the title reveal itself, you got maybe the biggest applause out there," adding, "I've got to admit, I got some chills watching you."[44]

Tran's reception suggests that those whom Miller calls "true fans" might begin to participate more vigorously in the (admittedly uncivil) conversation that had emerged online around the sequel trilogy and shift it in new directions. Not that it's likely that the "trolls" are persuadable: they share much in common with the fundamentalists that Appiah describes as "counter-cosmopolitans": people who

Figure 13 Celebrating *Star Wars*. Daisy Ridley, John Boyega, Oscar Isaac, and Kelly Marie Tran at "Star Wars Celebration", Chicago, April 12, 2019. Tran, who had been attacked by toxic fans on the internet, received a rousing round of applause when she appeared onstage, which brought her to tears. Photo by Daniel Boczarski. Getty Images.

believe they are in possession of the one truth and aren't interested in questioning or talking about it. And if you can't persuade them, then you need to find a way to keep them apart and limit the damage they can cause (admittedly a tall order in this era of globalized, instantaneous social media).[45] Or, as Rian Johnson suggested when responding to hate speech directed at Tran, "A few unhealthy people can cast a big shadow on the wall." Johnson went on to say, "But over the past 4 years I've met lots of real fellow SW fans. We like & dislike stuff but we do it with humor, love & respect. We're the VAST majority, we're having fun & doing just fine."[46]

8

Fallibilism

Star Wars begins with a failure. Princess Leia admits as much in the message to Obi-Wan Kenobi that she programs into R2-D2 at the beginning of *A New Hope*:

> General Kenobi, years ago you served my father in the Clone Wars. Now he begs you to help him in his struggle against the Empire. I regret that I am unable to present my father's request to you in person, but my ship has fallen under attack and I'm afraid my mission to bring you to Alderaan has failed.[1]

Luke becomes involved in the rebellion in order to help Obi-Wan remedy that failure. Princess Leia's message is the only time that the word "fail" or any of its derivatives is used in the film. As the larger story evolves across the Skywalker saga, however, those who follow the light side turn out to have an attitude toward failure that approximates what philosophers call *fallibilism*, "the sense" (as Kwame Anthony Appiah puts it in his book on cosmopolitanism) "that our knowledge is imperfect, provisional, subject to revision in the face of new evidence." Cosmopolitans, in Appiah's account, embrace the idea of fallibilism, because they believe that human beings can learn from the moments in which they are shown to be wrong and can increase the limits of their knowledge through the exchange of ideas with others. Indeed, trying, failing, correcting errors, and trying again become a crucial part of the learning process.

As counter-cosmopolitans, Darth Vader and the Empire have a rather different attitude toward failure. When Vader's fleet comes out of hyperspace in the first act of *The Empire Strikes Back* only to discover that "the Rebels are alerted to our presence," Vader tells the admiral in charge, "You have failed me for the last time," and chokes him to death using the Force. Later in the film, a similar fate greets the ship's captain who loses track of the *Millennium Falcon* in an asteroid field.[2] The First Order in the sequel trilogy seems to have the same attitude, as we can see in this passage from the novelization of *The Last Jedi*:

> True, Starkiller Base had then been destroyed, but Hux told himself that was merely an unfortunate setback—one that had been less a military defeat than the product of incompetence and treachery within the First Order. Those failures had been dealt with, or near enough. Most of those who had failed Hux and Supreme Leader Snoke had been vaporized with the base; those who'd escaped punishment would get what they deserved soon enough.

Two pages earlier, however, we've learned that Leia has learned the light-side attitude toward imperfection. One of her lieutenants wonders, "So what would General Organa do," and ("fortunately" the text tells us) knows the answer: "She'd say perfect information is a luxury you can rarely afford. All you can do is make the best decision with whatever imperfect information you do have."[3]

If imperfection is a fact of human existence, then the idea of fallibilism suggests that we must learn how to turn imperfection from a liability into a strength. We might remember Martha Nussbaum's invocation of the "complexity and mysteriousness" of the world, "its flawed and imperfect beauty," which conventional philosophical discourse can have difficulty capturing. The imperfections in the special effects and in the sets that Lucas was able to construct in 1977 bothered him over the years and led him to use emerging digital effects technologies to bring those films closer to his original vision in the "Special Editions" and gave him the confidence to attempt the grand storytelling that he imagined for his prequel trilogy. "Because of the digital technology," he said in an interview with *Cinefex* in 1999,

> I was able to think about a much grander, more epic scale—which is what I wanted it to be. Most people thought of *Star Wars* as being epic and grand, but it wasn't—it was just an illusion. I didn't have very many resources to do the kinds of things I wanted to do back then, even though I was able to successfully give the impression that that was what I had done. But with this one, I have actually been able to—in a much more concrete way—make it be on a large scale.

Cinefex described Lucas's technique for *The Phantom Menace* as the use of "minimal live-action sets … expanded to many times their actual size by the application of pioneering virtual backlot technology."[4] Abrams would adopt a slightly different approach to the idea of imperfection in *The Force Awakens* and *The Rise of Skywalker*, preferring the visual style of the original trilogy to that of the prequels. Oscar Isaac, who plays Poe Dameron in the sequel trilogy, put it this way in Lev Grossman's *Vanity Fair* article "Star Wars: The Rise of Skywalker, The Ultimate Preview": "It's the things that you can't anticipate—the imperfections. … It's very difficult to design imperfection, and the imperfections that you have in these environments immediately create a sense of authenticity. You just believe it more." According to Grossman, "It's that something, the presence and the details and the analog imperfections of a real nondigital place, that makes Star Wars so powerful."[5]

Imperfection—and learning how to make use of it—has thus always been a crucial element in both the style and the substance of *Star Wars*. The authoritativeness with which Yoda trains Luke in *The Empire Strikes Back* seems to have lulled many fans into thinking that Yoda was infallible. Yoda's famous dictum—"Try not. Do. Or do not. There is no try."—is a response to Luke's defeatist attitude after his X-wing sinks into the swamps of Dagobah. When Luke says that he'll give raising the X-wing "a try," Yoda's response indicates that he detects a timidity within Luke's idea of "trying." After Luke is unable to perform the feat because, he says, "it's too big," Yoda utters what has become an equally famous line—"Size matters not."—closes his eyes, concentrates, and raises the X-wing to dry land. Luke exclaims, "I can't believe it," and Yoda replies, "That is why you fail." Success, Yoda, suggests depends on self-belief and a determination to act resolutely—to act more forcefully than mere "giving it a try" would imply. You either get something done or you don't. There are no points, it seems, for trying. But there's also no doing without trying. Fear of failure leads to inaction. As it turns out, the completion of Luke's training occurs near the end of *The Rise of Skywalker*, well after he has become a Jedi master and even after he has become one with the Force: it is the moment when he finally raises an X-wing from underwater in order to give Rey what she needs in order to face Palpatine.

Yoda, however, is far from infallible. In *Revenge of the Sith*, he fails to defeat Darth Sidious in their climactic lightsaber duel and must be rescued by Bail Organa, to whom he says, "Into exile I must go. Failed, I have." In *The Empire Strikes Back*, he fails to convince Luke that it is more important to complete his training than to attempt to rescue Han and Leia and the droids from Darth Vader's clutches, imploring Luke as he leaves to "remember your failure in the cave." Yoda's failure here turns out to be a fortunate development, however, because it is Luke's decision to disobey his master that sets in motion a chain of events that ultimately leads to the redemption of Darth Vader and the defeat of the Emperor. The novelization of *The Last Jedi* makes this point explicit. At a moment when Leia finds herself fearing the prospect of failure, she remembers what her brother had taught her:

> On this point, Luke had explained, he had rejected the teachings of the Jedi. The Order had forbidden emotional attachments, warning that they left a Jedi vulnerable to the lures of the dark side. And indeed, it was a love curdled into jealousy and possessiveness that had led their father, Anakin Skywalker, into darkness and despair.
>
> But Luke had disagreed with Yoda and Obi-Wan Kenobi that Anakin was lost to the light. He had insisted that the very emotional entanglements that had led Anakin to become Darth Vader might also draw him back—entanglements such as the stubborn love between a father and son, each of whom had thought the other lost.
>
> Luke had been right—and ignoring his teachers had saved him, the Alliance, and the galaxy.[6]

The fans who were the most vocal critics of *The Last Jedi* were dismayed to find that it depicted a discouraged Luke Skywalker who had failed to reconstitute the Jedi Order and had hidden himself from his sister and the Resistance for reasons unknown: perhaps to do penance; perhaps to save the galaxy from the consequences of his inability to live up to the mantle of hero; perhaps to try to return to the legendary first Jedi temple order to learn from his mistakes.

What Luke believes he has discovered through his meditations on the planet Ahch-To is the Jedi's history of failure. He tells Rey:

> Now that they're extinct, the Jedi are romanticized—deified. But if you strip away the myth and look at their deeds, from the birth of the Sith to the fall of the Republic the legacy of the Jedi is failure. Hypocrisy. Hubris. ...

Luke points out that "at the height of their powers," the Jedi "allowed Darth Sidious to rise, create the Empire, and wipe them out," adding, "It was a Jedi Master who was responsible for the training and creation of Darth Vader."[7]

A vocal group of *Star Wars* fans has contended that Rian Johnson betrayed George Lucas's legacy by depicting a broken Luke Skywalker, who (as Rey puts it to herself in the novelization) had somehow come to reject not only "the legacy of the Jedi," but "his own legacy as well."[8] This contention ignores not only the increasing emphasis on failure in the original trilogy and then the prequel trilogy, but also Lucas's own preliminary plans for the sequel trilogy, which began with the idea that Luke had gone into seclusion. Lucasfilm VP and executive creative director Douglas Chiang prepared some portraits of an aged Luke Skywalker in preparation for a meeting with George Lucas on January 16, 2013. In *The Art of Star Wars: The Last Jedi*, Chiang describes the impetus behind the portraits and other materials prepared by a team of "Visualists" for this preproduction meeting:

> At this point in the story, thirty years after the fall of the Empire, Luke has gone to a dark place. He always had this potential dark side within him being that his father was Darth Vader. So he is really struggling with that. He ended up secluding himself in this Jedi temple on a new planet. Gradually, over the arc of the movie, he recovers his vitality and comes back to himself.[9]

Appropriately, in perhaps an inadvertent nod to Lucas's early career with Zoetrope, Christian Alzmann, senior art director at ILM, created renderings of Skywalker that were "inspired by Marlon Brando's character in *Apocalypse Now*, Colonel Kurtz."[10]

Lucasfilm made the decision early on not to use the treatments for the sequel trilogy that it had acquired from George Lucas, so that the screenwriters for Episode VII could give their imaginations free rein—at least as free as one can be when creating something called "Episode VII" that was going to be bringing back characters from the previous six episodes. Rian Johnson was given similar freedom for Episode VIII. In an interview with the *New York Times* that appeared two months before the release of *The Last Jedi*, Johnson said that as a kid "*Star Wars* was everything" and that he was surprised by the fact that the entire sequel trilogy had not yet been mapped out fully by Lucasfilm:

> I had figured there would be a big map on the wall with the whole story laid out, and it was not that at all. I was basically given the script for "Episode VII;" I got to watch dailies of what J. J. was doing. And it was like, where do we go from here? That was awesome.

Although Lucasfilm did not dictate that the film had "to contain certain plot points, or that certain things have to be achieved by its end," Johnson recognized that his freedom to imagine was constrained by the film's place as "the second film in a trilogy. The first film got these characters here. This second movie has to dig into and challenge these characters."[11]

Although *The Last Jedi* begins with a heroic sacrifice by members of the Resistance—and one in particular whose death will motivate her sister, Rose, to seize the opportunity to become a hero—the film's attitude toward failure is lighthearted rather than dour. *The Force Awakens* ended with what seemed to be a portentous moment: Rey finally locating Luke Skywalker and tentatively, imploringly holding out to him the lightsaber that he had lost on Bespin in *The Empire Strikes Back*. In *The Last Jedi*, Johnson goes back to that moment and then takes it in a direction that neither Rey nor the audience can foresee. Hamill's Luke takes it in his metallic prosthetic hand; Rey steps back; Luke looks at it, as Rey looks on expectantly. The music swells and then abruptly stops to signal a crucial moment. And then, with his nonmechanical left hand, Luke tosses the lightsaber over his shoulder nonchalantly and stalks away. It's not what she—or we—expected.

Luke adopts a sardonically playful attitude toward failure that disguises the depths of his despair. The film's signature one-liner—"Every word in that sentence was wrong."—appears three times. Luke says it to Rey before her first lesson in the ways of the force; Rey paraphrases it back before her second lesson; and Luke repeats it to Kylo Ren before the climactic encounter, which constitutes his final teaching moment in the film. Being wrong seems to be the starting point on the journey to wisdom. But as the relationship between Luke and Rey develops, we also see a parallel relationship develop between Rey and Kylo Ren, who had told her, during their showdown at the climax of *The Force Awakens*, "You need a teacher! I can show you the ways of the Force!" Rey refuses him then, but as *The Last Jedi* progresses, we are left to wonder whether her disappointment in Luke might drive him to seek Ren's tutelage.

Luke's account of what happened on the fateful night when he lost Ben Solo to the dark side is an account of multiple failures: first, his failure to see the dark-side building in Ben, just as Yoda had failed to see the workings of the dark side all around him and Obi-Wan had failed to see the growing presence of the dark in Anakin in the prequel trilogy; second, his failure to control his immediate instincts, leading him to ignite his lightsaber above the sleeping boy; and finally, his recognition that he has failed as a teacher: "The last thing I saw were the eyes of a frightened boy whose master had failed him." Rey, growing ever wiser, tries to reframe Luke's sense of failure: "You failed him," she says, "by thinking his choice was made. It wasn't." She makes it clear that she still believes that Ren can be turned from the dark side (even though she had earlier told Luke that "there is no light left in Kylo Ren").

The sequel trilogy reveals that Luke has tried to follow the last instruction that he was given by Yoda in *Return of the Jedi*: "Pass on what you have learned, Luke ... There is ... another ... Sky ... Sky ... walker." In one of the surprise moments in *The Last Jedi*, Leia manages to use the Force to levitate herself back to the Resistance's flagship through the vacuum of space after she has been blown out of it by a missile blast from Kylo Ren's wingmate, suggesting that she has had training in the use of the Force. This development is confirmed by a flashback scene in *The Rise of Skywalker* in which Luke describes Leia's training and why she decided, at the end, to leave her lightsaber behind. Almost despite himself, Luke passes on what he has learned to Rey during their short time together in *The Last Jedi*. In lines that were cut from the film but appear in the novelization, Luke complains after finding Rey looking at the ancient Jedi books, "This is my nightmare. A thousand wannabe younglings showing up on my doorstep, hoping they're the Chosen Whoevers, wanting to know how to lift rocks." Later he tells her, "The Force is not a power you have. ... It's not about lifting rocks. It's the energy between all things—a tension, a balance that binds the universe together." Except that—at what will no doubt turn out to be a watershed moment in galactic history—it turns out that sometimes it *is* about lifting rocks, as Rey uses her increasing facility with the Force to lift a pile of rocks that have been blocking the escape route for the surviving members of the Resistance.[12]

The scene shows us that Luke still had something to learn, despite the world-weariness that leads him to tell Rey that it's time for the Jedi to end, a position that he reverses at the climax of the film. The completion of Luke's own education begins when Rey asks him to rethink the way in which he failed Kylo Ren, but is completed by a surprise visit from none other than his old teacher, Yoda. It seems that Luke hasn't entirely followed Yoda's final instruction to "pass on what you have learned," perhaps because he never fully understood it. Like the film's audience, Luke is unaware that Rey has taken the ancient Jedi texts before leaving Ahch-To, and he goes to burn down the tree in which they are stored—only to be interrupted by Yoda's manifestation as a Force Ghost. "I'm ending all of this," he tells Yoda. "The tree, the texts, the Jedi. I'm going to burn it all down." At the moment of truth, however, he falters, so it falls to Yoda, who is powerful even as a Force Ghost: concentrating with his eyes closed, Yoda lifts his finger and a strike of lightning sets the tree aflame. Luke is appalled, but Yoda giggles and stamps his feet before saying, "Ah Skywalker. Missed you have I." He is still the master instructing a neophyte.

Even this late in the game, Luke's first impulse is to discern the wrong lesson. "So it *is* time," he ventures, "for the Jedi to end." Facing away from Luke and toward the tree, Yoda replies, "Time it is," before pausing and then turning around to continue with a rather different idea in mind: "for you to look past a pile of old books." Yoda had told Luke in *Empire* to "unlearn what you have learned," but all these years later, that isn't any easier: "The sacred Jedi books!" Luke protests. And then Yoda scolds him gently. Here's how the novelization dramatizes the scene:

> Read them, have you? Page-turners they were not. Wisdom they held, but that library contained nothing the girl Rey does not already possess.
>
> Yoda shook his head, and Luke felt very much like the Padawan he had been, so many years ago in the bogs of Dagobah. His master was disappointed, and he was embarrassed.
>
> "Skywalker," Yoda said. "Still looking to the horizon. Never here, now. The need in front of your nose."
>
> The little Jedi Master reached out with his cane, to rap Luke's nose with it.
>
> "I was weak, unwise," Luke said.
>
> "Lost Ben Solo, you did," Yoda said, gently but firmly. "Lose Rey, we must not."[13]

The scene proves to be an epiphany for Luke and changes the apparent meaning of the film's title (see Figure 14).

At the climax of the film, Luke plays the role that Han Solo played at the end of *A New Hope*: he appears unexpectedly to save the day. In this case, however, saving the day means not a resounding victory, but rather distracting Kylo Ren long enough to give the Resistance time to escape. (The film is, after all, the second film in the trilogy, occupying the downbeat role played earlier by *The Empire Strikes Back*.) This moment is one of a number of Johnson's reworkings of moments from the original trilogy, and once again he propels the narrative in an unexpected direction. The film, which has already shown us an amped-up version of the lightsaber battle that takes place in the Emperor's throne room in *Return of the Jedi*, now builds toward another climactic lightsaber duel—which turns out to be something other than an actual lightsaber duel, because Luke is only there as

Figure 14 Luke and Yoda watching the sacred Jedi tree burn. Yoda (as a Force Ghost): "Time it is … for you to look past a pile of old books." Luke: "The sacred Jedi books!" Yoda: "Read them, have you? Page-turners they were not. Wisdom they held, but that library contained nothing the girl Rey does not already possess." This lighthearted moment dramatizes *The Last Jedi*'s portrayal of fallibilism. Photo credit: Lucasfilm. *Star Wars: Episode VII—The Last Jedi*, directed by Rian Johnson © 2017 Walt Disney Pictures/Lucasfilm. All rights reserved.

a Force apparition. It is at this climactic moment that Luke has the opportunity to repeat his one-liner:

> Kylo and Luke regarded each other, their lightsabers humming between them. Each methodically adjusted his stance, eyes locked on the other. Around them drifted flakes of salt, light as ash.
>
> "I failed you, Ben," Luke said. "I'm sorry."
>
> "I'm sure you are," Kylo replied. "The Resistance is dead. The war is over. And when I kill you, I'll have killed the last Jedi." He waited to see what his former Master would say, bracing to defend against a lightning-fast strike. But Luke simply raised an eyebrow.
>
> "Amazing," he said. "Every word of what you just said was wrong. The Rebellion is reborn today. The war is just beginning. And I will not be the last Jedi."[14]

The recurrence of the line made audiences wonder whether this might turn out to be another teaching moment: would it be possible for Kylo Ren to recognize his error and return to the light side? What is the meaning of Luke's final line, "See you around kid"?[15]

If the Skywalker saga turns on the fraught relationships between parents and their children, *The Last Jedi* is also about the fraught nature of the relationship between teacher and student, an idea that Lucasfilm began to explore in earnest in the "High Republic" narratives that began to appear in 2021.[16] The end of Yoda's exhortation to Luke on Ahch-To offers a melancholy lesson about the nature of being a teacher. Part of it involves renouncing the pretense to authority and infallibility. But there's something else as well:

> "Heeded my words not did you," Yoda said. "'Pass on what you have learned.' Wisdom, yes. But folly also. Strength in mastery, hmm. But weakness and failure, yes. Failure most of all. The greatest teacher failure is." And then he sounded faintly regretful: "We are what they grow beyond. That is the true burden of all Masters."[17]

Yoda's final words provide a fitting way of understanding what Lucasfilm has achieved in making the transition to its second generation. The lesson of failure and the lesson that teachers must ultimately give way to their students are lessons embodied in George Lucas's decision to turn Lucasfilm over to a new generation of filmmakers.

This exemplary moment from Johnson's *Last Jedi* resonates with some of the symbolic choices that Abrams makes in the two films that he directed for the sequel trilogy. From its very first scenes, *The Force Awakens* presents characters who are haunted by the past: in the first piece of spoken dialogue, Lor San Tekka tells Poe Dameron, "This will start to make things right. I've traveled too far, and seen too much, to ignore the despair in the galaxy." A few scenes later, we meet the scavenger Rey, who lives in the wreckage of the past, literally (she survives by salvaging bits and pieces from a downed Star Destroyer and lives in the ruins of an Imperial AT-AT walker) and symbolically (she is haunted by visions of a moment from the past in which she was left abandoned on the desert world of Jakku). Later we learn that Kylo Ren is haunted by his failure to be as powerful in the dark side of the Force as his legendary grandfather, Darth Vader. Appropriately, at one of the climactic moments of *The Rise of Skywalker*, the two fight a lightsaber duel on top of the wreckage of the second Death Star from *The Return of the Jedi* (see cover image). "It felt like going back to a haunted house," Abrams said in an interview with *Entertainment Weekly*. "This is a story of people having to grapple with the burden the prior generation dumps on those that follow. So literally returning to this wreck of the past and having to fight it out felt like an obvious metaphor, but also felt incredibly cinematic."[18] It's a metaphor that's doubly metaphorical, giving us an insight into the burdens faced not only by the characters in the sequel trilogy, but also by that trilogy's makers.

9

Moral Compass

Growing up with the prequel trilogy, my kids found the mythology of the Jedis, with their lightsabers and seemingly magical power to manipulate objects and people, irresistible. As they grew older, however, they became fascinated by the Sith and their mythology; they loved the now noncanonical stories about Darth Revan, Darth Malak, and Darth Nihilus that animated the two *Knights of the Old Republic* games. They loved the red lightsabers. When the "Princess Jedi" started playing the online game *Star Wars: The Old Republic*, he completed the story several times, mastering each of the dark-side characters and playing the "Sith Warrior" and "Sith Inquisitor" classes with special relish. I don't think he ever bothered to play a Jedi (see Figure 15). He and his brother found the dark-side characters of the expanded universe to be much more charismatic than the Jedi, in the same way, I suppose, that Milton's Satan is charismatic in *Paradise Lost*.

The dark side is an ever-present part of the Force in Star Wars. The goal of the Jedi is not to eradicate the dark side, but rather to keep it in check and there by "to bring balance to the force." What the Jedi seek to eradicate is the Sith, who are dedicated to letting the dark side run rampant. In the *Star Wars Archives* volume devoted to the prequel trilogy, Lucas described the Force as "split into two: the

Figure 15 Princess Jedi grows up and grows dark. As my kids grew up, they became fascinated with the lore and characters of the Sith as a result of playing the games *Knights of the Old Republic, Knights of the Old Republic II: The Sith Lords,* and *Star Wars: The Old Republic*. They developed a particular fondness for Darth Revan, whose Hasbro Black Series lightsaber the former "Princess Jedi" holds here. They were delighted to see Revan enter the new canon via an oblique reference on page 175 of Pablo Hidalgo's reference book *Star Wars: The Rise of Skywalker: The Visual Dictionary* (2019), where the third Sith Trooper legion is designated "Revan." Photo credit: Cyrus R. K. Patell.

positive/light side, and the negative dark side."[1] As Lucas developed his ideas about the workings of the Force for the prequel trilogy, he gave this conception a biological basis, rooting the Force in entities that he called "Whills and midi-chlorians." The midi-chlorians—which Lucas conceived as a combination "of mitochondria in living organisms and photosynthesis in plants"—made it into *The Phantom Menace*. The Whills, the one-celled organisms that were present in Lucas's thinking in the early drafts for the first movie, had to wait for *Rogue One* for even an oblique mention.[2] According to Lucas, "The one-celled organisms have to have a balance. You have to have good ones and bad ones otherwise it would extinguish life. And if they go out of balance, then the dark side takes over."[3] Lucas then transfers this conception of biological balance onto human psychology: "The dark side is greedy and possessive. Greedy people want everything, and when they get everything, they're insecure, constantly afraid that somebody's going to take it away from them. Fear is the doorway to the dark side."[4] For Lucas, the opposite of fear is compassion: "If you're not afraid and you're willing to jump into the river to save a baby, regardless of the consequences, that's compassion. That's the good side of the Force."[5] The sequel trilogy turns out to rely on a very similar conception of what constitutes moral behavior. Only it isn't a baby that needs saving: it's a droid.

Just before the release of *The Last Jedi*, Daisy Ridley told an interviewer for *Rolling Stone* magazine that her "favorite thing" about the character Rey is "her strong moral compass":

> Rey is just a young girl going through something. My favorite thing about [her] is that strong moral compass. Even having grown up quite lonely, she meets people and immediately tries to do the right thing. BB-8 is a hilarious annoyance, [but] she is going to take down two guys to try and protect him. But anyone I know would

do that! If you meet someone and they're alone and then someone else tries to steal them, you're obviously going to get involved. It's just what people do.[6]

Ridley's comments assume, of course, that the droid *is* a "someone" worthy of dignity and protection—which is not a view shared universally in the *Star Wars* universe, though, as we've seen, it is used as one way of differentiating the "good guys from the bad guys." According to J. J. Abrams, "The idea was to tell a tale of a young woman who was innately powerful, innately moral, innately good, but also struggling with her place in the world and forced to fend for herself in every way."[7]

How does *The Force Awakens* establish Rey as "innately" powerful, moral, and good? The first scenes in the film establish who the "bad guys" are—Kylo Ren, Captain Phasma, and the First Order, who are willing to massacre civilians in their quest to obtain the location of Luke Skywalker—and "the good guys": Lor San Tekka who is aligned with the Jedi and with the Skywalkers; Poe Dameron, described in the crawl as Leia's "most daring pilot"; his droid, BB-8, in whom he places his trust and his hope that their mission can be completed; and FN-2187, a stormtrooper who refuses to fire on the villagers and will soon be rechristened "Finn."

A match cut establishes a visual and thus thematic connection between Finn in his dirty helmet and Rey, dressed roughly like a Tusken Raider, with goggles seemingly fabricated from the lenses of a stormtrooper's helmet, salvaging parts from a crashed starship. There is no music, just the sounds of scavenging, and we don't even know if she is human. But as soon as she lifts her goggles, we see that she is a young woman. She drains the last of her water accompanied by the sounds of a plaintive flute, as her theme music begins. According to Abrams, "The idea was to continue the story and to begin with this young woman who felt like Luke Skywalker was a myth." Composer John Williams said in an interview that Rey's theme was written to illustrate the empathy that he felt for this girl who, "when we first meet her," is "alone … without her parents."[8]

We see Rey dragging her salvage, cleaning it, and then trading it in for food rations—and receiving just one-quarter portion for it from the threatening boss Unkar Plutt. We see her speed home across the sunset on a lonely desert landscape and then scratch a line on the metal of a wall, as if she is keeping count of something important. There are a lot of scratched lines. We see her cook that little portion and then eat it outside, pausing to put on an old Rebel pilot's helmet, establishing a connection between her and the good guys of the original trilogy. The camera pulls back to reveal that she is living alone in the wreck of an old Imperial walker.

Only then does she hear—and run to save—BB-8, grabbing her staff and facing down a menacing masked figure. Her first lines explain to BB-8, "That's just Teedo. Wants you for parts. He has no respect for anyone." Then she fixes his antenna and asks him where he comes from: "Classified? Really? Me too. Big secret." (How true that turns out to be!) After giving him directions to Niima Outpost, she takes him in when he seems to be afraid to venture on his own. And with that, the basic contours of her character are established: she's on her own, forced to be self-reliant; she's strong and not afraid; and she has respect for others. These character traits are reinforced in her second set of scenes, when she tells BB-8, "Don't give up hope. He still might show up, whoever it is you're waiting for, Classified. I know all about waiting." In response to the droid's chirping query, she says, "My family. They'll be back. One day." When she refuses to trade BB-8 for sixty portions of food, her moral compass is established. It turns out to be a bonus that she can fly the *Millennium Falcon* and escape Jakku with BB-8 and Finn. She has a fan's appreciation for the history of the Falcon (even if she gets the number of parsecs in the notorious Kessel Run wrong), and Han Solo immediately recognizes her as a worthy companion.

The film's establishment of Rey's "strong moral compass" (and its suggestion that both Poe and Finn are also morally worthy) draws on the ideas that Lucas articulated in his interview with Bill Moyers in 1999:

> What these films deal with is the fact that we all have good and evil inside of us and that we can choose which way we want the balance to go. "Star Wars" was made up of many themes. It's not just a single theme. One is our relationship to machines, which are fearful but also benign. They're an extension of the human, not mean in themselves. The issues of friendship and your obligation to your fellow man and to other people that are around you, that you have control over your destiny, that you have many paths to walk down and [that] you may have a great destiny. If you decide not to walk down that path, your life might not be as satisfying as if you wake up and listen to your inner feelings and realize what it is that you have a particular talent for and what contributions you can make to society.[9]

Rey's scenes during the first act of *The Force Awakens* establish that she is self-reliant and believes in a brighter future despite her downtrodden circumstances. She regards BB-8 as a "person" (in the legal sense of someone who has rights), and she treats him with respect and friendship, a sign that she is powerfully aware of her obligations to those around her. She values family, in large part because it's something that she doesn't have. And she embodies hope.

At the same time, however, there is a darkness within Rey that she must combat in order to be able to have control of her destiny. As played by Daisy Ridley, Rey exudes a fierceness in her facial expressions whenever she is threatened or when she fights. Astute listeners of *The Force Awakens* soundtrack noticed that, if Williams meant Rey's theme music to illustrate empathy, it also had thematic affinities with the music for Emperor Palpatine and for Kylo Ren.[10] When Luke's lightsaber calls to her from the recesses of Maz Kanata's castle in *The Force Awakens*, Rey has a vision that is full of images of dark-side violence and her own past grief. Later, when the lightsaber flies to her instead of Ren in the forest on Starkiller base, she not only fights with fierceness, but also instinctively adopts the forward-thrusting fighting style that we have seen only once before in the saga: when Palpatine reveals himself as a Sith to the Jedi who have come to arrest him. In *The Last Jedi*, Luke is appalled when her first training lesson leads her to venture in her mind straight to the island's source of dark-side energy:

LUKE: You went straight to the dark!
REY: That place was trying to show me something.
LUKE: It offered something you needed. And you didn't even try to stop yourself.

Later, Rey ventures physically into the dark-side area in search of answers about her parentage; it's a version of Luke's experience in the dark-side cave in *The Empire Strikes Back*, and the dark resonance of the experience is magnified when we realize that what we are seeing is actually a visualization of an account that she is giving to Kylo Ren through the Force bond that has been established between them. Even before it reveals her blood relation to Palpatine, *The Rise of Skywalker* raises the stakes by imbuing her with Force lightning powers that we've only seen the Emperor use and then showing us a Force vision in which she battles a dark-side version of herself, who wields a double-bladed red lightsaber akin to Darth Maul's. In other words, the darkness inside Rey is not trivial (see Figure 16).

Figure 16 Rey is fierce. In *The Rise of Skywalker*, Daisy Ridley's Rey is fierce and needs to train herself to control her anger (top) lest she turn into the dark-side version of herself (bottom) that is revealed to her in a Force vision. Photo credits: Lucasfilm. *Star Wars: Episode IX—The Rise of Skywalker* directed by J. J. Abrams © 2019 Walt Disney Pictures/Lucasfilm. All rights reserved.

When Luke appears as a Force ghost late in *The Rise of Skywalker*, he acknowledges that he knows the truth of her lineage—and that Leia knew it as well. Rey whispers in amazement: "She didn't tell me. [Pause.] She still trained me." Luke reveals it was "because she saw your spirit. Your heart. Rey, some things are stronger than blood." Rey's "spirit" is her innate moral compass, which in this case is not aligned with the legacy of her blood. The sequel trilogy's rhetoric of bloodlines links "blood" to Force power, but *The Rise of Skywalker* and indeed the saga as a whole tell us that blood is not destiny and that facing up to and defeating the darkness within us requires more than self-reliance. The triumph of the light requires networks of relationships, particularly familial ties and bonds of friendship. Even those, like Rey, who are born with a strong moral compass need the support of mentors, family, and friends in order to learn how to use it effectively.

Premiering just before the release of *The Rise of Skywalker*, *The Mandalorian*, which draws inspiration from the mythologies of rugged individualism dramatized by the classic Hollywood Western, also demonstrates the power and the necessity of networks of relationships. The Mandalorian "way" establishes bonds of kinship and obligation that turn out to be chosen rather than biological. The title character's moral compass is established not primarily through his devotion to "the way," however, but rather through his compassion for a foundling, who starts out as one of his bounties. Ironically, where *The Force Awakens* follows the earlier trilogies in using droids to establish where a character stands in the universe's moral order, *The Mandalorian* deliberately plays against those expectations. The title character hates droids and won't let them fly speeders that he needs to ride or work on his ship. Flashbacks indicate that he has been orphaned, his parents likely killed by an Imperial battle droid (which might account for his aversion). Self-reliance is not sufficient to establish moral compass in the *Star Wars* universe, but being drawn to protect the weak—in this case a fifty-year-old "child" who belongs to the same species as Yoda and is sought after by ex-Imperials—is a start. When an ex-New Republic shock trooper refers to the child as "your boy," the Mandalorian's moral compass is established. Rey won't trade BB-8 for food that she desperately needs; the Mandalorian won't leave the child to his fate despite the fact that this act of rescue will make the Mandalorian a pariah, transformed from bounty hunter into bounty, who takes on the mission of returning the child to his people—the Jedi.

More than simply establishing the title character's moral character by having him bond with the show's cute character (a role filled in *The Force Awakens* by BB-8), *The Mandalorian* draws on a symbolic pattern that emerges in Lucas's trilogies and that is emphasized in the sequel trilogy: the importance of family, friends, and community. "Your overconfidence is your weakness," Luke tells Emperor Palpatine on the second Death Star in *Return of the Jedi*. "Your faith in your friends is yours." The rhetoric of friendship marks the final scenes of *Return*. The Emperor taunts Luke by telling him that his "friends up there on the Sanctuary Moon are walking into a trap"; later he says, attempting to fill Luke with anger and hatred, "Your fleet is lost. And your friends on the Endor moon will not survive. There is no escape, my young apprentice. The Alliance will die … as will your friends."[11] The Emperor seems to believe that Luke's attachment to his "friends" is stronger than his attachment to the Alliance, ending his speech with the idea that he thinks will wound Luke the most. At the end of *The Rise of Skywalker*, Palpatine adopts a similar tactic with Rey but raises the stakes:

> Your master Luke Skywalker was saved by his father. The only family you have here is me. [Pause.] They don't have long: no one is coming to help them, and you are the one who led them here. Strike me down. Reign over a new empire, and the fleet will be yours. Only you have the power to save them. Refuse, and your new family dies.

Luke's and Rey's ability to defeat the Emperor depends not only on their friends' achievements, but also on those bonds of family—

largely adoptive in Luke's case, completely adoptive in Rey's—and their willingness to sacrifice themselves for them. Altruism thus proves to be an integral part of moral compass in the *Star Wars* films. Obi-Wan sacrifices himself when fighting Vader so that Luke, Leia, Han, and the droids can escape in *A New Hope*. Unwilling to fight his father to the death in *Return of the Jedi*, Luke avoids engaging in a climactic duel with him until Vader uncovers the existence of Luke's twin: "So … you have a twin sister. Your feelings have now betrayed her, too. Obi-Wan was wise to hide her from me. Now his failure is complete. If you will not turn to the dark side, then perhaps she will."[12] It is this threat that leads to the climax of *Return of the Jedi*: Luke defeats his father to save his sister. Luke has put himself in jeopardy by coming before the Emperor, and he doubles that jeopardy when he refuses to kill his father and throws away his lightsaber. But in refusing to kill Vader, Luke brings about Vader's redemption and thus the defeat of the Emperor. In the sequel trilogy, Luke will follow the model set by Obi-Wan, sacrificing himself so that the Resistance can survive. Indeed, in the sequel trilogy, the three main protagonists of the original trilogy—Luke, Han, and Leia—all sacrifice themselves for their heirs, as do Rey's parents. And those heirs are willing, in turn, to sacrifice themselves for those they love. Rey destroys Palpatine but has sacrificed herself in the process, her life energy drained by the fight. Her resurrection comes only because the redeemed Ben Solo follows his parents' example and sacrifices himself to bring her back.[13]

Like the two trilogies that preceded it, the sequel trilogy is all about finding one's way—and not just because the opening quest portion of *The Rise of Skywalker* involves locating "wayfinders," Sith "compasses" that lead to the hidden planet Exegol, where a resurrected Palpatine and his Sith Eternal cultists have been building the fleet that will bring about "the Final Order." "Why are *you* here," Luke asks Rey in *The Last Jedi*, after she discovers the ancient Jedi texts hidden in the hollow of a massive tree on Ahch-To. Rey answers: "Something inside me has always been there, but now it's awake. And I'm afraid. I don't know what it is or what to do with it, and I need help." Later she tells Luke: "I need someone to show me my place in all of this."

To find her way, Rey must rely not only on her strong, inborn moral compass, but also on the guidance of others like Luke and Leia. She must locate herself on a map of relationships, responsibilities, and duties. Like a good cosmopolitan, she learns to model her global—indeed, her galactic—obligations on her local relations with friends and mentors, who become her adoptive family. By the end of *The Rise of Skywalker*, she is sacrificing herself to save her friends, the Resistance, and the galaxy, all of which are part of the network of relations in which she has learned to place herself. The galaxy is her family now, a fact unwittingly validated by Palpatine's threat. Throughout all the films, the ways in which characters like Obi-Wan, Yoda, and Maz Kanata describe the Force resonate with the idea that it is a network that connects everything in the galaxy together. When we first learn about the Force in *A New Hope*, Obi-Wan describes it as "an energy field created by all living things. It surrounds us an penetrates us. It binds the galaxy together."[14] Anticipating what theorists like Bruno Latour today call "actor-network theory," Yoda tells Luke in *The Empire Strikes Back*, "You must feel the force around you. Here, between you … me … the tree … the rock … everywhere! Yes, even between the land and the ship!"[15] And in *The Force Awakens*, Maz Kanata tells Rey that the Force "moves through and surrounds every living thing. Close your eyes. Feel it: the light. It's always been there. It will guide you."

Part of the guidance that Rey requires will come from the Force as the films progress, but another part must come from the past, from the traditions of the Jedi, some of which were flawed and need revision, but some of which pave the way for the future. Despite what many critics and some fans have argued, *The Last Jedi* was not about disregarding the past, but rather about learning to place oneself in a workable relation to it.[16] "Let the past die. Kill it if you have to. That's the only way to become what you were meant to be." These are the words of Kylo Ren, the villain of *The Last Jedi*, not the perspective of the film, and they are words that Rey rejects when Ren repeats them to her after the death of Snoke. They also represent the attitude that Luke Skywalker has brought with him to exile: "It's time for the Jedi to end." By the end of the film, as we have seen, Luke has realized that this view is mistaken, and he tells Ren, "The Rebellion is reborn today, the war is just beginning, and I will not be the last Jedi." The immediate cut to Rey's using the Force to lift rocks and enable the Resistance survivors to escape shows just what and who Luke means. Before Luke goes out to face Ren, Leia laments, "I held out hope for so long, but I know my son is gone." Luke responds: "No one's ever really gone." He's talking about his nephew Ben Solo, but his words apply to himself as well: meeting Rey has enabled him to become once again the Luke Skywalker that he once was.

Maz Kanata tells Rey in *The Force Awakens*, in words that prove to be prophetic, "Dear child. I see your eyes. You already know the truth. Whomever you're waiting for on Jakku, they're never coming back. But there's someone who still could. ... The belonging you seek is not behind you. It is ahead." But rather than have Rey reject the past, Maz urges Rey to make productive use of it: "The saber. Take it." At that point in her story, Rey is unable to heed the lightsaber's call. But at the end of *The Rise of Skywalker*, she has found her place. She knows her history, and she is at peace with the sacrifice that her parents have made: "My parents were strong," she tells Palpatine in their final confrontation. "They saved me from you." When she returns to Tatooine in the last scene of the film to pay homage to her teachers, Luke and Leia, by burying their lightsabers in the sands of the Lars homestead where Luke was raised, she tells a wanderer who comes by that her name is "Rey Skywalker." Choosing to adopt the surname of her teachers is not a rejection of her parents, but a validation of their desire to reject Palpatine and all he represents. It's poetic justice that the victory of the house of Skywalker is complete when a Palpatine becomes its heir.

We see that Rey's training as a Jedi is now complete, when she turns on the lightsaber that she has constructed (see Figure 17). It pays homage to her past, because it is built from the staff that she carried as a scavenger and continues to wield throughout the sequel trilogy. Its rotating switch is unique in the annals of *Star Wars* lightsabers. And the color of its blade is not the blue or green of Obi-Wan, Anakin, Luke, and Leia. It is yellow, the color used by the guards who protect the Jedi Temple in the *Clone Wars* television series.[17] Armed with that innate moral compass strengthened by the network of relationships she has developed, Rey has indeed found her "place in all of this." She is Rey Skywalker, guardian of the Jedi past—and its future.

Figure 17 Rey's skills are complete. In the final scene of *The Rise of Skywalker*, Rey looks at the lightsaber that she has constructed out of the staff that she has carried throughout the sequel trilogy, its yellow blade a color not seen before in a *Star Wars* film. Photo credit: Lucasfilm. *Star Wars: Episode IX—The Rise of Skywalker* directed by J. J. Abrams © 2019 Walt Disney Pictures/Lucasfilm. All rights reserved.

Notes

Introduction

1. Aftab 2008, n.p.
2. Throughout this book, I will use the term *Star Wars* in italics to indicate the entire *Star Wars* enterprise, which I describe below as a "shared universe." I will refer to the first *Star Wars* film, known simply as "*Star Wars*" when it was released, by the name that George Lucas gave to it subsequently: *A New Hope*. I will occasionally refer to that film as "Episode IV" or "the 1977 film" when appropriate.
3. Kline, vii.
4. See Dewey 1926.
5. Qtd. in Maitland 63.
6. Machen, 261, 263.
7. D. Brooks, n.p.
8. I will also mention other Lucasfilm productions such as *THX 1138*, *American Graffiti*, and the Indiana Jones film and television series along the way where appropriate, but *Star Wars* is clearly Lucasfilm's major achievement and the reason that Disney purchased the company.
9. Dargis 2017, n.p.
10. The definition comes from Borojević 2017, who notes that it "was first coined by Ben Vincent in a 1976 study by Robert Silvey, and was then further researched by psychologist David Cohen and psychiatrist Stephen A. MacKeith (1992)."
11. Rogers 2018, n.p.
12. Rogers 2015, 129.
13. Bouzereau, 34.
14. Rogers 2019, n.p.
15. Rogers 2015, 122, 124.
16. Fagles, 22.
17. Lusted, 9.

18 Tompkins, 6. Tompkins finds herself surprised and somewhat appalled to discover that Indians play a relatively minor role in the Western imaginary, at least insofar as Indians are people. "It was bizarre. Either I had managed to see seventy-five to eighty Western films that by chance had no serious representations of native people in them, or there was something wrong with the popular image of Westerns. I remembered the Indians in Cooper's novels—Uncas, Chingachgook, Hardheart—ethnographically incorrect, maybe, but still magnetic, compelling. There were no such characters in the movies I had watched. Logic would suggest that in his flight from women and children, family life, triviality, and tameness, the Western hero would run straight into the arms of the Indian, wild blood brother of his soul, but it doesn't happen. Indians are repressed in Westerns—there but not there—in the same way women are" (9).
19 Reiman, n.p.
20 Dawson, n.p.
21 For a promising start, see Lomax 2018.
22 See Patell 2015.
23 Appiah 2006b, 30.
24 Greenblatt 1995, 226.
25 Greenblatt 1995, 227.
26 Nussbaum 1990, 3.
27 Kennedy quoted in Rogers 2015, 129.
28 Rogers 2018, n.p.
29 Appiah 2005, 259.

Chapter 1

1 Bradatan 2017, n.p.
2 Heath 6–7.
3 Althusser 1971, 162.
4 Althusser 1971, 222–4.
5 Nussbaum 1990, 3–4.
6 Wartenberg, 1–2.
7 See Nussbaum 2002.
8 Wartenberg, 2.
9 Wartenberg. 2.
10 Wartenberg, 4–5.
11 Mulhall, 6.
12 Wartenberg, 3–4.
13 Chieffo, n.p.

14 Plantinga, 2.
15 Plantinga, 8.
16 Sinnerbrink, 86.
17 Shenk, 3:20.
18 Plantinga, 5–6.
19 Clifford, 7.
20 Graff, 54.
21 Davis, 17.
22 Althusser 1969, 231.
23 Hall, 104.
24 Fish, 14–16.
25 Jauss, 22, 23, 26.
26 Patches 2015, n.p.
27 Becker et al., 1:12:30.
28 Becker et al., 1:13:10.
29 See Lepitak for Lippincott's reflections on why the marketing campaign worked in 1977 and how things are different now with the advent of social media.
30 Polo 2015, n.p.
31 *Star Wars: Episode IV—A New Hope* (1977), written and directed by George Lucas, © Lucasfilm.
32 Becker et al., 1:10.25.
33 Becker et al., 1:11.26.
34 Nussbaum 1995, 12.
35 Nussbaum 1995, 10.
36 Scharf, n.p.
37 Bean, n.p.

Chapter 2

1 Moyers 199 n.p.
2 Bouzereau, 12.
3 Caro 2005, n.p.
4 Herr 61, 244.
5 Moyers 1999, n.p.
6 Moyers 1999, n.p.
7 Moyers 1999, n.p.
8 Kline 15; Rinzler 2007, 4.
9 Rinzler 2007, 3.
10 Rinzler 2007, 4.
11 Jenkins, 31.

12 Moyers 1999, n.p.
13 Rinzler 2007, 4.
14 Rinzler 2007, 4.
15 Jenkins, 36.
16 Qtd. in Jenkins, 36.
17 Jenkins, 37.
18 Campbell 1972, 30.
19 National Air and Space Museum, "Star Wars: The Magic of Myth," online exhibition, https://airandspace.si.edu/exhibitions/star-wars/online/sw-unit1.htm
20 Henderson, 4.
21 Henderson, 6.
22 Isaacson, xix.
23 Smith 1986, 4–5. For an excellent scholarly account of the history and significance of ILM, see Turnock.
24 Vaz and Duignan, 6.
25 Shay 1980, 8.
26 Smith 1986, 7.
27 Vaz and Duignan, 7.
28 Brooker 2009, 35.
29 Vaz and Duignan, 7.
30 Walt Disney Company 2012, n.p.
31 Cieply, B1.
32 Wookieepedia, "Holocron."
33 Zakarin 2018, n.p.
34 Cameron, 109.
35 Rose, n.p. See Iger 173–88 for the Disney perspective on the acquisition of Lucasfilm.
36 Shepherd 2017, n.p.
37 Baruh 2020a, Episode 2: "Legacy," 5:39.
38 Baruh 2020a, Episode 2: "Legacy," 6:15.
39 Baruh 2020a, Episode 2: "Legacy," 6:50.
40 Baruh 2020a, Episode 2: "Legacy," 11:57.
41 Dargis 2017, n.p.
42 Sager, 134.
43 Breznican 2015, n.p.
44 Bouzereau, 236.
45 Bouzereau, 297.
46 Liptak 2018, n.p.
47 Rebel Force Radio interview.
48 Handy 2015b, n.p.

49 Szostak 2017, 23.
50 See Dyer and De Semylen 2020 for a list of "101 Mando Easter Eggs" that pay homage to all forms of *Star Wars* storytelling.
51 See Guynes and Hassler-Forest, *Star Wars and the History of Transmedia Storytelling* (2018) for assessments of the significance of the ways in which the *Star Wars* became a transmedia phenomenon that created a broadly influential template for other popular culture franchises.
52 Baruh 2020b, 42:10. Rodriguez reports his own response: "And I just thought: these are my people!"
53 *Citizens United v. Fed. Election Commission*, 558 U.S. 310, 314 (2010).
54 Greenfield, xi–xii, 209, 3.
55 Ratcliffe, 9.

Chapter 3

1 You can find that Lego video here: https://youtu.be/wUlliAUvcfU.
2 Duncan, 41.
3 Fagles, 24.
4 Fagles, 19, 21, 23, 22.
5 Barnes, 92.
6 Kenny, xxxii.
7 Heath, ix–x.
8 Heath, xxxvii.
9 Heath, 5, 9.
10 Heath, 39–40.
11 Heath, 10.
12 Heath, 12, 18.
13 Heath, 18.
14 Heath, xxx.
15 Heath, 18–19.
16 Heath, 29.
17 Bouzereau, 35.
18 Hamill, 2016, 16:55.
19 Blondell, 89.
20 Heath, 21.
21 *Star Wars: Episode IX—The Rise of Skywalker* (2019), directed by J. J. Abrams, written by Chris Terrio & J.J. Abrams, from a story by Derek Connolly & Colin Trevorrow and J.J. Abrams & Chris Terrio. © Lucasfilm.
22 Patterson 2020, 25:49.
23 Campbell 1990, 84; Patterson, 1:31:17.
24 Heath, xxxiii.

25 Patterson, 1:36:48.
26 Rinzler 2013, 7.
27 Rinzler 2013, 277.
28 Bouzereau, 34.
29 Bouzereau, 168.
30 X3 Productions, v.
31 X3 Productions, xi.

Chapter 4

1   P. Brooks, 62.
2   See Hayward, 243–53.
3   Higgins, 10.
4   Neale, 169.
5   Neale, 185.
6   Hamill, "Oxford Union," 7:41.
7   P. Brooks, 42.
8   Lusted, 65.
9   Cameron, 92. See also Bouzereau, 27.
10 Hibberd 2019a, n.p.
11 See Horton 2019 for a summary of the changes, including usefully annotated video and a simultaneous comparison of the versions that highlights the changes in timing.
12 *Star Wars: Episode I—The Phantom Menace* (1999), written and directed by George Lucas, © Lucasfilm.
13 Block, n.p.
14 Stuever, n.p.
15 Lusted, 46.
16 Tompkins, 228.
17 Bouzereau, 76.
18 Houser et al., issue 1, 10.
19 Lucasfilm 2018, n.p.
20 Young 2012, n.p.
21 Baver 2019a, n.p.

Chapter 5

1   Henderson, 55.
2   Walzer 2003, n.p.
3   Rinzler 2007, 17.
4   Burr, n.p.
5   Lasch, 21.

6   Carter, 707, 714.
7   Becker et al., 1:19:00.
8   Lukes, 73. The account of US individualism that follows draws on the analysis I present in Patell 2001.
9   Bouzereau, 35.
10 Bouzereau, 59.
11 Cameron, 114.
12 Bouzereau, 187.
13 Bellah et al. 1996, 21.
14 Bellah et al. 1996, 20.
15 Bellah et al. 1996, 334.
16 Bellah et al. 1996, 20–1.
17 Jameson, 105–6.
18 Bellah et al. 1996, 21, 294.
19 Bellah et al. 1991, 19, 10, 15.
20 Cameron, 110.
21 Bouzereau, 80.
22 Bouzereau, 187.
23 Turner, 1–2, 37.
24 Bouzereau, 267.
25 Ratcliffe, 9.
26 Cameron, 116.
27 Cameron, 116.
28 Murdock, 3.

Chapter 6

1   Bouzereau, 39.
2   Hamill, "Oxford Union," 36:25. Hamill offers a slightly different account of the genesis of the Ewoks: "Originally, the concept was we were supposed to visit a planet of Wookiees, and they said from the budgetary point of view, it would be way too expensive to make all those costumes. And then George said, 'Well, we'll just make them really tiny. Let's make small Wookiees.'"
3   Bouzereau, 281.
4   Asimov, 435.
5   On the origins and nature of English Luddism, see Bailey 1998 and Dinwiddy 1986.
6   Ellis, 1.
7   Bouzereau, 292.
8   Arendt, 19.
9   Arendt, 7.

10 Arendt, 121.
11 Arendt, 151, 309.
12 Arendt, 151.
13 Bouzereau, 268.
14 Bouzereau, 39.
15 Arendt, 210.
16 Handy 2015a, 146.
17 Fordham, 44.
18 Fordham, 63.
19 Sciretta, n.p. It's worth noting that the extensive use of the Stagecraft system was first revealed at a November 2019 panel called "Women of Lucasfilm." Deborah Chow, who directed the third episode of *The Mandalorian* ("The Sin"), discussed using the system for her upcoming Disney+ series about Obi-Wan Kenobi's life after the fall of the Jedi. See also Epstein 2019 and Baver 2019b.
20 Marilyn Butler (2012) highlights the extent of Shelley's engagement with contemporary debates about "vitalism" in "*Frankenstein* and Radical Science," originally published in 1993 in the *Times Literary Supplement*.
21 Čapek, 21.
22 Daniels, 11–12.
23 Chapter 17 of the novelization of *Solo* by Mur Lafferty includes a poignant scene between Lando and the last vestiges of L3's individual consciousness that depicts the pain that L3 feels as she loses her individuality and merges fully with the *Falcon*'s software.
24 Bouzereau, 16.
25 Bouzereau, 9.
26 Bouzereau, 43.
27 The fifth episode of *The Mandalorian*, "The Gunslinger" (directed by Dave Filoni), pays ironic homage to this scene. Set on Tatooine after the death of Jabba the Hutt and the consequent loss of bounty hunting as a local industry, the episode shows us the cantina's business failing, nearly empty, with its human bartender replaced by a droid.
28 Daniels, 84, 87.
29 Daniels, 263.
30 Daniels, 13.
31 Luceno, 93.
32 Wu, 117.
33 Kaczynski, n.p.
34 Haraway, 72. Haraway's invocation of "Star Wars" here refers not to the films but rather to the derisive nickname given to Ronald Reagan's proposed Strategic Defense Initiative in the 1980s by Senator Ted Kennedy.

SDI, as far as Kennedy and many others were concerned, was space fantasy. In 2019, the Microsoft Corporation was awarded a ten-year contract to overhaul the US military's cloud computing systems. The name of the project was the Joint Enterprise Defense Infrastructure, JEDI, for short—no doubt a coincidence. See Conger et al.
35 Bouzereau, 34.
36 The stage directions in the first trilogy's scripts use the terms "light saber" and "laser sword" interchangeably, but characters never use the term "laser sword." The older, disaffected Luke finally uses the term "laser sword" disparagingly in *The Last Jedi* as he tries to convince Rey that he is not the answer to the Resistance's problems.
37 Bouzereau, 34, 292.
38 Bouzereau, 59.
39 Bouzereau, 292.
40 Leane, n.p.
41 Luceno et al., 14.
42 Johnston, 296.
43 Soule et al., 15.
44 Asimov, 435.
45 Mander, 350.

Chapter 7

1 Zahn 2017, 95.
2 Ueda 1994, 171.
3 Lee, 18–19.
4 Ueda 1994, 139.
5 American Association of Colleges and Teacher Education, 264.
6 Ravitch and Vinovski, 121.
7 Appiah 2006b, xiii; Hollinger, 85.
8 Hamill, 2016, 1:00.
9 Hamill, 2016, 1:04.
10 LaVorgna, n.p.
11 Scherstuhl, n.p.
12 Johnston, 328–9.
13 Lussier, n.p.
14 D'Acy and Tyce's relationship is described in *Star Wars: The Rise of Skywalker: The Visual Dictionary* (Hidalgo, 78).
15 Bouzereau, 216.
16 Appiah 2006b, xix.
17 Appiah 2006b, 137–53.

18 Sunstein, 65–6.
19 Read Chapter XVIII of Hobbes's *Leviathan* on the rights of the sovereign, and you'll find a vision of authority that could well have been written by Emperor Palpatine. The Empire's vision of authority seems "nuts" because the *Star Wars* films have used a variety of narrative devices to persuade us that it is. Hobbes's *Leviathan* is, after all, a classic of Western political theory, and its views have never been dismissed out of hand.
20 Brooker 2009, 69.
21 Becker et al., 2:24:41; qtd.in Brooker, 83.
22 Appiah 2006a, 52.
23 Appiah 2006b, 111.
24 Appiah 2006b, 113.
25 Ratcliffe, 9.
26 Rogers 2015, 129.
27 Becker et al., 2:23:30.
28 Vaz 1997, 15.
29 Vaz 1997, 17.
30 Vaz 1997, 30.
31 Associated Press, n.p.
32 Brooker 2002 provides evidence that not *all* rabid *Star Wars* films hated Lucas's revisions. For example, one fan told him: "Even as a little girl I noticed the slightly gray boxes around the TIE fighters and X-Wings. I loved the scene, don't get me wrong, but the obvious signs of special effects nagged at me like a mosquito by my ear. When I first viewed ANH of the SE, I was amazed. I kept walking up to the screen and attempting to find the touch-up lines, but there were none ... The same proved true for Hoth, it was refreshing not to see any lines on ships or have to see through the dashboard."
33 Brooker 2002, 85–6.
34 See the fourth chapter of Brooker 2002.
35 See, for example, Priest 2019, who argues that the sequel trilogy lacks Lucas's "daring": "Disney's cautiousness has led to good-but-never-great Star Wars movies. And that's why I will always take the bad dialogue and incredible moments of the prequels over a Star Wars trilogy that has neither."
36 Yuhas, n.p.
37 Yuhas, n.p.
38 Yuhas, n.p.
39 BBC Newsnight, n.p.
40 Raftery, n.p.
41 Holland 2018, n.p.

42 Miller, 2018a, n.p. Miller's original article generated so much online hate mail that he wrote a follow-up in which he concluded, "The response to this article demonstrated that there's a core section of the *Star Wars* fandom that is rotten. And it's amplified by pervasive social media harassment and vocal far-right abusers. Anyway, thanks for proving my point, trolls."
43 Loughery, n.p.
44 Yahoo Entertainment, n.p.
45 See Appiah 2006b, 152–3.
46 Holland 2018, n.p.

Chapter 8

1   Bouzereau, 37.
2   Bouzereau, 143, 189.
3   Fry, 28, 26.
4   Shay 1999, 16, 23.
5   Grossman, 82.
6   Fry, 72.
7   Fry, 146.
8   Fry, 146.
9   Szostak, 19.
10 Szostak, 28.
11 Itzkoff, n.p.
12 Fry, 92.
13 Fry, 195.
14 Fry, 303.
15 Fry, 305.
16 For example, two of the central Jedi characters in Claudia Gray's novel *Into the Dark* (2021) find themselves questioning the putative infallibility of the Jedi order. Orla Jareni has chosen to become a Wayseeker, "a Jedi who would operate independently of dictates of the Jedi Council" (18), charting her own, independent knowledge of the Force because she has come to believe that "*the Jedi Order and I no longer … see eye to eye*" (39, italics and ellipsis in original). Even more troubled is Jedi Master Cohmac Vitus, still traumatized by the death years earlier of his own master during a mission, a death for which Cohmac still feels responsible. Revisiting the general vicinity of that mission brings to light emotions that the Order has taught him to set aside and bury. "It's ridiculous," he comes to believe. "They command that master and apprentice spend years together, working as a partnership, as close as any family could possibly be, and then they expect

us not to become attached. I never thought about it before—I never had to—but now I can't escape how unfair it is. Worse than unfair. It's wrong" (260).
17. Fry, 195.
18. Hibberd 2019b, 37.

Chapter 9

1. Duncan 2010.
2. Duncan 209.
3. Duncan 210.
4. Duncan 210, 217.
5. Duncan 217.
6. Hiatt 2017, n.p.
7. Hiatt 2019, n.p.
8. "The Sound of a Galaxy" (starwars.com).
9. Moyers 1999, n.p.
10. Kleinman, n.p.
11. Bouzereau, 296, 306.
12. Bouzereau, 311.
13. In the climactic fight of *The Rise of Skywalker*, Palpatine also uses the rhetoric of "sacrifice," but it is a dark, perverted version of what the heroes do. Palpatine wants to be ritually sacrificed—his body destroyed—so that his spirit can gain in power. His "sacrifice" is an act of selfishness, in contrast to the altruism of the sacrifices that Obi-Wan, Han, Luke, Leia, Rey, her parents, and Ben all make.
14. Bouzereau, 35.
15. Bouzereau, 178. Ellipses in original. On actor-network theory, see Latour.
16. See, for example, Dockterman; Goldberg; and Rougeau.
17. See *The Clone Wars*, season five, episode 20, "The Wrong Jedi."

Bibliography

Aftab, Kaleem (2008). "Eric Rohmer: Father of the New Wave," *The Independent* (March 21). https://www.independent.co.uk/arts-entertainment/films/features/eric-rohmer-father-of-the-new-wave-798616.html

Althusser, Louis (1969). *For Marx*. Trans. Ben Brewster. New York: Random House.

Althusser, Louis (1971). *Lenin and Philosophy and Other Essays*. Trans. Ben Brewster. New York: Monthly Review Press.

American Association of Colleges and Teacher Education (1973). "No One Model American: A Statement on Multicultural Education," *Journal of Teacher Education* 24.4, 264–5.

Anonymous (1839). "The Course of Civilization." *US Magazine and Democratic Review* 6, 208–11.

Anonymous (1841). "Catholicism." *Boston Quarterly Review* 4, 320–39.

Appiah, Kwame Anthony (2005). *The Ethics of Identity*. Princeton, NJ: Princeton University Press.

Appiah, Kwame Anthony (2006a). "The Case for Contamination." *New York Times Magazine* (January 1), 30–7, 52.

Appiah, Kwame Anthony (2006b). *Cosmopolitanism: Ethics in a World of Strangers*. New York: Norton.

Arieli, Yehoshua (1964). *Individualism and Nationalism in American Ideology*. Cambridge, MA: Harvard University Press.

Asimov, Isaac (1990). *Robot Visions*. New York: Penguin Books.

Associated Press, (2004). "Lucas Talks as 'Star Wars' Trilogy Returns." https://www.today.com/popculture/lucas-talks-star-wars-trilogy-returns-wbna6011380

Bailey, Brian J. (1998). *The Luddite Rebellion*. New York: New York University Press.

Barnes, Jonathan (2000). *Aristotle: A Very Short Introduction*. Oxford: Oxford University Press.

Baruh, Bradford (dir.) (2020a). *Disney Gallery: Star Wars: The Mandalorian*. Lucasfilm.
Baruh, Bradford (dir.) (2020b). *Disney Gallery: Star Wars: The Mandalorian: The Making of Season 2*. Lucasfilm.
Baver, Kristin (2019a). "SWCC 2019: 9 Things We Learned from *The Mandalorian* Panel." Starwars.com (April 14). https://www.starwars.com/news/swcc-2019-9-things-we-learned-from-the-mandalorian-panel
Baver, Kristin (2019b). "Meet the Women Working behind the Scenes of Star Wars." Starwars.com (December 19). https://www.starwars.com/news/meet-the-women-working-behind-the-scenes-of-star-wars
BBC Newsnight (1999). "George Lucas on Toxic Fandom and *The Phantom Menace*" (Interview with Kirsty Wark). https://youtu.be/9fN2gypFa-I
Bean, Travis (2020). "Post-Cinema: The Revolutionary Storytelling of 'Star Wars: The Rise of Skywalker.'" *Forbes* (March 21).
Becker, Edith, and Kevin Burns, dir. (2004). *Empire of Dreams: The Story of the "Star Wars" Trilogy*. Written by Ed Singer. Prometheus Entertainment in Association with Fox Television Studios and Lucasfilm.
Bellah, Robert N., Richard Madsen, William M. Sullivan, Ann Swindler, and Steven M. Tipton (1991). *The Good Society*. New York: Knopf.
Bellah, Robert N., Richard Madsen, William M. Sullivan, Ann Swindler, and Steven M. Tipton (1996). *Habits of the Heart: Individualism and Commitment in American Life* (1985). Updated ed. Berkeley and Los Angeles: University of California Press.
Block, Alex Ben (2012). "5 Questions with George Lucas: Controversial 'Star Wars' Changes, SOPA and 'Indiana Jones 5.'" *Hollywood Reporter* (February 9). https://www.hollywoodreporter.com/heat-vision/george-lucas-star-wars-interview-288523
Blondell, Ruby (ed. and trans.) (2002). *Sophocles: King Oidipous*. Newburyport, MA: Focus Publishing.
Borojević, Jelena (2017). "An Intimate Adaptation," in Gilad Padva and Nurit Buchweitz (eds.), *Intimate Relationships in Cinema, Literature and Visual Culture*. New York: Palgrave Macmillan. 65–74.
Bouzereau, Laurent (1997). *Star Wars: The Annotated Screenplays*. New York: Del Ray.
Bradatan, Costica (2017). "Philosophy Needs a New Definition." *Los Angeles Review of Books* (December 17).
Bradshaw, Peter (2017). "40 Years of *Star Wars*—Why the Blockbuster Saga Is the Greatest Soap Opera in the Galaxy." *The Guardian* (May 12).
Breznican, Anthony (2015). "How Luke Skywalker Lured J.J. Abrams into Directing *Star Wars: The Force Awakens*." *Entertainment Weekly*. Web.

https://ew.com/article/2015/08/12/star-wars-luke-skywalker-hooked-jj-abrams/

Brooker, Will (2002). *Using the Force: Community, Creativity, and Star Wars Fans*. New York: Continuum.

Brooker, Will (2009). *Star Wars*. London: Palgrave Macmillan.

Brooks, Dan (2018). "How Lucasfilm Reimagined Classic Moments in *Star Wars Galaxy of Adventures*." starwars.com (November 30). https://www.starwars.com/news/lucasfilm-reimagined-classic-moments-star-wars-galaxy-of-adventures-exclusive

Brooks, Peter (1995). *The Melodramatic Imagination: Balzac, Henry James, and the Mode of Excess*. Rev. ed. New Haven, CT: Yale University Press.

Bryce, James (1910). *The American Commonwealth*. Rev. ed. New York: Macmillan.

Burr, Ty (2005). "Complete transcript of Ty Burr's Interview with the Legendary Filmmaker." *Boston.com* (October 25). http://archive.boston.com/ae/movies/lucas_interview/

Butler, Marilyn (2012). "Frankenstein and Radical Science." Rpt. in Mary Shelley, *Frankenstein: Norton Critical Edition*. Ed. J. Paul Hunter. 2nd ed. New York: Norton, 404–16. Originally published in the *Times Literary Supplement*, April 9, 1993.

Cameron, James (2018). *James Cameron's Story of Science Fiction*. San Rafael CA: Insight Editions.

Campbell, Joseph. (1972). *The Hero with a Thousand Faces*. Rpt. Princeton, NJ: Princeton University Press.

Campbell, Joseph. (1990). *The Hero's Journey: Joseph Campbell on His Life and Work*. Ed. Phil Cousineau. New York: HarperCollins.

Čapek, Karel (1961). *R.U.R. and the Insect Play*. Trans. Claudia Novack. New York: Penguin Classics.

Caro, Mark (2005). "'*Star Wars*' Inadvertently Hits Too Close to U.S.'s Role." *Chicago Tribune*. May 18. Web.

Carson, Rae (2020). *The Rise of Skywalker*. New York: Del Rey. [Based on characters created by George Lucas; screenplay by Chris Terrio & J. J. Abrams; based on a story by Derek Connolly & Colin Trevorrow and Chris Terrio & J. J. Abrams.]

Carter, Jimmy (2006). "Address to the Nation on Energy Policy," Washington, DC, July 15, 1979, in Ted Widmer (ed.), *American Speeches: Political Oratory from Abraham Lincoln to Bill Clinton*. New York: Library of America. 705–14.

Chieffo, Mary (2019). Twitter thread (December 25). https://twitter.com/marythechief/status/1209734911013244929

Cieply, Michael (2012). "Disney Is Buying Lucasfilm." *New York Times* (October 30): B1.
Clifford, James (1991). "The Transit Lounge of Culture," *Times Literary Supplement* (May 3), 7–8.
Conger, Kate, David E. Sanger, and Scott Shane (2019). "Microsoft Wins Pentagon's $10 Billion JEDI Contract, Thwarting Amazon," *New York Times* (October 26).
Daniels, Anthony (2019). *I Am C-3PO: The Inside Story*. New York: DK Publishing.
Davis, David Brion (1999). *The Problem of Slavery in the Age of Revolution, 1770–1823*. 2nd ed. Oxford: Oxford University Press.
Dargis, Manohla (2017). "Review: 'Star Wars: The Last Jedi' Embraces the Magic and Mystery." *The New York Times* (December 12).
Dawson, Delilah S. (2019). Twitter feed (December 21). https://twitter.com/DelilahSDawson/status/1208216244433932288
Dewey, John (1926). "The Historic Background of Corporate Legal Personality," *Yale Law Journal* 35, 655–73.
Dinwiddy, J. R. (1986). *From Luddism to the First Reform Bill: Reform in England 1810–1832*. Oxford: Oxford University Press.
Duncan, Paul (2020). *The Star Wars Archives: Episodes I–III, 1999–2005*. Köln, Germany: TASCHEN Books.
Dyer, James, and Nick de Semlyen (2021). "101 Mando Easter Eggs." *Empire* (February). 54–9.
Ellis, John (1975). *The Social History of the Machine Gun*. New York: Pantheon.
Epstein, Adam (2019). "The Filmmaking Technology behind 'The Mandalorian' Is Straight Out of the Star Wars Universe." *Quartz* (November 23). https://qz.com/1754288/disney-is-trying-to-revolutionize-filmmaking-with-the-mandalorian/
Fagles, Robert "Greece and the Theater," in *Sophocles: The Three Theban Plays* New York: Penguin. 13–30.
Fish, Stanley (1980). *Is There a Text in This Class? The Authority of Interpretive Communities*. Cambridge, MA: Harvard University Press.
Fordham, Joe (2016). "The Spirit of '77," *Cinefex* 145. 43–77.
Fry, Jason (2018). *The Last Jedi: Expanded Edition*. New York: Random House [Based on characters created by George Lucas; based on a story by Rian Johnson.]
Gans, Herbert J. (1988). *Middle American Individualism: The Future of Liberal Democracy*. New York: Free Press.
Goldberg, Matt (2019). "'The Rise of Skywalker' Ending Is Emblematic of the Film's Biggest Problem." *Collider* (December 27). https://collider.com/rise-of-skywalker-review/
Graff, Gerald (1990). "Teach the Conflicts," *South Atlantic Quarterly* 89, 51 –68.

Gray Claudia (2015). *Journey to Star Wars: The Force Awakens: The Lost Stars*. New York: Del Rey.

Gray, Claudia (2021). *Star Wars: The High Republic: Into the Dark*. New York: Lucsasfilm Press.

Greenblatt, Stephen (1995). "Culture," in Frank Lentricchia and Thomas McLaughlin (eds.), *Critical Terms for Literary Study*. 2nd ed. Chicago: University of Chicago Press. 225–32.

Greenfield, Kent (2018). *Corporations Are People Too: (And They Should Act Like It)*. New Haven: Yale University Press.

Grossman, Lev (2019). "Tour de Force." *Vanity Fair* (Summer): 82–103. Reprinted online as "Star Wars: The Rise of Skywalker, The Ultimate Preview" (https://www.vanityfair.com/hollywood/2019/05/star-wars-cover-story).

Guynes, Sean, and Dan Hassler-Forest (2018). *Star Wars and the History of Transmedia Storytelling*. Amsterdam: Amsterdam University Press.

Hall, Stuart (1985). "Signification, Representation, Ideology: Althusser and the Post-Structuralist Debates," *Critical Studies in Mass Communication* 2, 91–114.

Hamill, Mark (2016). "Mark Hamill | Full Q&A | Oxford Union." Oxford Union https://youtu.be/_5Iv_sazoGg

Handy, Bruce (2015a). "An Empire Reboots," *Vanity Fair* (June), 92–103, 145–7.

Handy, Bruce (2015b). "J.J. Abrams on the Secret Movie References He Snuck into *Star Wars: The Force Awakens*." vanityfair.com (May 6). https://www.vanityfair.com/hollywood/2015/05/jj-abrams-star-wars-extended-interview

Haraway, Donna L. (1985). "A Manifesto for Cyborgs: Science, Technology, and Socialist Feminism in the 1980s," *Socialist Review* 80, 65–108.

Hayward, Susan (2018). *Cinema Studies: The Key Concepts*. 5th ed. New York: Routledge.

Heath, Malcolm (ed. and trans.) (1996). *Poetics* by Aristotle. New York: Penguin Books.

Henderson, Mary (1997). *Star Wars: The Magic of Myth*. New York: Bantam Books.

Herr, Michael (1991). *Dispatches*. Rpt. New York: Vintage International.

Hiatt, Brian (2017). "Daisy Ridley: 'The Last Jedi' Interview" *Rolling Stone* (13 December). https://www.rollingstone.com/movies/movie-features/daisy-ridley-the-last-jedi-interview-123474/

Hiatt, Brian (2019). "The Writer and Director on the Challenge of Ending the Saga, Fan Criticism, and Respecting George Lucas' Vision." *Rolling Stone* (November 21). https://www.rollingstone.com/movies/movie-features/star-wars-jj-abrams-secrets-of-skywalker-912362/

Hibberd, James (2019a). "Disney+ Version of *A New Hope* Changes Iconic *Star Wars* Scene." *Entertainment Weekly* (November 12). https://ew.com/movies/2019/11/12/disney-new-hope-han-greedo-macklunkey/

Hibberd, James (2019b). "The War to End All Wars." *Entertainment Weekly* (December): 32–9.

Hidalgo, Pablo (2019). *Star Wars: The Rise of Skywalker: The Visual Dictionary*. New York: DK Publishing.

Higgins, Scott (2016). *Matinee Melodrama: Playing with Formula in the Sound Serial*. New Brunswick, NJ: Rutgers University Press.

Hobbes, Thomas (1996). *Leviathan*. Ed. Richard Tuck. Rev. ed. Cambridge: Cambridge University Press.

Holland, Luke (2018). "Why Are (Some) Star Wars Fans So Toxic?" *The Guardian* (June 7). Web. https://www.theguardian.com/film/2018/jun/07/kelly-marie-tran-rose-why-are-some-star-wars-fans-so-toxic

Hollinger, David A. (2000). *Postethnic America: Beyond Multiculturalism*. Tenth Anniversary ed. New York: Basic Books.

Horton, Alex (2019). "The Han and Greedo Shooting Scene Changed Again (and Probably Not the Way You Wanted)." *Washington Post* (November 13). https://www.washingtonpost.com/arts-entertainment/2019/11/13/han-shot-greedo-disney-plus-maclunkey/

Houser Jody et al. (2019). *Star Wars: TIE Fighter*. New York: Marvel Comics.

Iger, Robert (2019). *The Ride of a Lifetime: Lessons Learned from 15 Years as CEO of the Walt Disney Company*. New York: Random House.

Isaacson, Walter (2011). *Steve Jobs*. New York: Simon & Schuster.

Itzkoff, Dave (2017). "The Fate of 'The Last Jedi' Is in His Hands." *New York Times* (September 15).

Jameson, Fredric (1988) "On Habits of the Heart," in Charles H. Reynolds and Ralph V. Norman (eds.), *Community in America: The Challenge of "Habits of the Heart*. Berkeley and Los Angeles: University of California Press. 97–112.

Jauss, Hans Robert (1982). "Literary History as a Challenge to Literary Theory," in Timothy Bahti (trans.), *Towards an Aesthetic of Reception*. Minneapolis: University of Minnesota Press. 3–45.

Jenkins, Garry (1999). *Empire Building: The Remarkable Real Life Story of Star Wars*. Rev. ed. New York: Citadel Press.

Johnston, E. K. (2016). *Star Wars: Ahsoka*. Los Angeles and New York: Lucasfilm Press.

Kaczynski, Ted (1997). "Unabomber's Manifesto." Web. https://www.washingtonpost.com/wp-srv/national/longterm/unabomber/manifesto.text.htm.

Kenny, Anthony (ed. and trans.) (2013). *Poetics* by Aristotle. Oxford: Oxford

Kleinman, Jake (2019). "'Force Awakens' Music Teased a Huge Palpatine Twist in 'Rise of Skywalker.'" *Inverse* (December 26). https://www.inverse.com/article/61993-rise-of-skywalker-easter-eggs-palpatine-is-rey-grandfather-music-themes-predicted-it

Kline, Sally (ed.) (1999). *George Lucas: Interviews.* Jackson, MI: University Press of Mississippi.
Lafferty, Mur (2018). *Solo: A Star Wars Story: Expanded Edition.* New York: Del Rey.
Latour, Bruno (2005). *Reassembling the Social: An Introduction to Actor-Network-Theory.* Oxford: Oxford University Press.
LaVorgna, Bria (2018). "Doctor Aphra Creator Kieron Gillen, Co-Writer Si Spurrier Discuss What's Next for the Fan Favorite Rogue." star wars.com (April 26). https://www.starwars.com/news/doctor-aphra-creator-kieron-gillen-co-writer-si-spurrier-discuss-whats-next-for-the-fan-favorite-rogue.
Leane, Rob. "*Star Wars*: A History of Lightsaber Design." *Den of Geek!* Web. https://www.denofgeek.com/movies/lightsabers/36763/star-wars-a-history-of-lightsaber-design
Lee, Erika (2006). "A Nation of Immigrants and a Gatekeeping Nation: American Immigration Law and Policy," in Ueda 2006, 5–35.
Lepitak, Stephen (2015). "Star Wars Marketing Man Charles Lippincott on the Real Force behind the Franchise's Success." *The Drum* (December 1). Web. https://www.thedrum.com/news/2015/12/01/star-wars-marketing-man-charles-lippincott-real-force-behind-franchises-success
Liptak, Andrew (2018). "Solo Demonstrates That the *Star Wars* Expanded Universe Hasn't Been Forgotten." *The Verge* (May 31). https://www.theverge.com/2018/5/31/17408544/solo-star-wars-story-expanded-universe-ac-crispin-novels
Lomax, Tara (2018). "'Thank the Maker!' George Lucas, Lucasfilm, and the Legends of Transtextual Authorship across the Star Wars Franchise." In Guynes and Hassler-Forest. 35–48.
Loughrey, Clarisse (2019). "Why There's Still Hope for the Star Wars Fandom Yet." *The Independent* (April 23). https://www.independent.co.uk/arts-entertainment/films/features/star-wars-celebration-chicago-the-rise-of-skywalker-kelly-marie-tran-a8878151.html
[Lucasfilm] (2018). "The Mandalorian First Image, Directors Revealed." Starwars.com (October 4). https://www.starwars.com/news/the-mandalorian-revealed.
Luceno, James (2017). *Catalyst: A Rogue One Novel.* New York: Del Rey.
Luceno, James, and David West Reynolds, Ryder Windham, Jason Fry, and Pablo Hidalgo (2018). *Star Wars: The Complete Visual Dictionary (New Edition).* New York: DK Publishing.
Lukes, Stephen (1973). *Individualism.* Oxford: Basil Blackwell.
Lussier, Germain (2019). "Star Wars Has Been Hiding a Gay Couple in Plain Sight." *Gizmodo* (September 30). https://io9.gizmodo.com/star-wars-has-been-hiding-a-gay-couple-in-plain-sight-1838634202

Lusted, David (2003). *The Western*. New York Routledge.
Machen, Arthur W., Jr. (1911). "Corporate Personality." *Harvard Law Review* 24.4, 253–67.
Maitland, F. W. (2003). *State, Trust and Corporation*. Ed. David Runciman and Magnus Ryan. Cambridge: Cambridge University Press.
Mander, Jerry (1978). *Four Arguments for the Elimination of Television*. New York: William Morrow.
Masters, Kim (2019). "'Star Wars' Uncertainty Extends to Kathleen Kennedy's Disney Future." *The Hollywood Reporter* (November 20). https://www.hollywoodreporter.com/heat-vision/star-wars-uncertainty-extends-kathleen-kennedys-disney-future-1256357
Milton, John (1886). *Paradise Lost* (1674). Ed. Robert Vaughan. Chicago and New York: Belford, Clarke & Co.
Moyers, Bill (1999). "The Mythology of 'Star Wars' with George Lucas." Interview transcript. Web. https://billmoyers.com/content/mythology-of-star-wars-george-lucas/
Mulhall, Stephen (2016). *On Film*. 3rd ed. New York: Routledge.
Murdock, Maureen (1990). *The Heroine's Journey: Woman's Quest for Wholeness*. Boston, MA: Shambhala Press.
Neale, Steve (2000). *Genre and Hollywood*. London: Routledge.
Nussbaum, Martha (1990). *Love's Knowledge: Essays on Philosophy and Literature*. New York: Oxford University Press.
Nussbaum, Martha (1995). *Poetic Justice: The Literary Imagination and Public Life*. Boston: Beacon Press.
Nussbaum, Martha (2002). "Patriotism and Cosmopolitanism," in Nussbaum, *For Love of Country*, Joshua Cohen (ed.). Boston, MA: Beacon Press. 3–21.
Patches, Matt (2015). "*Star Wars* Mastermind George Lucas: Movies Don't Have to Make Sense." esquire.com (April 17). https://www.esquire.com/entertainment/movies/news/a34459/george-lucas-star-wars-saga-experimental-roots/
Patell, Cyrus R. K. (2001). *Negative Liberties: Morrison, Pynchon, and the Problem of Liberal Ideology*. Duke University Press.
Patell, Cyrus R. K. (2015). *Cosmopolitanism and the Literary Imagination*. New York: Palgrave Macmillan.
Patterson, Debs (dir.) (2020). *The Skywalker Legacy*. Lucasfilm.
Plantinga, Carl (2009). *Moving Viewers: American Film and the Spectator's Experience*. Berkeley: University of California Press.
Polo, Susan (2015). "Stephen Colbert and George Lucas Talk *Star Wars*, Wooden Dialogue and *Howard the Duck*." polygon.com (April 18). https://www.polygon.com/2015/4/18/8448685/stephen-colbert-george-lucas-tribeca-talk.

Priest, David (2019). "The New Star Wars Trilogy Is Worse than the Prequels." *CNet* (October 11). https://www.cnet.com/news/the-new-star-wars-trilogy-is-worse-than-the-prequels/.

Raftery, Brian (2017). "Jar Jar Binks Breaks Out." wired.com (July 15). https://www.wired.com/2017/07/ahmed-best-jar-jar-binks-new-podcast/

Ratcliffe, Amy (2018). *Star Wars: Women of the Galaxy*. New York: Chronicle Books.

Ravitch, Diane, and Maris Vinovski (eds.) (1995). *Learning from the Past: What History Teaches Us about School Reform*. Baltimore, MD: The Johns Hopkins University Press.

Reaves, Michael, and Steve Perry (2007). *Death Star*. New York: Random House.

Rebel Force Radio, "Dave Filoni: Growing Up with *Star Wars*" (https://youtu.be/xB0tMecj51s).

Reiman, Tom (2019). "'The Mandalorian': Werner Herzog Calls the Series 'Cinema Back at Its Best.'" *Collider* (November 14). https://collider.com/the-mandalorian-werner-herzog-cinema/

Rinzler, J. W. (2007). *The Making of Star Wars*. New York: Del Rey.

Rinzler, J. W. (2013). *The Making of Star Wars: Return of the Jedi*. New York: Del Rey.

Rogers, Adam (2015). "The Force Will Be with Us. Always." *Wired* (December), 120–9.

Rogers, Adam (2019). "The *Wired* Guide to *Star Wars*." Web. https://www.wired.com/story/guide-star-wars/

Rose, Charlie (2015). "Interview with George Lucas." https://charlierose.com/videos/23471

Rougeau, Michael (2019). "Star Wars: Episode IX Swerves Hard to Retcon the Last Jedi's Story." *Gamespot* (December 19). https://www.gamespot.com/reviews/star-wars-episode-9-the-rise-of-skywalker-review-a/1900-6417383/

Sager, Mark (2015–2016). "The Golden Child." *Esquire* (December–January): 134–41.

Sandel, Michael J. (1998). *Liberalism and the Limits of Justice*. 2nd ed. Cambridge: Cambridge University Press.

Scharf, Zack (2020). "Ian McDiarmid Says Original 'Rise of Skywalker' Script Confirmed Palpatine Clone, but Reveal Got Cut." *Indiewire* (March 3). https://www.indiewire.com/2020/03/ian-mcdiarmid-original-rise-of-skywalker-script-palpatine-clone-1202215067/

Scherstuhl, Alan (2019). "The Best Star Wars Character of This Millennium Is a Lesbian Archaeologist." *Slate* (April 12). https://slate.com/culture/2019/04/star-wars-comics-doctor-aphra-best-star-wars-character.html.

Sciretta, Peter (2019). "How Lucasfilm's New 'Stagecraft' Tech Brought 'The Mandalorian' to Life and May Change the Future of TV." *Slashfilm* (November 20). https://www.slashfilm.com/the-mandalorian-stagecraft/

Shay, Don (1980). "Of Bog Planets, Ice Planets, and Cities in the Sky." *Cinefex* 2, 4–23.

Shay, Don (1999). "Return of the Jedi." *Cinefex* 78. 15–32.

Shenk, Jon (dir.) (2001). *The Beginning: Making Episode I.* Lucasfilm.

Shepherd, Jack (2017). "*Star Wars: The Last Jedi* Director Rian Johnson Speaks about George Lucas's Reaction to Movie." *The Independent* (December 13). https://www.independent.co.uk/arts-entertainment/films/news/star-wars-the-last-jedi-rian-johnson-george-lucas-reaction-review-a8108126.html

Smith, Thomas G. (1986). *Industrial Light and Magic: The Art of Special Effects.* New York: Ballantine Books.

Soule, Charles, Giuseppe Camuncoli, Cam Smith, and David Curiel (2017). *Darth Vader* #1 (August). New York: Marvel Worldwide.

"Sound of a Galaxy, The" (2016). starwars.com. https://www.starwars.com/video/the-sound-of-a-galaxy-inside-the-star-wars-the-force-awakens-soundtrack

Stuever, Hank (2015). "George Lucas: To Feel the True Force of 'Star Wars,' He Had to Learn to Let It Go." *Washington Post* (December 5). https://www.washingtonpost.com/lifestyle/style/george-lucas-to-feel-the-true-force-of-star-wars-he-had-to-learn-to-let-it-go/2015/11/27/d752067a-8b1f-11e5-be8b-1ae2e4f50f76_story.html?utm_term=.825585d3bc94

Sunstein, Cass R. (2016). *The World According to Star Wars.* New York: HarperCollins.

Szostak, Phil (2017). *The Art of Star Wars: The Last Jedi.* New York: Abrams.

Tocqueville, Alexis de (1961). *Democracy in America.* 2 vols. Trans. Henry Reeve. New York: Schocken.

Tocqueville, Alexis de (1969). *Democracy in America.* Ed. J. P. Mayer. Translated by George Lawrence. Garden City, NY: Doubleday-Anchor.

Turner, Frederick Jackson (1947). *The Frontier in American History.* New York: Henry Holt.

Turnock, Julie A. (2015). *Plastic Reality: Special Effects, Technology, and the Emergence of 1970s Blockbuster Aesthetics.* New York: Columbia University Press.

Ueda, Reed (1994). *Postwar Immigrant America: A Social History.* New York: Bedford.

Ueda, Reed (ed.) (2006). *A Companion to American Immigration.* Malden, MA: Blackwell.

Vaz, Mark Cotta (1997). "Star Wars Trilogy: Every Old Is New Again," *Cinefex* 69, 15–24, 29–30.

Vaz, Mark Cotta, and Rose Duignan (1996). *Industrial Light & Magic: Into the Digital Realm.* New York: Ballantine Books.

Walt Disney Company (2012). "Disney to Acquire Lucasfilm." YouTube (October 30). https://youtu.be/QIkqX5fG_tA

Walzer, Michael (2003). "The United States in the World—Just Wars and Just Societies: An Interview with Michael Walzer." *Imprints*. 7.1. Web.

Wartenberg, Thomas E. (2007). *Thinking on Screen: Film as Philosophy*. New York: Routledge.

Wookieepedia (n.d.). "Holocron." https://starwars.fandom.com/wiki/Holocron/Legends

Wu, Cheng-Tsu (ed.) (1972). *"Chink!": A Documentary History of Anti-Chinese Prejudice in America*. New York: World Publishing.

X3 Productions (2012). *Star Wars: Identities Exhibition Catalog*. Lucasfilm.

Yahoo Entertainment (2019). "Kelly Marie Tran Talks about Her Emotional Moment at Star Wars Celebration 2019" (April 12). https://youtu.be/3OUl2PZToek

Young, Bryan (2012). "The Cinema Behind *Star Wars*: *The Good, the Bad, and the Ugly*." starwars.com (December 17). https://www.starwars.com/news/the-cinema-behind-star-wars-the-good-the-bad-and-the-ugly

Young, Bryan (2015). "The Cinema Behind *Star Wars*: *2001: A Space Odyssey*." starwars.com (July 20). https://www.starwars.com/news/the-cinema-behind-star-wars-2001-a-space-odyssey

Yuhas, Alan (2020). "Why 'Star Wars' Keeps Bombing in China." *New York Times* (January 14).

Zahn, Timothy (2017). *Star Wars: Thrawn*. New York: Random House.

Zakarin, Jordan (2018). "Inside Lucasfilm's Top Secret *Star Wars* Database (Fandom Files #13)." SyFy.com (January 15). https://www.syfy.com/syfywire/inside-lucasfilm%E2%80%99s-top-secret-star-wars-database-fandom-files-13

Index

2001: A Space Odyssey 30, 36, 143, 144, 147

Abrams, J. J. 37, 56–9, 81, 120, 203, 208
   aesthetics of 140–1, 193
   on Daniels 146–7
   depiction of technology 139
   on droids 144, 146–7
   and imperfection 193
   and LGBTQIA+ representation 167
   and Next-Gen Lucasfilm 56, 58–9, 61
   on plot of *Rise of Skywalker* 81, 120, 203
   and post-cinema 38–9
   on Rey's character 208
   as screenwriter for *Force Awakens* 125
   and sequel trilogy arc 181, 203
   on Williams 61–2
Academy Award 51
Ackie, Naomi 127
action figures 13, 57, 64
Ackbar, Admiral (character) 165
Acropolis 72
Aeschylus 92
aesthetics 23, 24, 29, 96
   and special effects 141, 177

African American Studies 25
agency 42, 89–90, 129, 133, 147, 153–4, 160, 186
Agents of S.H.I.E.L.D. 130. *See also* Marvel
Ahsoka. *See* Tano, Ahsoka. *See also Star Wars* novels
Alien (film series) 22, 150. *See also* Ridley Scott
aliens 31, 93, 99, 131, 161, 168. *See also* anthropocentrism, nonhumans
   Chinese as, in US 153
Allen, Woody 21
Althusser, Louis 18–19, 27
Alworth, Andrea 180
Alzmann, Christian 196
American Association of Colleges and Teacher Education 163–4
American Graffiti (film) 31, 44–5, 51, 110, 219 n.8
American Historical Association 118–9
American Studies 25, 119
American Zoetrope 44, 196
Amidala, Padmé (character) 83–4, 123
animatic 64
anthropocentrism 161. *See also* nonhumans

Index

Aphra, Doctor Chelli Lona (character) 147, 168–9
Apocalypse Now (film) 41–2, 44, 196
Appiah, Kwame Anthony 11, 14, 165, 170, 173–4, 189–91
apprentice 80, 84, 89, 214
Arendt, Hannah 137–41
   anagnorisis 76
   Aristotle 18, 20, 24, 37 (*see also* hamartia, hubris, katharsis, reversal and recognition, tragedy)
   methodology 72–3
   Nichomachean Ethics 73
   Poetics 18, 67, 72–5, 76, 77, 80, 88–9
Arnt, Michael 59, 124
artificial intelligence 130, 144–8
Asimov, Isaac 132, 160
Associated Press 177
attachment 83 195, 214. *See also* emotion, love
Auman, Brandon 169
Austin v. Michigan Chamber of Commerce (1990) 64
auteurism 1–2, 6, 8
   Herzog as
   Lucas and 64, 179

Balboa, Rocky (character) 133
Barnes, Jonathan 73
Bean, Travis 38–9
Beckett, Tobias (character) 104
Bellah, Robert 114–16
Best, Ahmed 187–8
betrayal 75–6, 196, 215
BFI Film Classics series (books) 51, 172
Black Power movement 163
Blade Runner (film) 21. *See also* Scott, Ridley

Blau, Patty 177
Bliss, Zorii (character) 127
The Blob 150–1
Boba Fett 64, 107
Boczarski, Daniel 190
The Borg (*Star Trek* characters) 149–50, 152–3
bounty hunters 93, 107, 147
Boyega, John 190
Bradatan, Costica x, 5, 18
Brando, Marlon 196
The Bride of Frankenstein (film) viii, 142–3, 148
Brooker, Will 51, 172, 175, 180, 183–4
Brooks, Peter 95, 97
Buck Rogers (film serial) 33, 112, 185
Bulloch, Jeremy 107
Burroughs, Edgar Rice 46

Calrissian, Lando (character) 43, 145, 187
Cameron, James 55, 98, 114
Campbell, Joseph 36, 61–2, 72, 75
   The Hero with a Thousand Faces 46–7, 87–8, 121
   The Hero's Journey 81
   masculinist bias of 127
   Murdock on 123–4
Cantina, Mos Eisley. *See under Star Wars* places
Čapek, Karel 141–2, 148. *See also R. U. R.*
Carson, Rae 39
Carter, Jimmy 111–12, 118
catharsis. *See* katharsis
censorship: of *Rise of Skywalker* 169
characters. *See also* identity
   empathy and 39, 91
   identifiable for audience 97
Chee, Leeland 54

Chewbacca (character) 14, 31, 51, 54, 92, 98, 108, 121, 132, 162, 183, 187
Chiang, Douglas 196
Chieffo, Mary 23
childhood 42, 46, 61–2, 187–8
children 17, 56, 75, 164, 167, 174–5, 180, 183–4, 187, 202. *See also* younglings
China
    Cultural Revolution 184
    Star Wars in 184–5
Chinese
    US discrimination against 153
chivalric romance 31, 77
Chow, Deborah 56, 226 n.19
Christie, Gwendolyn 126
Churchill, Winston 14
cinematic-aesthetic devices 24–5
cinematic technique. *See also* aesthetics, music; special effects
    cinematography 48
    color 24
    composition 24
    editing 2, 99–101
    flashback 68, 199, 213
    framerate 50
    gesture 24
    jump cut 68
    lighting 24
    match cut 208
    mise-en-scène 6
    montage 24
    mood 24–5 (*see also* emotion)
    performance 24
    plot 38
    props 63, 136
    scroll 32–3
    VistaVision 50
    visualization 141, 211

Citizens United v. Federal Election Commission (2010) 3, 64–5
Civil Rights movement 162
class 25–6, 153–4, 162
Clifford, James 25
cloning 151. *See also under* Palpatine, Emperor Sheev. *See also Attack of the Clones*
Coffee with Kenobi (podcast) 169
cognition 24
Colbert, Stephen 32–3
comedy 42, 72, 74, 104, 187
communism 150–2
communitarian 110, 113–14
community 7, 27–9, 102, 111, 152, 166, 180, 214
Colbert, Stephen 32–3
Cold War 42, 150–2
Columbia University: International House 182, Low Library 67
The Conversation (film) 44
Cooper, James Fenimore 102, 220 n.18
Coppola, Francis Ford 6, 44–5
cosmopolitanism 9–10, 161–90, 170–2, 173–4. *See also* cultural purity, multiculturalism
    Appiah on 14–15, 170, 173–4, 191
    and contamination 173–4
    conversation, importance of for cosmopolitanism 9–10, 14–15, 48, 51, 170–2, 173
    and cultural purity 173–4, 181–3
    difference from pluralism 166
    and knowledge 48
    opposed to moral relativism 166–7
    and multiculturalism 166–7
    and multidisciplinarity 47–8
    and reading 10–11
    and Rey 216
    Star Wars promotion of 9

cosplay. *See under Star Wars fandom*
Cotta, Mark 50, 176
counter-cosmopolitanism 170
   See also cosmopolitanism; fundamentalism
Court, U.S. Supreme 3, 64–5
Cowboys and Indians. *See* Hollywood Western
Cronkite, Walter 112
Cruise, Tom 181
cultural purity 173–4, 181–3
   See also cosmopolitanism; multiculturalism
cultural studies 9, 25–6, 154
culture 10–12, 30, 48, 91, 117, 120, 173–4. *See also* cultural purity
   future, in *Star Trek* 144
   of narcissism in US 111
   popular 25, 109, 118, 149, 152, 160
   and storytelling 139
   US 120, 127, 149, 152–4, 156
   wars 162–6
   Western 129, 134
   women in 124
The Culture of Narcissism (book) 111
cyborg 148–56, 160. *See also* hive mind; robot
   and *Frankenstein* 143
   and hybridity 148–9
   lightsaber as 159–60
   monstrosity of 148–9, 156
   in *A New Hope* 36
   partial identity 155
   Rise of Skywalker 155–6
   in US culture 149–50, 153, 156

Da Vinci, Leonardo 48
D'Acy, Commander (character) 169
Daniels, Anthony 144, 146
Dargis, Manohla 57–8

Darth Malak (character) 205
Darth Nihilus (character) 205
Darth Revan (character) 205–6
Darth Vader. *See* Vader, Darth
Dashit, Cos (character) 41
Davis, David Brion 26–7
Dawson, Delilah S. 8
death. *See also* sacrifice
   and Anakin Skywalker 83–4, 170
   caused by Vader 192
   of Chewbacca in EU 162
   of Death Star soldiers and workers 94, 106
   of Empire 106
   Finn saved from 126
   of Greedo 98
   of Jabba the Hutt 226 n.27
   in Luke Skywalker's vision 85
   of Mace Windu 89
   of Obi-Wan Kenobi 77, 89, 215
   of Paige Tico 197
   of Snoke 217
   threats against Ahmed Best 187
   threats against Matt Miller 188
   in the Western 7
   of Yoda 120
Death Star. *See under Star Wars places*
democracy 72, 153, 169
   Lucas on 41
   Nussbaum on 36–7
Del Rey Books 32
destiny 88–91, 113–14, 186, 210, 213
   and biology 91, 213
   and family 82, 213
   vs. free will 89–90
   Han Solo on 114
   of a Jedi 86
   Lucas on 43, 210
   and Oedipus 88
   Vader on 113

Dionysus, Festival of 72
Disney
   acquisition of Lucasfilm 52–3, 180, 183, 222 n.35
   classic movie adaptations 42
   Expanded Universe 53, 61, 162
   on Lucas 52
   Interactive Studios 93
   Lucas's dispute with 55–6
   revision of *A New Hope* on Disney+ 100–1, 174
Doctor Aphra. *See* Aphra, Doctor Chelli Lona
Dooner, P. W. 153
droids 143–8, 208
   Abrams on droids 144, 146–7
   differentiation from robot 144–6
   as index to moral compass 144, 207–8, 213
   portrayal of C-3PO 146–7
Dune (novel) 46
Dykstra, John 49–51, 172
Dykstraflex 50–1

Eastwood, Clint 107
Edlund, Richard 49
education 25, 163–5, 199
Ellis, John 135
emotion 39, 76. *See also* katharsis
   and film reception 23
   music and 35
   as persuasion technique 25
the Empire 6, 36. *See also* Death Star *under* Star Wars places
   and anthropocentrism 20, 162
   capital of 60
   and counter-cosmopolitanism 192
   and dark side of the Force 117
   Darth Sidious and 85, 196
   destruction of Jedi Order 76, 85
   fall of 106
   and hive mind 151
   ideology of 162, 169, 171–2
   Obi-Wan's description of 157
   and order 107, 117
   personification by Darth Vader 139
   rebellion against 18, 94, 191
   TIE fighters of 31, 51, 106–7, 228 n.32 (*see also* Star Wars comic books)
Empire Building: The Remarkable Real Life Story of Star Wars (book) 44–5
Empire of Dreams: The Story of the Star Wars Trilogy 31–2, 35, 112, 172, 176
Entertainment Weekly (magazine) 58, 203
epic 33, 79, 134, 193
   and tragedy 74–5
E.T. The Extraterrestrial (film) 130
   See also Spielberg, Stephen
Eteocles 71
Euripides 92
exile and return 87–9, 171

Fagles, Robert 6–7, 71–2
fairy tale
   Star Wars as 30, 42, 46
fallibilism 191–203
   Appiah on 170, 191
   and special effects 193
   thematic 194–6, 198–203
family 56, 79, 82, 84, 91, 173, 188, 209–10, 213–4, 216. *See also* fatherhood, motherhood
   Palpatines 81–2
   Skywalker 54, 79–80, 81–2, 208
fatherhood 43, 58, 67–71, 75–7, 79, 87–90, 157, 181–2, 191, 195–6, 214–15

Famuyiwa, Rick 56
fate 71, 84, 88, 89–90. *See also* destiny
  Lucas on 43
Favreau, Jon 7, 37, 56, 64, 107
Fellini, Federico 45
Fett, Boba (character) 64, 107
Filoni, Dave 37, 45, 56–7, 61, 64
Finnegans Wake (novel) 46
First Amendment (U.S. Constitution) 3, 65
Fish, Stanley 27–9, 171
Flash Gordon
  character 45–6
  Flash Gordon Conquers the Universe (film) 33–4
  serials 33–4, 46, 153
Flix (character) 169. *See also* LGBTQIA+
the Force 129
  dark side of 47, 82, 83–4, 85, 87–8, 173, 198, 200
  ghost 86, 200
  Han Solo's view of 113–14
  Lucas on 114
  midi-chlorians and 55
  Obi-Wan Kenobi's view of 118, 126
  and technology 139
  Vader and 129, 139
  vision 82, 83, 118, 203, 211
  and the Whills 55
  Yoda's view of 114
Frankenstein (film) 142–3, 148, 155. *See also Bride of Frankenstein*
Frankenstein (novel) 142–3, 148, 155, 226 n.20
Frankenstein, Victor (character) 148, 155
Frazer, James George 46
free will. *See under* destiny
fundamentalism 170, 173, 189. *See also* cosmopolitanism

future 36, 85, 144, 154
  of cinema 39
  knowledge of, in tragedy 71
  of Lucasfilm 52
  in science fiction 31
  in the sequel trilogy 81–2, 210, 216–7
  of *Star Wars* 52, 167, 183–4
futurism 30

gender 25, 153–4, 186
Gillen, Kieron 168
Gnosticism 117
The Godfather (film) 44
Goldberg, Matt 174
The Golden Bough: A Study in Comparative Religion (book) 46
The Good Society (book) 116–17
Graff, Gerald 25–6
Gray, Claudia 219 n.16
Great Britain 25–6, 112
Greedo (character) 98–102
Greenblatt, Stephen 11–12, 94–5, 171
Greenfield, Kent 65
Grossman, Lev 193
Grimm's Fairy Tales 42, 46

Habits of the Heart: Individualism and Commitment in American Life (book) 114–15, Jameson on 116
Hall, Stuart 27
hamartia 82–6. *See also* Aristotle
Hamill, Mark 77, 86, 97, 131–2, 136, 197, on sexuality 167–8
Hanson, Lisa 184
Haraway, Donna 154–5, 226 n.34
Harrison, Frazer 59
Harry Potter novel series 60
Harvard Law Review 3
Hasbro Black Series (toys) 206

Heath, Malcolm 73–4, 76, 82–3
Hemingway, Ernest 14
Henderson, Mary 47–8, 109
Hera Syndulla (character) 123
Herbert, Frank 46
Herr, Michael 42
Herzog, Werner 1, 7
Hidalgo, Pablo 206
The Hidden Fortress (film) 145
Higgins, Scott 96
hive mind 149–56
Hobbes, Thomas 228 n.19
Holland, Luke 188
Hollinger, David 166
Hollywood Western 26, 98–9, 102–4, 118–21, 213
  and Greedo controvery 99–103
  influence on *Star Wars* 63, 98, 107–8
  Lucas on 98, 111, 120
  Lusted on 7
  and melodrama 96–7
  moral code of 98
  psychological turn in history of 98
  and rugged individualism 118, 121, 213
  as a shared universe 6–7
  sidekick in 121
  and *Solo* 103–4
  Tompkins on 103, 220 n.18
  and US cultural mythology 98
  and Vietnam War 42
The Home and the World (novel and film) 21
Homer 11
horizon of expectations 29, 30–6, 144, 185
Howard, Bryce Dallas 56–7
Howard, Ron 61
hubris 80, 82–6, 89, 130, 195
The Human Condition 137–41

humor 104–5, 190. *See also* comedy, satire
  in *The Hidden Fortress* 145
Hutchinson, James 69
Hux, General (character) 192

identity
  categories of identity in *Star Wars* 168
  collective 26
  and cosmopolitanism 9, 14–15
  cyborg 149, 154–5
  ethnic 163
  formation of 90–1
  individual 22, 113
  and individualism 113, 117
  of Kylo Ren/Ben Solo 88
  politics 165
  in social psychology 14
  and *Star Wars: Identities* exhibition 14–15, 90–1
  and technology 134, 149
  and US immigration 163
ideology 7, 25–9, 129, 154
  Althusser on 19, 27
  associative nature of 7, 27, 154
  definition of 26–7
  and film 23, 25
  of individualism 116, 171–2
  and interpretive community 7, 27–8
  operations of 27–8
  and *Star Wars: Identities* 91
  and technology 129, 160
Iger, Robert 52–3, 60
ILM. *See* Industrial Light and Magic
Indiana Jones film series 219 n.8
Indigenous Studies 25
individualism 109–27. *See also* ideology
  Lasch on 111

liberal 109–18, 127, 148, 164, 171
and masculinity 152
ontological 112–13, 118–19
rugged 109, 118–21, 122, 126, 127, 131, 152, 213
and technology 132
individuality 133, 148–50, 152–3, 156
individuals 3, 19, 27, 42, 112–13, 115, 117, 144, 149–50, 152, 163, 166
Industrial Light and Magic 4, 49–51, 64, 139, 222 n.23. *See also* Dykstra, John; acquisition by Disney, 52
art for sequel trilogy 196
Dykstraflex 50–1
and Special Editions 176–7
Stagecraft system 141, 226 n.19
injustice
Star Wars fans on 188
inspiration 4, 14, 17–18, 33–4, 46–8, 53, 57, 60, 63, 66, 97–8, 107, 127, 146, 153, 156, 175, 189, 196, 213
intentionality 8, 78, 86
and auteurism 8
intentions
authorial 29, 42
corporate 130
good 70, 84, 160
and technology 160
interdisciplinary 25, 48. *See also* multidisciplinary
interpretive communities 27–9
Invaders from Mars (film) 150
Invasion of the Body Snatchers (film) 150
irony. *See also* reversal and recognition
dramatic 69–71, 84, 104

in Lucas's career 172–3
situational 76
Isaac, Oscar 190, 193
Isaacson, Walter 48

Jabba the Hutt (character) 64, 99, 124, 140, 157, 178, 226 n.27
Jameson, Fredric 116
Jauss, Hans Robert 29, 171. *See also* horizon of expectations
Jedi
ancient books in sequel trilogy 125, 199–201, 215
on attachment 195
as artisans 136, 145, 157–9
belief system 89, 169, 195, 205
destruction of 76, 85, 151–2
enmity with Sith 75, 82, 84, 104
failure of 85, 171, 174, 195–6
and fallibilism 86, 200–1
female 121, 125
and the Force 113, 120, 129
and Force healing 125
on freedom 89
future of 202, 217–18
and heroism 136
and individualism 136, 156
influence of 90
justice and 6, 157
legend of the "Chosen One," 70, 173
lightsabers of 136, 145, 157–9
Luke Skywalker on 195, 200
in *The Mandalorian* 214
mythology of 183
Obi-Wan Kenobi on 6, 157
in Old Republic 6, 157
and Order 66, 151–2
as pacifists 89
reconstitution of 113
restrictions 83, 195

and revenge 86–7
Rey as most powerful 125
Rey's belief in 85
and Separatists 147
survivors in exile 87
and technology 136–7, 145
Temple 158, 195, 196, 218
training 82, 84–5
Jeffress, Jerry 51
Jenkins, Garry 44–6
Jenkins, Patty 56
Jobs, Steve 48–9
Johnson, Rian 56–8, 61–3, 79–81, 181, 190, 196–7, 201, 203
  on *A New Hope* 62
Joyce, James 46
justice
  Anakin Skywalker's view of 170
  Jedi Knights and 6, 157
  in the Hollywood Western 102
  melodrama and 96
  poetic 36–7, 218
  Rawls, theory of 113

Kaczynski, Ted 153–4
Kanata, Maz (character) 118, 126, 211, 216–17
Karloff, Boris x, 143, 148
Kasdan, Lawrence 59, 125, 140
katharsis 20, 67, 74–5. *See also* Aristotle, tragedy
Kazanjian, Howard 86
Kennedy, Anthony 64
Kennedy, Kathleen 13, 52–4, 65–6, 175–6, 186
  and Abrams 58–9
  on women in *Star Wars* 121–2, 124–5
Kennedy, Ted 226 n.34
Kenny, Anthony 73

Kenobi, Obi-Wan (character) 6, 37, 47, 70, 75, 78, 98, 113, 121, 123, 161, 169, 175, 191
  and Darth Vader 76–8, 139, 149, 155
  in Death Star 104–5
  death of 77, 89, 215
  duel with Anakin 71, 120, 170, 173
  exile of 85, 87
  failure of 198
  lightsaber of 158, 218
  on the lightsaber 87, 157
  Luke disagrees with 194–5
  view of the Force 118, 216
Kershner, Irvin 1, 77
King Features 45
Kline, Sally 1
Krazy Glue 183
Kubrick, Stanley 30–1, 36, 144
Kurosawa, Akira: *The Hidden Fortress* 145, *Rashomon* 21
Kurtz, Gary 32, 42, 44–6, 125
Kylo Ren. *See* Ren, Kylo

Land, Edwin 48
Lasch, Christopher 111
Latour, Bruno 216
Lee, Erika 163
legal cases: *Austin v. Michigan Chamber of Commerce* (1990) 64, *Citizens United v. Federal Election Commission* (2010) 3, 64–5
legislation: McCarran-Walter Act (1952) 162–3, Nationality Act (1965) 163
Leia, Princess. *See* Organa, Leia
LGBTQIA+: characters in *Star Wars* 167–9, Studies 25
liberal individualism. *See* individualism

liberalism 9, 35, 109–10. *See also* individualism
lightsaber 87
   of Anakin Skywaker 218
   construction of 136–7, 158–9
   cyborg nature of 159–60
   of Darth Vader 158, 159
   Han Solo view of 136–7, 145, 157, 158, 211, 227 n.36
   and kyber crystal 158–60
   of Leia Organa 86, 90, 137, 218
   of Luke Skywalker 136–7, 145, 157, 158, 211, 218, 227 n.36
   of Obi-Wan Kenobi 158, 218
   Obi-Wan Kenobi view of 87, 157
Lippincott, Charles 32
Liszt, Franz 34
The Lone Ranger 98, 121
The Lord of the Rings
   films 130
   novels 46
love 8, 23, 44, 57, 78, 82, 84–5, 124, 130–2, 140, 144, 146, 167, 175, 179, 181, 183, 189–90, 195, 205, 215
Lucas, George. *See also* Lucasfilm, *Star Wars* influences
   as auteur 1–2, 64, 179
   biography, before *Star Wars* 41–7, 172–3
   on character 91
   cultural influences 46–7
   and Daniels 146
   on destiny as an idea 210
   Disney, dispute with 55–6
   Disney, sale to 52–3, 168, 180
   and droids 144–5
   and early conception of Luke Skywalker as girl 125–6
   and exile and return 87
   and Expanded Universe 53–4, 60
   on the Force 114, 207
   on Hollywood Western 98, 111
   and horizon of expectations 30–3
   as inspiration 56–8, 175–6
   and Joseph Campbell 36, 46–7, 61–2, 123
   on Kubrick's *2001* 30–1
   on Leia Organa 123
   and melodrama 38, 97
   as mentor 45
   on morals 210
   and music for *Star Wars* 34–5, 97
   on mythology 98
   on narrative in *Star Wars* 25, 120
   and paracosm 5
   and pedagogy 14
   personal investment in *Star Wars* 13
   and philosophical thinking 4
   and prequel trilogy narrative 90
   on racism in *Phantom Menace* 187–8
   and revision of Greedo scene 98–102
   and rugged individualism 120–2
   sequel trilogy treatments 55, 196
   and shared universe 5, 65
   on the Sith 117
   and Special Edition revisions 174–9
   and special-effects innovation 49–51, 140, 174–8, 193
   on technology 131–2
   and tragedy 70, 86–7
Lucas, Sr., George Walton 43
Lucasfilm. *See also American Graffiti*; Indian Jones; Kennedy, Kathleen; Industrial Light and Magic; *THX 1138*

acquisition by Disney 52–3, 56, 100, 179–80, 183, 203
agenda of 175, 184, 185
archives 140
and conventions 14
as corporate person 64–6
as corporation 2–5, 65–6
and cosmopolitan approach to knowledge 48
Daniels, treatment of 146–7
development of 64, 75
and Expanded Universe 53–4, 93
fan reactions to 15, 29, 181, 186, 188
founding of 44–5
and LGBTQIA+ characters 167
and licensing 13
marketing 32
Next-Gen 37, 52–66, 185, 203
non-Star Wars films 219 n.8
and pedagogy 14
responsibility to Lucas's legacy 175–6, 184
and sequel trilogy production 196–7
and sequel trilogy treatments by Lucas 196–7
and shared universe development 6, 13, 22
and Special Editions 177
Story Group 13, 53
and technological innovation 49
and transmedia 29, 202
Lucifer 134
Luddism 132–3, 137, 147, 225 n.5. *See also* technophobia
Luke Skywalker. *See* Skywalker, Luke
Lukes, Steven 113
Luminara Unduli (character) 121
Lusted, David 7, 97, 102

machine 43, 109, 131, 133, 135–6, 138–9, 142–4, 148–9, 152, 155–6, 210. *See also* technology, technophobia
machine gun 135–6. *See also* technophobia
The Mandalorian (television series) 7–8, 57, 62–3, 64, 107, 141, 147, 213–14, 226 n.19, 226 n.27
Manichean 94, 97, 104
Marx, Karl 27
Marxism 19, 25, 26
Millennium Falcon 31, 77, 104, 113, 118, 132, 145, 192, 209. *See also* Chewbacca; Solo, Han
melodrama 93–108
  Brooks on 95
  Higgins on 96
  in Hollywood films 96–7, 107–8
  and Manichean view 94
  and music 36
  Neale on 96–7
  origins 95
  use by Lucas 38, 104–6
  Western genre 101–3, 108
memory 23, 62, 72, 134, 175
mentoring 6, 43–6, 78, 91, 104, 213, 216. *See also* teacher
monomyth 46–7, 62, 87, 127, 171. *See also* Campbell, Joseph
moral compass 205–18
  and altruism 214–15
  droids as index to 144, 207–8, 213
  and family 214–18
  in *The Mandalorian* 213–14
  Rey's 207–13, 216
Mos Eisley Cantina. *See under Star Wars* places
motherhood 71, 83, 88, 123, 182

Mothma, Mon (character) 143
Moyers, Bill 41–3, 45, 112, 184–5, 210
Mullhall, Stephen 22
multiculturalism 9, 29, 161–2, 164–7, 174
multidisciplinarity 47–8, 51
Murdock, Maureen 123–4
music. *See also* Williams, John
   in 1970s films 35
   Appiah on 11, 14
   Aristotle on 74
   as artistic discipline in filmmaking 48
   as cinematic-aesthetic device 24–5
   and emotion 34–6
   in *The Force Awakens* 208, 209, 211
   in *The Last Jedi* 197
   and melodrama 95–7
   and opening crawl 34
   and persuasion 38
   Twentieth-Century Fox theme 30
   of Vader's introduction 36
multiculturalism. *See also* cosmopolitanism, universalism
   vs. cosmopolitanism 9, 165–7
   and "culture wars," 162–4
   in education 164–5
   and Hart-Celler Act 162
   immigration policy 163, Lucas and, 47
   and McCarran-Walter Act 162–3
   and pluralism 9, 164, 165–7
   and Rebellion 165
   in sequel trilogy 29, 174
   in *Star Wars* universe 161–2
myth 41–3, 46–7, 87, 102–3. *See also* monomyth
   classical Greek 72–3
   Star Wars as 47–8, 61–2, 75, 79–82
   Western as 98
   women and 124

narrative 6, 9, 11, 14, 20, 23–4, 38, 42, 47–8, 69, 72, 74, 79, 87–9, 129, 174, 189, 201–2. *See also* plot
Nationality Act (1965) 163
National Air and Space Museum 14, 47, 109
nation
   and immigration 162
   memory of 72
   will of 111
nationalism 9, 72. *See also* cosmopolitanism
nationality 163
nature 154
nature vs. nurture 90
Neale, Steve 96
Nihilus, Darth (character) 205
Nixon, Richard 41, 110–11
nonhumans 98, 146, 153, 161–2, 165
nostalgia 6, 184
novelization 32, 39, 70, 192, 195–6, 199–200, 226 n.23
Nozick, Robert 110
Nussbaum, Martha 12–13, 20–2, 36–7, 192

Obama, Barack 65, 165
The Odyssey (epic) 11
Oedipus Rex see Sophocles
Orca (character) 169. *See also* LGBTQIA+
Organa, Leia (character) 31, 69, 75, 86, 102, 108, 137, 144, 147, 183, 194–5, 199, 208, 212, 215
   character traits of 123, 126
   daughter of Padmé Amidala 123

and dramatic irony 69
in Expanded Universe 61
and fallibilism 191–2, 195
as hero 123–4
as Jedi 86, 90, 121
Jedi training of 195, 199
lightsaber of 86, 90, 137, 218
as mentor 91, 125, 212, 216, 217
mother of Ben Solo 84, 217
music for 35
relationship to Darth Vader 69, 79
relationship to Han Solo 84, 102
relationship to Luke Skywalker 69, 78–9, 84, 121
in sequel trilogy 126, 195, 199
originality
as revision 46
in Romanticism 45

padawan 78, 123, 169, 200. *See also* apprentice
Palpatine, Emperor Sheev (character) 106, 157, 201 211, 228 n.19, 230 n.13
as clone 38
and dark side of the Force 47, 83, 87–8
as Frankenstein figure 155
Lucas's early ideas about 41, 111
relationship to Anakin Skywalker/Darth Vader 83–4, 89, 157, 159, 169
relationship to Luke Skywalker 89, 214
relationship to Rey 80, 86, 89, 120, 156, 211, 214–18
in sequel trilogy 38, 80–1, 84, 89, 120, 156, 211, 214–18
Sunstein on 171–2
panegyric 11, 94
pantomime 95

paracosm. *See under* shared universe
Paradise Lost 134–5, 205
parentage 80–2, 88, 91, 181–2, 202, 209, 211, 213, 215, 217–18
particularity 9, 12, 20, 26, 45, 47–8, 98, 166, 210. *See also* cosmopolitanism
Pascal, Pedro 107
past 7, 23, 30, 39, 46, 50, 72, 81, 85, 105, 156, 184, 190, 200–1, 203, 211, 216–18
patriarchy 127, 152
pedagogy 14
Pegg, Simon 181
Perry, Steve 93
person 10, 48
    artificial 141
    and class 145
    corporate 2–3, 64–5
    Daniels on 146
    development of a 90–1
    droids as 162, 210
    third- narrative 106
personality 15, 91
photography 50, 61
physics 158
Picasso, Pablo 14
Planet 31, 33, 35–6, 47, 53, 55, 60, 91, 94, 120, 125, 129–30, 132, 139. 145, 150–1, 155
Plantinga, Carl 23
Plato 18, 21, 43, 134
plot 8, 38–9, 54, 70–1, 73, 76, 79, 82, 95–6, 103, 176, 185, 197
pluralism 9, 164, 165–7. *See also* individualism, liberalism, multiculturalism
Plutt, Unkar (character) 145, 181, 209
Poetics. See under Aristotle
poetry 7–8, 11, 25, 44, 72–4, 75–6, 79, 90, 134

Paradise Lost 134–5, 205
Poetic Justice (Nussbaum) 12–13,
    20–2, 36–7, 192
politics 3, 25, 30, 36–7, 64, 72, 74,
    109–11, 113–15, 119, 154–5,
    163, 165, 170, 173
Pollock, Tom 44
Polynices 71, 78
Princess Leia. *See* Organa, Leia
Prometheus 142
Prowse, David 77

Ralston, Ken 31
Ralston, Mark 136
The Ramayana (epic) 11
Ray, Nicholas 96
Ray, Satyajit 21
reader-response theory 28–9. *See also*
    interpretive communities
Reagan, Ronald 112, 118, 226 n.34
Rebel Alliance 36, 106–8, 112, 172,
    192, 214
    chaotic nature of 107
Rebels (television series). *See Star
    Wars: Rebels*
Reeves, Michael 93
Ren, Kylo (character) 43, 199 208, 217
    cinematic treatment of 38, 208
    and combat 120, 126, 137, 198,
        201–2
    connection to Force 79–80, 198
    and dyad (Force Twin) 81–2
    and fallibilism 202–3
    hubris of 80
    music for 211
    relationship to Luke Skywalker
        17, 84–5, 198–9, 200–2, 217
    relationship to Palpatine 17, 84
    relationship to Rey 80–1, 85–6,
        120, 126, 137, 198–9, 211
    relationship to Snoke 79–80, 85
    view of Darth Vader 80, 88
    as villain 208, 217
    the Resistance 17, 90, 106, 126, 169,
        195, 197, 199, 201–2, 215–17
Revan, Darth (character) 205–6
revolution
    in cinema (post-cinema) 38
    in communications technology 134
    Cultural, in China 184
    English 95
    in special effects 50, 132, 141
Rey. *See* Skywalker, Rey
reversal and recognition 20
    in *Star Wars* original trilogy 67–9
    in *Star Wars* prequel trilogy 76–8
rhetoric 11, 23–4, 213–14
Ridley, Daisey 126, 186, 190, 207–8,
    210, 212
Rimbaud, Arthur 26
robot 143, 184
    in *Agents of S.H.I.E.L.D.* 130
    Daniels on 146
    Darth Vader resemblance to 70
    vs. "droids," 144–6
    in first *Star Wars* trailer 31
    and *Frankenstein* 148
    as labor 141–2
    in opening scenes of *A New Hope*
        36
    origins of 141–2
    in *Transformers* films 130
Rogers, Adam 5–6, 175–6
Rogue One: A Star Wars Story (film)
    33, 123, 145, 160
Rohmer, Eric 1
Roosevelt, Theodore 14
Rowling, J. K. 60
rugged individualism. *See under*
    individualism
R.U.R.: Rossum's Universal Robots
    (play) 141–4, 148

sacrifice 78, 82, 126, 197, 215–17, 230 n.13
same-sex relationships. *See LGBTQIA+*
Sandel, Michael 114, 117
satire 11, 94
Scanlan, Neal 140–1
Scherstuhl, Alan 168–9
Schwarzenegger, Arnold 131
Scott, Ridley 21–2. *See also Alien*
science 19, 21, 29–33, 46, 73, 112, 130, 144, 150
science fiction 21, 46, 130, 144, 150, 179
    and the horizon of expectations 29–33
Sebulba (character) 101
Secura, Aayla (character) 121
self 10, 12, 85, 87, 94, 99, 102, 111, 117, 153, 168, 194, 209–10, 213. *See also* individualism, individuality, individuals
    selfishness 117
    selflessness 168
sentimentality 130, 145
Shakespeare, William 11, 56, 72
shared universe 3–8, 13–14, 38–9, 64–5, 186, 188, 219 n.2
    classical Greek tragedy as 89–92
    fandom and 179, 186–8
    and paracosm 5–6
Shaw, George Bernard 142
Sheen, Martin 42
Shelley, Mary 142, 148
Singapore 169
Sinnerbrink, Robert 24
Sirk, Douglas 96
Sith 75, 97, 173. *See also* Palpatine, Emperor Sheev; Vader, Darth
    appeal of 205–6
    as counter-cosmopolitans 170
    destiny, conception of 89
    enmity with Jedi 75, 82, 84, 104
    Eternal cultists 215
    ideology 82, 89, 117, 155, 169–70, 205
    influence of 90
    lightsaber construction 159
    lightsaber, double-bladed 82
    as materialists 118
    Obi-Wan's view of 170
    Palpatine reveals himself to be 211
    and planet Exegol 120, 125
    throne 156
    troopers 206
    wayfinders 215
Skywalker, Anakin (character) 43, 75. *See also* Vader, Darth
    as "Chosen One," 70, 173
    and combat 71, 78, 120, 170
    compared to George Lucas 173
    compared to Luke Skywalker 90–1
    and dark side of the Force 84, 173, 198
    and fate 71, 89
    and hamartia 83–4
    hubris of 83, 84
    and ideology of empire 170
    lightsaber of 218
    as pilot 151
    as podracer 101
    pre-teen 180
    relationship to Obi-Wan Kenobi 71, 78, 120, 170, 173
    relationship to Padmé Amidala 83
    relationship to Palpatine 83–4, 89
    and slavery 80
    in *The Story of Anakin Skywalker* (video short) 68–9
    transformation of 47, 70, 78, 87, 155, 195

Skywalker, Luke (character) 31, 37, 47, 58, 108, 146, 161–2, 183
- as Campbell's hero 121
- and change 43, 47, 86, 90, 112–13, 120, 186
- character traits of 43, 86
- and combat 120, 157, 169, 215
- compared to Anakin 90–1
- as cyborg 156–7
- daughter of Padmé Amidala 123
- and Death Star 129, 135
- destiny of 113, 120
- and dramatic irony 69
- in Expanded Universe 61
- and fallibilism 84–5, 174, 191, 195–6, 200–1
- fan identification with 180, 186
- and friendship 214
- Hamill on 167–8
- as hero 123–4
- as Jedi 86, 90, 121
- on Jedi beliefs 195, 200
- Jedi training of 114, 136, 169, 194
- lightsabers of 136–7, 145, 157, 158, 211, 227 n.36
- as mentor 84–5, 91, 125, 174, 200–2, 211, 214–16
- redemption of 86
- McQuarrie's early sketches of 125–6
- music for 35, 211
- relationship to Ben Solo/Kylo Ren 17, 84–5, 198, 200–2, 217
- relationship to Darth Vader 67–9, 75–7, 84, 89, 120, 157, 169, 170, 215–16
- relationship to Obi-Wan Kenobi 6, 77, 87, 98, 118, 139, 191, 195
- relationship to Han Solo 98
- relationship to Leia Organa 69, 78–9, 84, 121
- relationship to Padmé Amidala 123
- relationship to Palpatine 89
- relationship to Rey 84–6, 156, 194, 197–9, 209, 211, 214–16, 218
- relationship to Yoda 89, 114, 194, 195, 198–200, 202
- in sequel trilogy 17, 84–6, 90, 125, 156, 194, 196–202, 208, 211–17, 227 n.36, 230 n.13
- and storytelling 17–18

Skywalker, Rey (character) 32, 43, 84–6, 90–1, 118, 120, 125–6, 137, 156–7, 181, 194–201, 203, 207–18
- character arc 81
- and dark side of the Force 82
- and dyad (Force Twin) 81–2
- and family 217
- and Jakku 80, 203, 209, 217
- lightsaber of 218
- relationship to Kylo Ren 80–1, 85–6, 120, 126, 137, 198–9, 211
- relationship to Palpatine 80, 86, 89, 120, 156, 211, 214–18
- "Rey from Nowhere," 80
- and Tatooine 217–18

slavery 55, 80, 101, 138, 141, 150, 166
Smith, E. E. ("Doc") 46
Smith, Greg 24
Smith, Thomas G. 49–50
Snoke (character) 79–80, 85, 192, 217
socialism 110, 154
Socrates 18, 26, 43, 134
Solo: A Star Wars Story (film) 34, 61, 103–4, 141, 145
Solo: A Star Wars Story (novelization) 226 n.23
Solo, Ben (character) 202, 217. *See also* Ren, Kylo

as apprentice 84, 200
and dark side of the Force 85, 198, 200
death of 215
and dyad (Force Twin) 81–2
exile and return 88
redemption of 81–2, 215
as tragic hero 81–2
Solo, Han (character) 75, 108, 147, 183, 194, 201, 215. *See also* *Solo: A Star Wars Story*
and change 43
as damsel in distress 124
death of 82, 188, 215
and the Force 113–14
and friendship 14
in *Galaxy of Adventures* 14
and Greedo controversy 98–104
and Jabba the Hutt 140
in *Han Solo: Imperial Cadet* comic 107
and Hollywood Western 98, 120–1
on lightsabers 157
McQuarrie's early sketches of 126
and *Millennium Falcon* 132, 145
as parent 82, 84
and Rey 126, 210
in Special Editions 140
as tragic hero 78, 82
Sophocles 68, 92
in Aristotle's *Poetics* 79
Oedipus Rex 67, 69, 71–2, 76, 78, 82–3, 88, 92
South China Morning Post (newspaper) 185
Spalko, Irina (character) 168
special effects 31, 49–50, 132, 139–140, 176–180. *See also* Dykstraflex, Industrial Light and Magic

Academy Award for 51
aesthetics of 141, 176
blue-screen photography 50
digital 141, 178, 193
green screen 141, 177
practical 24–5, 141
spectacle 31, 71, 76, 161, 176. *See also* Aristotle
spectatorship 23, 36–7, 72
Spielberg, Steven 2, 130
Star Trek 129–31, 147
Deep Space Nine 149, 150
Discovery 23, 150
First Contact 152
Next Generation 144, 149
Voyager 144, 149
Star Wars characters. *See* individual character names by surname
Star Wars comic books 180
Captain Phasma 127
Dark Empire 54
Darth Vader 159–60, 168
Doctor Aphra 147, 168
Han Solo: Imperial Cadet 107
TIE Fighter 106–7
Star Wars, Episode I: The Phantom Menace (film) 55, 83, 101, 167, 184, 207
fan critique 180–1, 187–8
hive mind 151
mood 24–5
Pegg critique 181
special effects 140, 193
Star Wars, Episode II: Attack of the Clones (film) 83, 151. *See also* hive mind
Star Wars, Episode III: Revenge of the Sith (film) 69–71, 83–4, 151, 155, 170, 173, 194
Star Wars, Episode III: Revenge of the Sith (novelization) 70

Index

Star Wars, Episode IV: A New Hope
(film) 29–33, 62, 87, 104, 131,
157, 180, 191, 201, 215, 216
availability 62
melodrama 38, 94, 97
Special Edition 99–102, 177
tragedy 76–9
Star Wars, Episode IV: A New Hope
(novelization) 32
*Star Wars, Episode V: The Empire
Strikes Back* (film) 33, 89, 114,
147, 169, 194, 216
reversal and recognition 67–9, 76–8
*Star Wars, Episode VI: Return of the
Jedi* (film) 17–18, 60, 81, 86–7,
120, 131–2, 136, 139, 157, 170,
198–9, 214, 215
against Campbell model 123–4
original title 86–7
reversal and recognition 78–9
*Star Wars, Episode VII: The Force
Awakens* (film) 61, 78, 84,
118, 138–140, 171, 188–9,
193, 197–8, 203, 208, 210–11,
213–14, 216–17
Lucas dispute over 55–6
women and 124–7
Star Wars, Episode VIII: The Last Jedi
(film) 58, 90, 156, 189, 192,
195–203, 211, 215–17, and
epic 80
and hamartia 84–5
Pegg on 181
storytelling in 17–18
women and 126–7
Star Wars, Episode VIII: The Last Jedi
(novelization) 192, 195, 199
*Star Wars, Episode IX: The Rise of
Skywalker* (film) 23–4, 38–9,
84–8, 91, 120, 125, 127, 137,
157–8, 199, 203, 211–18

Poetics and 80–2
sexuality and 167–9
visuals 193–4
*Star Wars, Episode IX: The Rise of
Skywalker* (novelization) 39,
196, 200–1
Star Wars fandom xiv, 5, 8, 188–9
and cosplay 14
Dawson on 8
and desire for narrative details
38–9
as interpretive community 29
Lucas on 187
participation in *Star Wars*
universe 13
pre-1977 32
response to Disney-era films 15
response to Special Editions 179,
229 n.42
toxic 186–8, 190
and white masculinity 186
Star Wars games 4
Battlefront II 106
Knights of the Old Republic 206
*Knights of the Old Republic II: The
Sith Lords* 206
Star Wars: The Old Republic 206
Tiny Death Star 93–94
Star Wars: Identities (exhibition) viii,
14–15, 90–1
Star Wars influences. *See also*
Campbell, Joseph; Hollywood
Western
cultural 41, 46–7, 72, 165
fairy tale 42
historical 111
Hollywood Western 97–8
individualism 114
mythological 41
personal 43–4
serials 33, 97

Star Wars: The Magic of Myth
   (exhibition) 14, 47–8, 109
Star Wars novels
   Aftermath 64
   Ahsoka 159, 169
   Catalyst 151
   Death Star 93–4
   Into the Dark 219 n.16
   Lost Stars 107
   Thrawn 161–2
Star Wars places
   Abbadon, Had 60
   Alderaan 94, 191
   Bespin 197
   Coruscant 60
   Death Star 17, 75, 77, 86, 93–4, 106–7, 118, 129, 138–9, 145, 151, 160–1, 203, 214
   Endor 18, 132, 214
   Exegol 120, 125, 215
   Geonosis 151
   Hoth 228 n.32
   Jakku 80, 203, 209, 217
   Mos Eisley Cantina 47, 93, 98–9, 103–4, 145–6, 157, 161–2
   Mustafar 173
   Naboo 151
   Rebel Base 94
   Starkiller Base 139, 192, 211
   Tatooine 47, 90, 145, 217–18
   Unknown Regions 162
   Yavin IV 165
Star Wars: Rebels (television series) 57, 60–1, 64, 106, 123, 161
Star Wars reference books
   The Complete Visual Dictionary (New Edition) 158
   Star Wars: The Rise of Skywalker: The Visual Dictionary (book) 206

Stevens, Wallace 171
storytelling 17, 43, 46, 139
   in Aristotle's *Poetics* 18
   Lucas and 52, 139, 193
   other *Star Wars* 57, 168, 223 n.50
   and philosophy 18–20, 37–9, 66
   and shared universe 6, 13
   transmedia 223 n.51
Swidler, Ann 114–16
Sunstein, Cass 170–1
Supreme Court, U.S. 3, 64–65
Syndulla, Hera (character) 123

Tagore, Rabindranath 21
Tanen, Ned 45
teacher 163, 180, 195, 198–9, 202–3, 217–18
teaching 164, 195, 198, 202
technology. *See also* special effects, technophobia
   Abrams and 139
   of Empire 18
   and the Force 139
   and identity 134, 149
   and ideology 129, 160
   and individualism 132
   and intentionality 160
   and mise-en-scène of *Star Wars* 36
technophobia 129–60. *See also* cyborg, Kaczynski, Ted; robot
   Jedi and 136–7
   in late-twentieth-century films 129–31, 149–50
   in *Paradise Lost* 134–5
   Plato and 134
   and rugged individualism 131–2, 135–6
   and technophilia 132
tekhne 73
Tekka, Lor San (character) 203, 208

television 7, 13–14, 23, 42, 53, 64, 68, 107, 111, 123, 130–1, 141, 147, 150, 152, 158, 160–1, 169, 218
Terminator (film series) 130, 143, 147, 187
Terrio, Chris 38, 81, 120
Them! (film) 150
The Thing (film) 150
Thrawn, Grand Admiral (character) 60, 106, 161–2
THX 1138 (film) 44, 144, 219 n.8
Tipton, Steven M. 114–16
tolerance 9, 164–7. *See also* individualism, pluralism
Tolkien, J. R. R. 46. *See also Lord of the Rings* (films)
Tolstoy, Leo 14
Tompkins, Jane 7, 103, 220 n.18
tragedy 20, 36–7, 67, 74, 87–9, 95, 171. *See also* Aristotle
  Fagles description of 6–7
  hero of 78, 81
  in medias res device 33
  as shared universe 6–7, 89
  in *Star Wars* original trilogy 79, 87
  in *Star Wars* prequel trilogy 70–1, 84, 87–8
tragic flaw. *See* hamartia
Tano, Ahsoka (character) 123, 159, 169
Tico, Paige (character) 126, 197
Tico, Rose (character) 147, 189, 197
TIE fighters. *See under* the Empire
Tran, Kelly Marie 186, 189–90
Transformers (film series) 130, 184
transmedia 64, 223 n.51
Tribeca Film Festival 32
Turner, Frederick Jackson 118
Tyce, Wrobie, Lieutenant (character) 169

Ueda, Reed 163
Unduli, Luminara (character) 121
United States 25–6, 41–2, 64–5, 70, 111, 114–15, 118–19, 153, 162, 166, 181–2, 185–6. *See also* Civil Rights movement, individualism, legislation
  audiences 162, 184
  cinematic history 97–8
  Congress 153
  cultural mythology 119
  culture 120, 127, 150, 154
  education 165–6
  immigration policy 162
  military 226 n.34
  political thought 109, 119
  politics 110, 112
  popular culture 109, 149, 152, 156
Universal Pictures 34, 143
Universal Studios 45
universalism 9, 48. *See also* cosmopolitanism, multiculturalism
University of Birmingham 26
University of Southern California 44
U.S. Supreme Court 3, 64–65

Vader, Darth (character) 31, 37, 68–9, 87, 90, 145, 147, 194. *See also* Skywalker, Anakin
  cinematic presentation of 38
  and combat 157
  as counter-cosmopolitan 192
  as cyborg 156
  in *Darth Vader* (comic) 159
  and dramatic irony 69
  failure, attitude toward 192
  and filming of *Empire Strikes Back* 77
  and the Force 129, 139

Hamill on 97
influence on Kylo Ren 80, 203
lightsaber of 158, 159
as machine
music for 35
as personification of Empire 139, 192
redemption of 84–5, 149, 195, 215
relationship to Leia Organa 69, 79
relationship to Luke Skywalker 47, 67, 69, 76–7, 89–90, 113, 120, 136, 156, 157, 169, 196
relationship to Obi-Wan Kenobi 85, 196, 215
relationship to Palpatine 159, 169
as tragic figure 70
as villain 38, 58, 70
Vanity Fair (magazine) 140, 193
Vaz, Mark Cotta 50, 176
Veitch, Tom 54
VHS tape 61–3, 179
video 47, 52–3, 62–4, 70, 75, 81, 140, 174, 181, 188
Vietnam War 41–2, 72, 112, 163, 185
villain 31, 38, 58, 96–7, 102–3, 149, 161, 217
violence 6, 89–90, 96, 98, 102–3, 211
The Virginian (novel) 102
VistaVision 50

Waititi, Taika 56
Walzer, Michael 110, 114
Warner Brothers 44
Wartenberg, Thomas 20–1
Watergate scandal 41, 72
Wayne, John 102

weaponry 87, 90, 130–2, 135–6, 157–60. *See also* lightsaber
Weathers, Carl 107
Wendig, Chuck 64
Western (genre) 102–3. *See also* Hollywood Western
Whale, James 143, 148
Wicked Witch of the West (character) 188
Williams, John 25, 35–6
    Abrams on 61
    on Lucas's ideas 35
    on Rey's theme 209
Windu, Mace (character) 89–90
Wister, Owen 102
Wittgenstein, Ludwig 116
Wren, Sabine (character) 120
writing 5–6, 7–8, 10–11, 18, 21, 42–5, 48, 52, 54, 59, 60, 64, 106, 124, 134, 146, 159, 168, 183, 209

xenophobia 173, 186

Yahoo Entertainment 189
Ying Xiao 185
Yoda (character) 85–7, 89, 113–4, 118, 120, 140, 158, 198–203, 213, 216
    and fallibilism 199–203
    on the Force 114
    Luke disagrees with 194–5
The Young Indiana Jones Chronicles (television series) 14
younglings 14, 158, 199. *See also* childhood, children

Zahn, Timothy 60, 75, 106, 161
Zoroastrianism 182–3

www.ingramcontent.com/pod-product-compliance
Lightning Source LLC
Chambersburg PA
CBHW060946230426
43665CB00015B/2080